JIM OTTAVIANI &

PRIMATES

The Fearless Science of Jane Goodall, Dian Fossey, and Biruté Galdikas

SQUARE
FISH

First Second
New York

PRIMATES

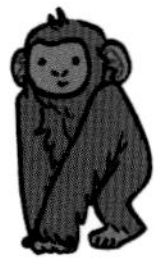

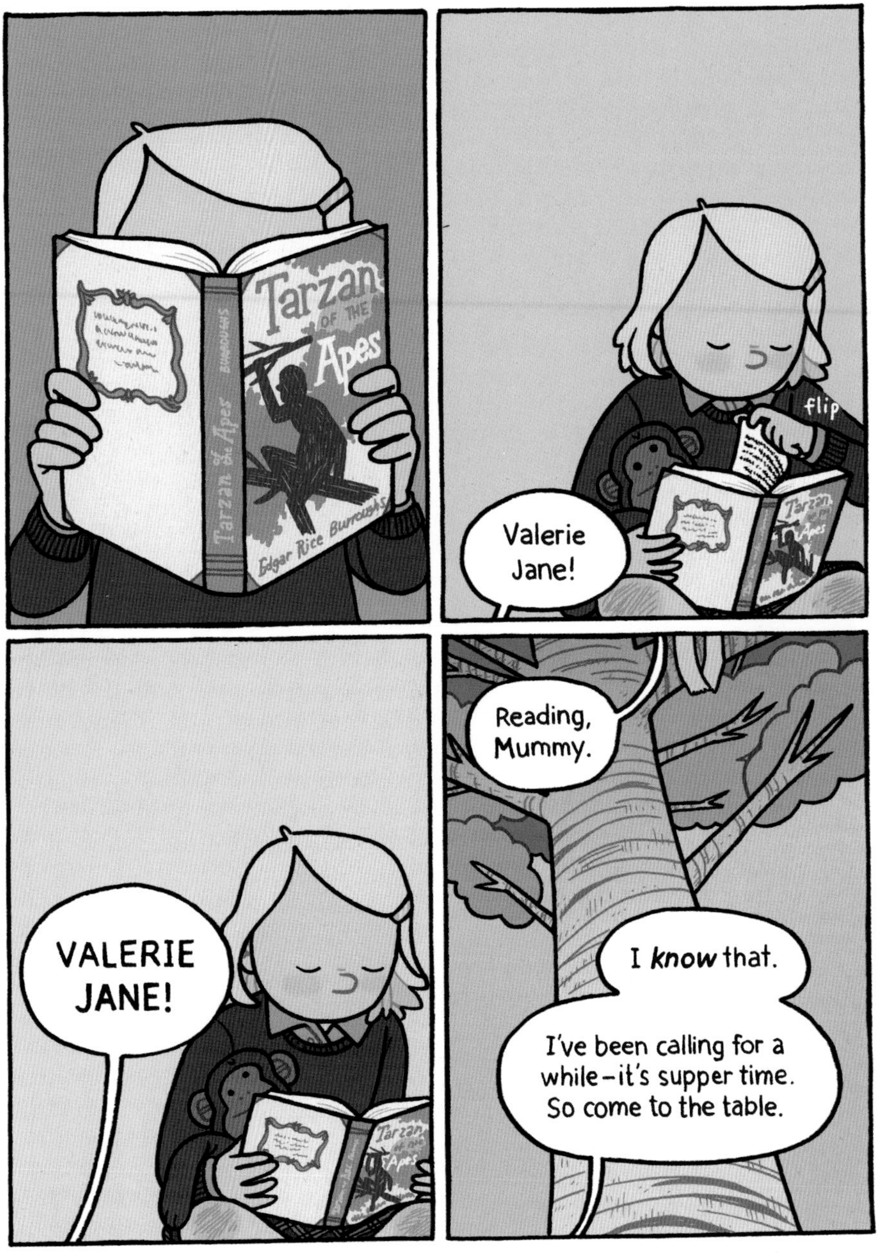
Tarzan of the Apes
BURROUGHS
Tarzan of the Apes
Edgar Rice Burroughs
flip
Valerie Jane!
VALERIE JANE!
Reading, Mummy.
I *know* that.
I've been calling for a while–it's supper time. So come to the table.

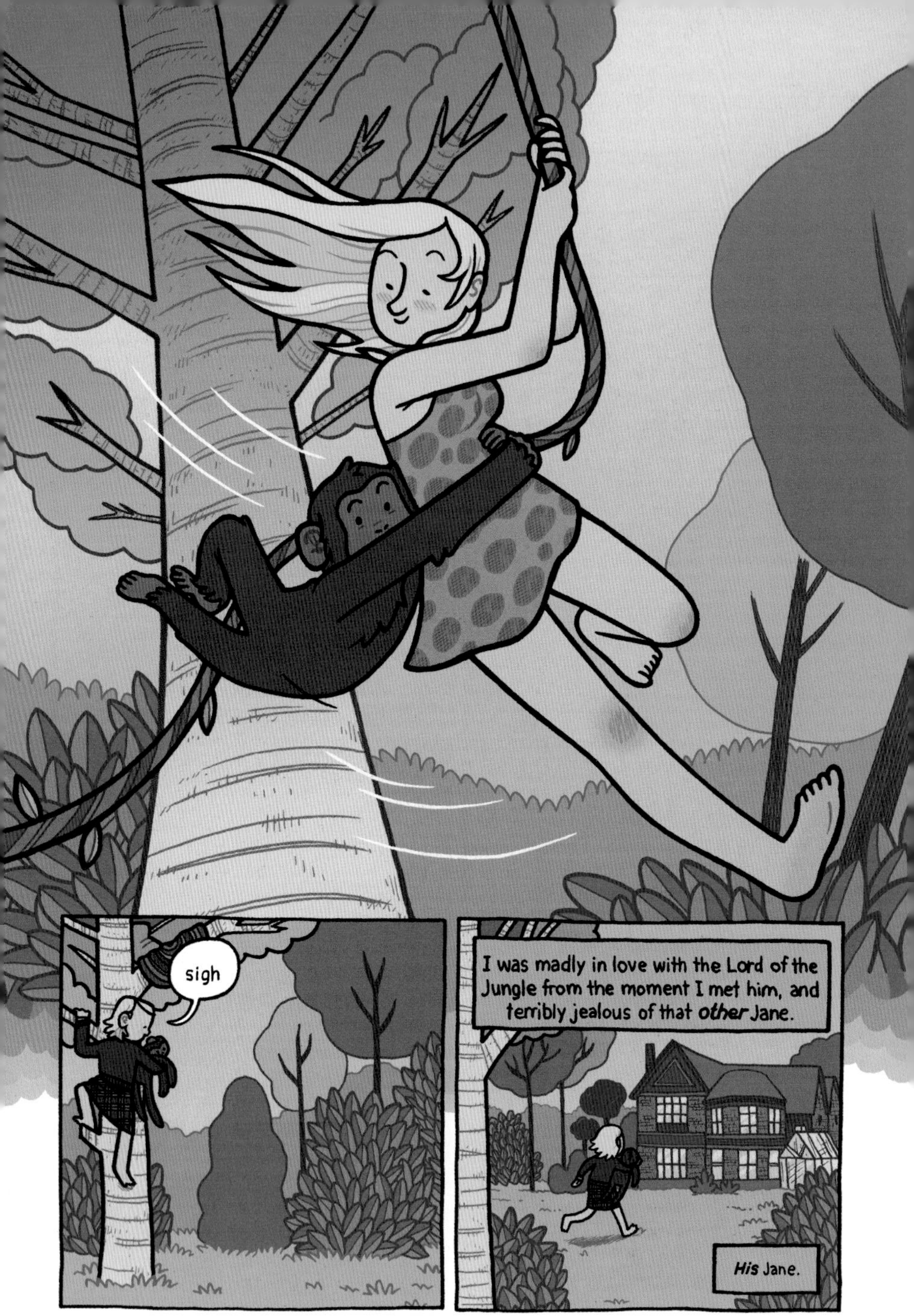
sigh
I was madly in love with the Lord of the Jungle from the moment I met him, and terribly jealous of that *other* Jane.
His Jane.

Part 1: But in my dreams, I did bigger things.

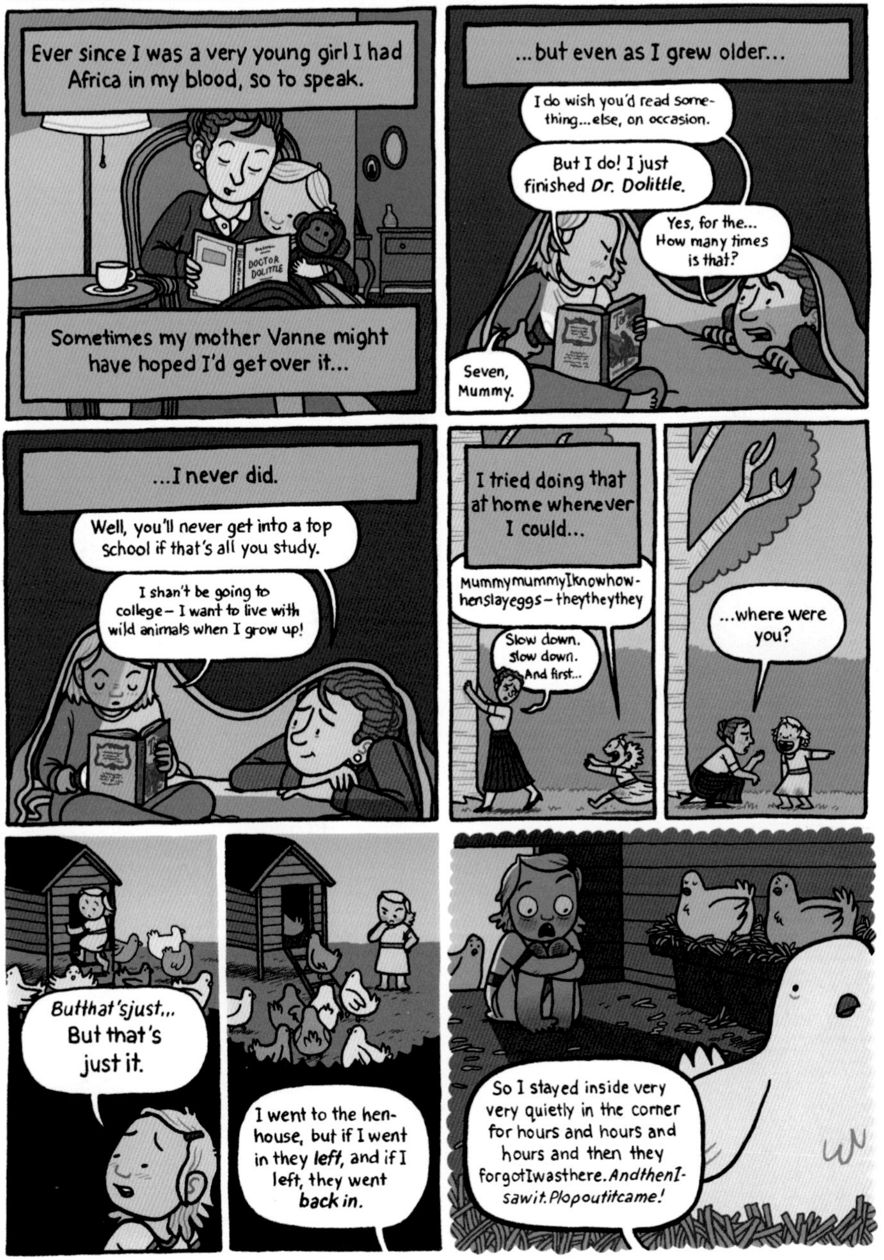
Ever since I was a very young girl I had Africa in my blood, so to speak.
DOCTOR DOLITTLE
Sometimes my mother Vanne might have hoped I'd get over it...
...but even as I grew older...
I do wish you'd read something...else, on occasion.
But I do! I just finished *Dr. Dolittle.*
Yes, for the... How many times is that?
Seven, Mummy.
...I never did.
Well, you'll never get into a top school if that's all you study.
I shan't be going to college– I want to live with wild animals when I grow up!
I tried doing that at home whenever I could...
MummymummyIknowhowhenslayeggs–theytheythey
Slow down. slow down. And first...
...where were you?
Butthat'sjust... But that's just it.
I went to the henhouse, but if I went in they *left,* and if I left, they went *back in.*
So I stayed inside very very quietly in the corner for hours and hours and hours and then they forgotIwasthere. *AndthenIsawit.Plopoutitcame!*

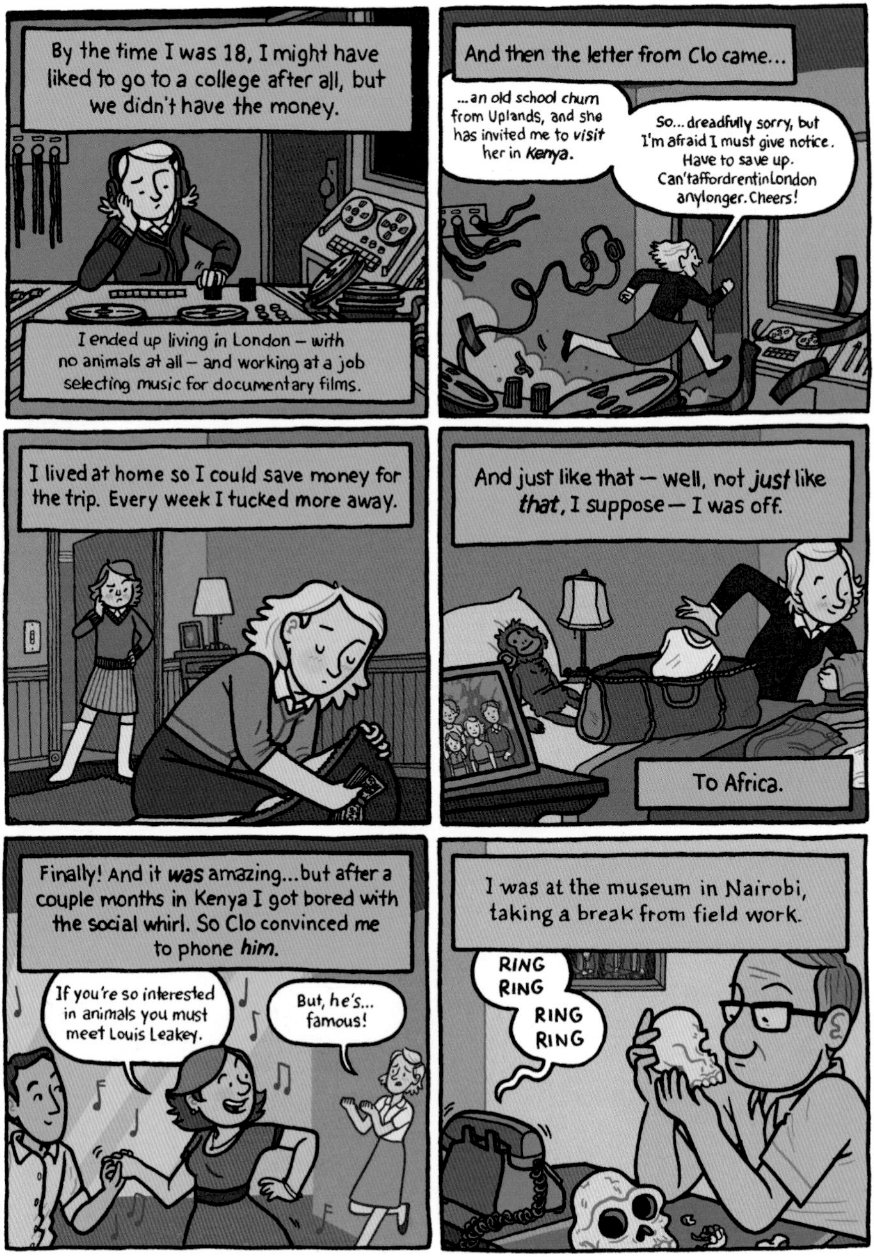
By the time I was 18, I might have liked to go to a college after all, but we didn't have the money.
I ended up living in London – with no animals at all – and working at a job selecting music for documentary films.
And then the letter from Clo came...
...an old school chum from Uplands, and she has invited me to *visit* her in *Kenya*.
So... dreadfully sorry, but I'm afraid I must give notice. Have to save up. Can'taffordrentinLondon anylonger. Cheers!
I lived at home so I could save money for the trip. Every week I tucked more away.
And just like that – well, not *just* like *that*, I suppose – I was off.
To Africa.
Finally! And it *was* amazing...but after a couple months in Kenya I got bored with the social whirl. So Clo convinced me to phone *him*.
If you're so interested in animals you must meet Louis Leakey.
But, he's... famous!
I was at the museum in Nairobi, taking a break from field work.
RING RING
RING RING

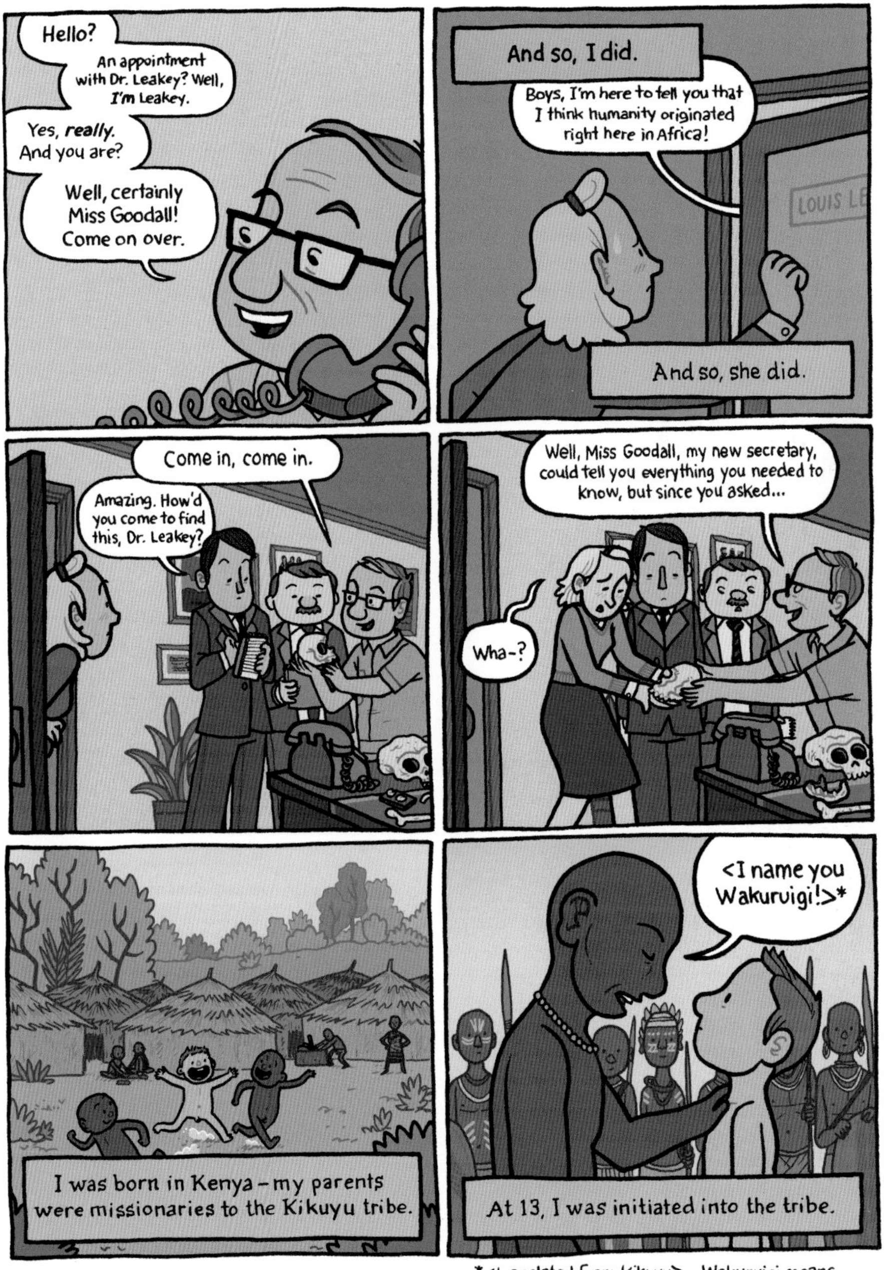
Hello?
An appointment with Dr. Leakey? Well, *I'm* Leakey.
Yes, *really*. And you are?
Well, certainly Miss Goodall! Come on over.
And so, I did.
Boys, I'm here to tell you that I think humanity originated right here in Africa!
LOUIS LE
And so, she did.
Come in, come in.
Amazing. How'd you come to find this, Dr. Leakey?
Well, Miss Goodall, my new secretary, could tell you everything you needed to know, but since you asked...
Wha-?
I was born in Kenya – my parents were missionaries to the Kikuyu tribe.
<I name you Wakuruigi!>*
At 13, I was initiated into the tribe.

*<translated from Kikuyu> – Wakuruigi means "Son of the Sparrow Hawk"

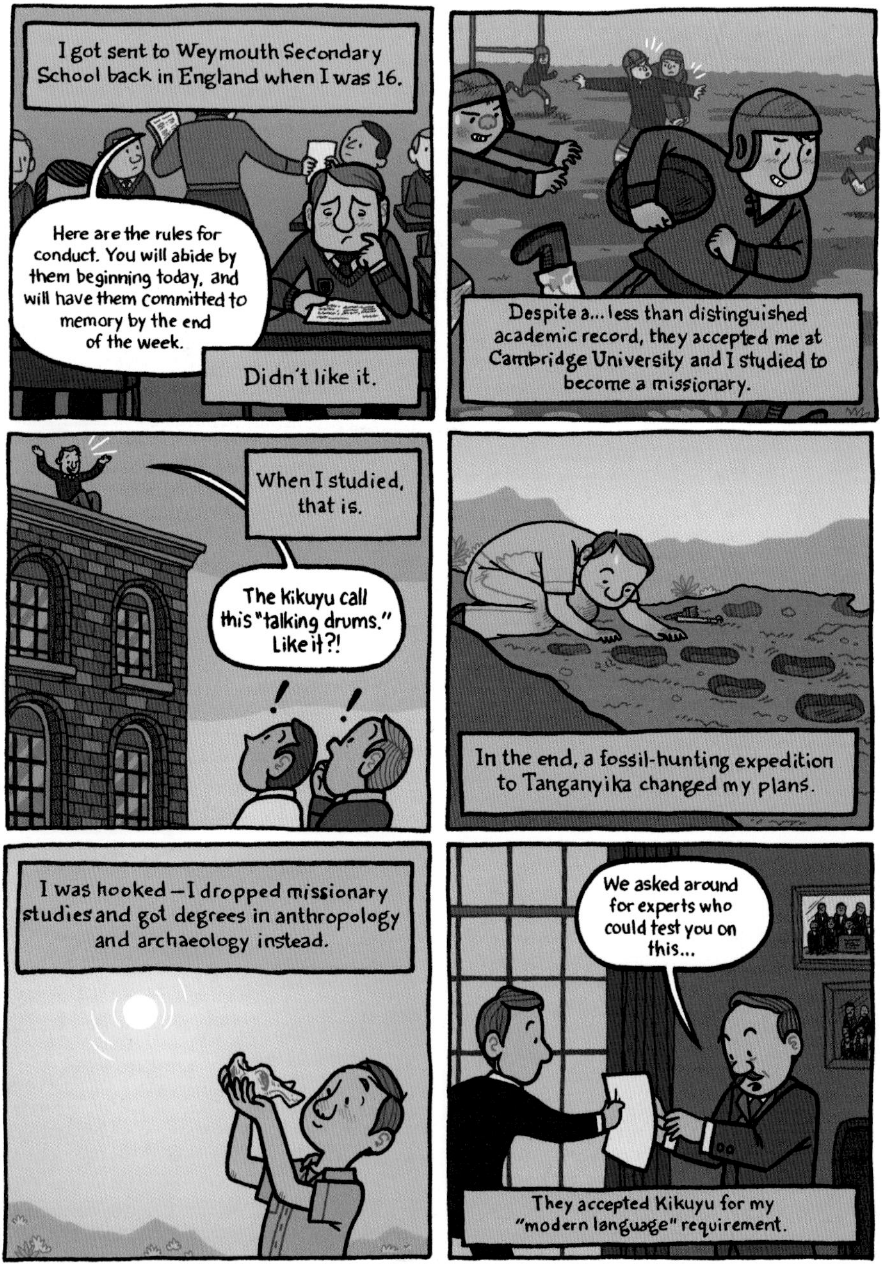
I got sent to Weymouth Secondary School back in England when I was 16.
Here are the rules for conduct. You will abide by them beginning today, and will have them committed to memory by the end of the week.
Didn't like it.
Despite a... less than distinguished academic record, they accepted me at Cambridge University and I studied to become a missionary.
When I studied, that is.
The Kikuyu call this "talking drums." Like it?!
! !
In the end, a fossil-hunting expedition to Tanganyika changed my plans.
I was hooked—I dropped missionary studies and got degrees in anthropology and archaeology instead.
We asked around for experts who could test you on this...
They accepted Kikuyu for my "modern language" requirement.

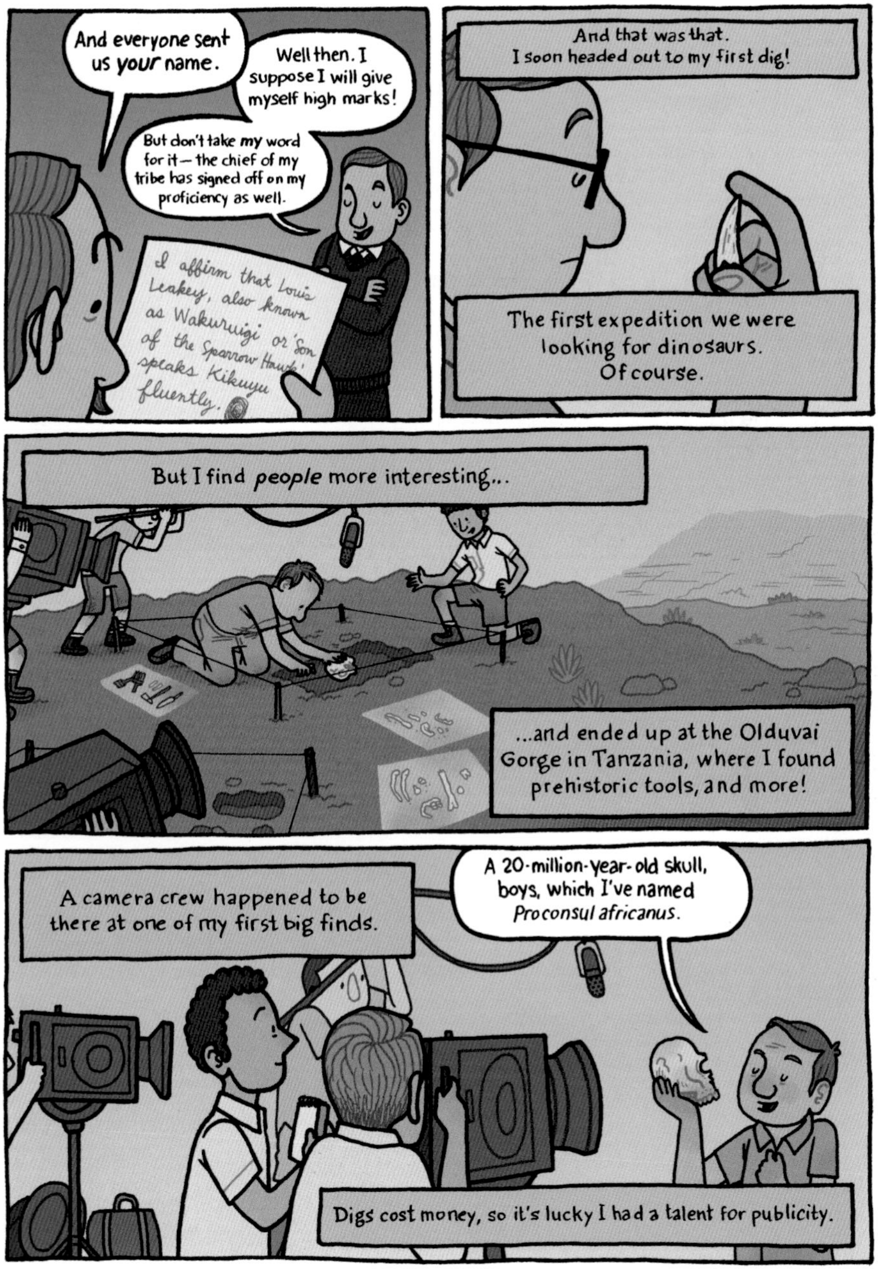

And everyone sent us *your* name.
Well then. I suppose I will give myself high marks!
But don't take *my* word for it—the chief of my tribe has signed off on my proficiency as well.
I affirm that Louis Leakey, also known as Wakuruigi or 'Son of the Sparrow Hawk' speaks Kikuyu fluently.
And that was that. I soon headed out to my first dig!
The first expedition we were looking for dinosaurs. Of course.
But I find *people* more interesting...
...and ended up at the Olduvai Gorge in Tanzania, where I found prehistoric tools, and more!
A camera crew happened to be there at one of my first big finds.
A 20-million-year-old skull, boys, which I've named *Proconsul africanus*.
Digs cost money, so it's lucky I had a talent for publicity.

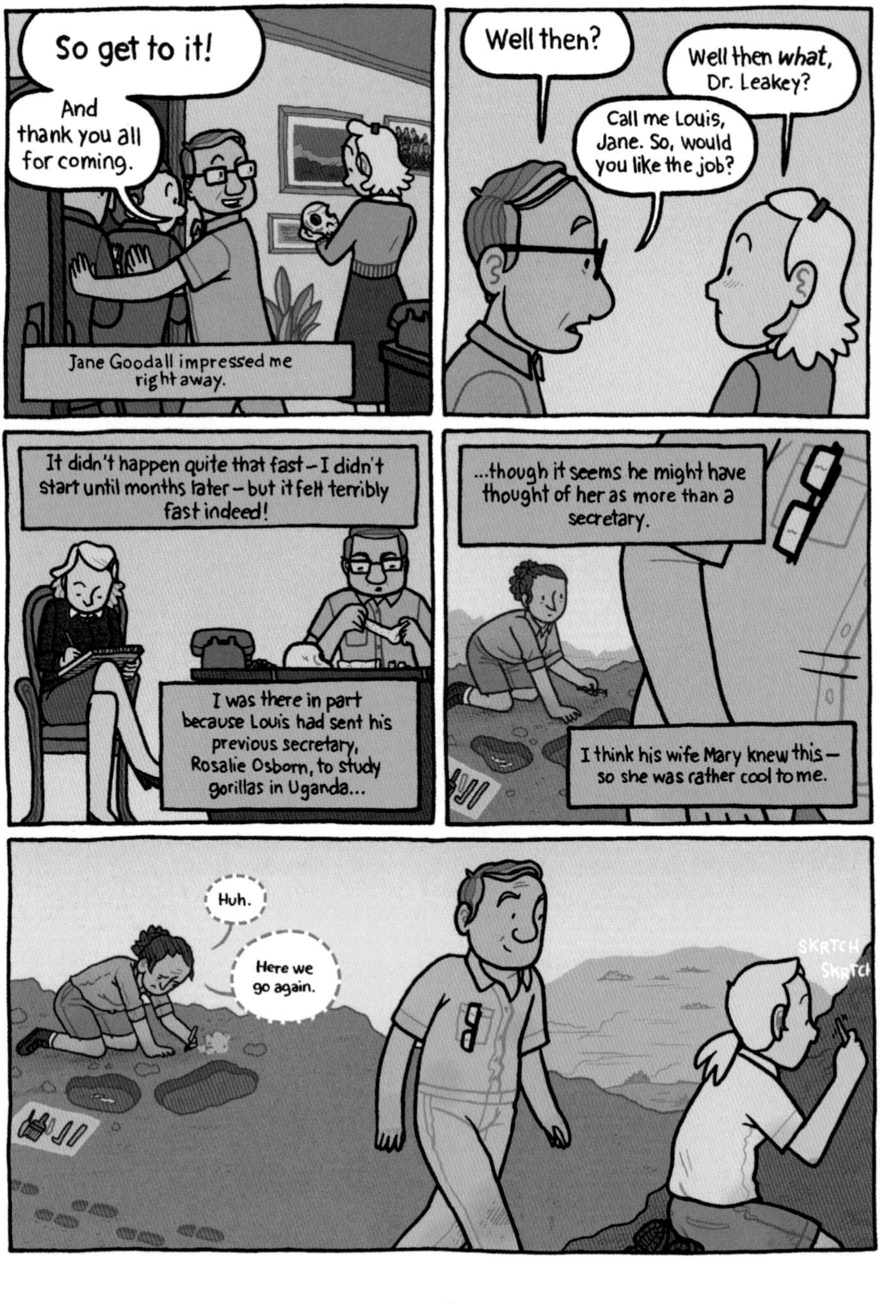
So get to it!
And thank you all for coming.
Jane Goodall impressed me right away.
Well then?
Call me Louis, Jane. So, would you like the job?
Well then *what*, Dr. Leakey?
It didn't happen quite that fast—I didn't start until months later—but it felt terribly fast indeed!
I was there in part because Louis had sent his previous secretary, Rosalie Osborn, to study gorillas in Uganda...
...though it seems he might have thought of her as more than a secretary.
I think his wife Mary knew this—so she was rather cool to me.
Huh.
Here we go again.
SKRTCH

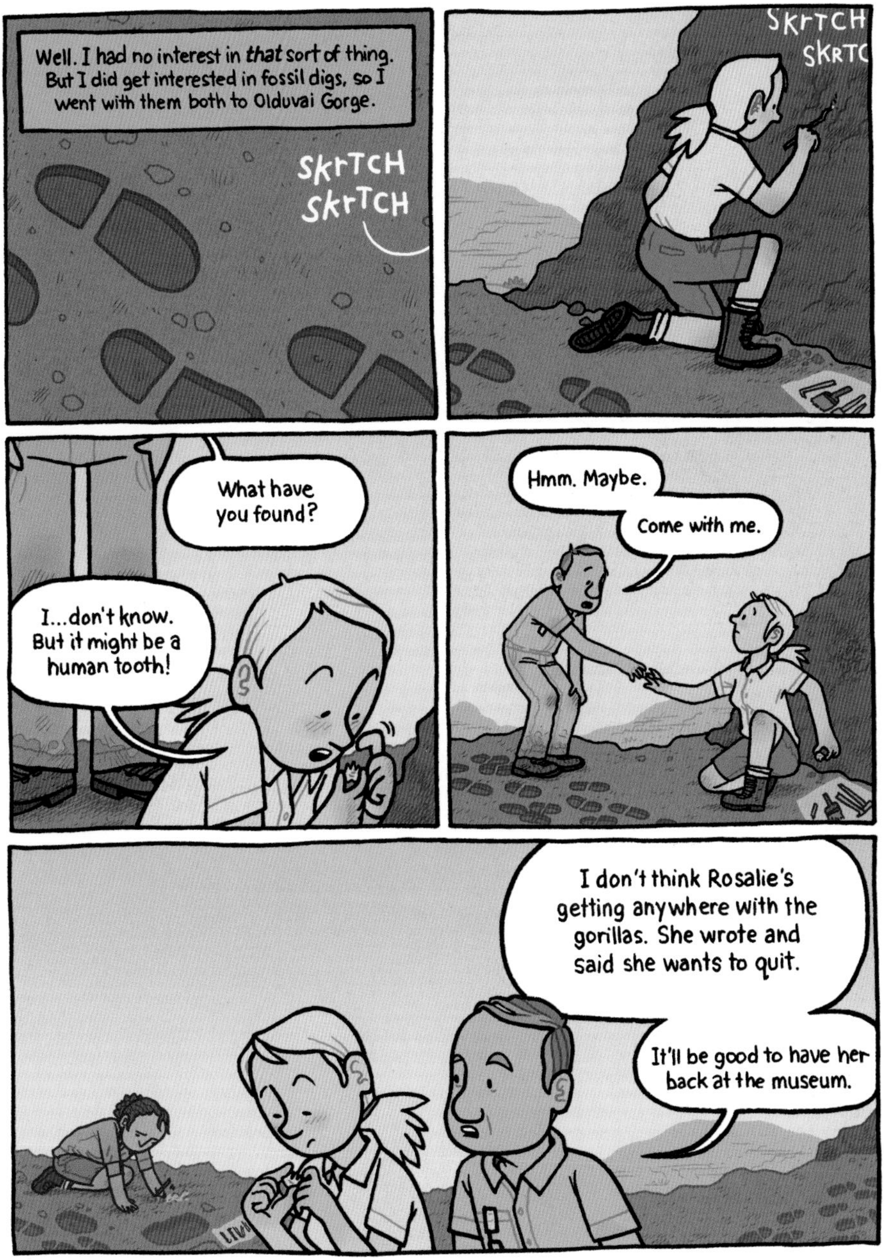
Well. I had no interest in *that* sort of thing. But I did get interested in fossil digs, so I went with them both to Olduvai Gorge.
SKrTCH
SKrTCH
SKrTCH
SKRTC
What have you found?
I...don't know. But it might be a human tooth!
Hmm. Maybe.
Come with me.
I don't think Rosalie's getting anywhere with the gorillas. She wrote and said she wants to quit.
It'll be good to have her back at the museum.

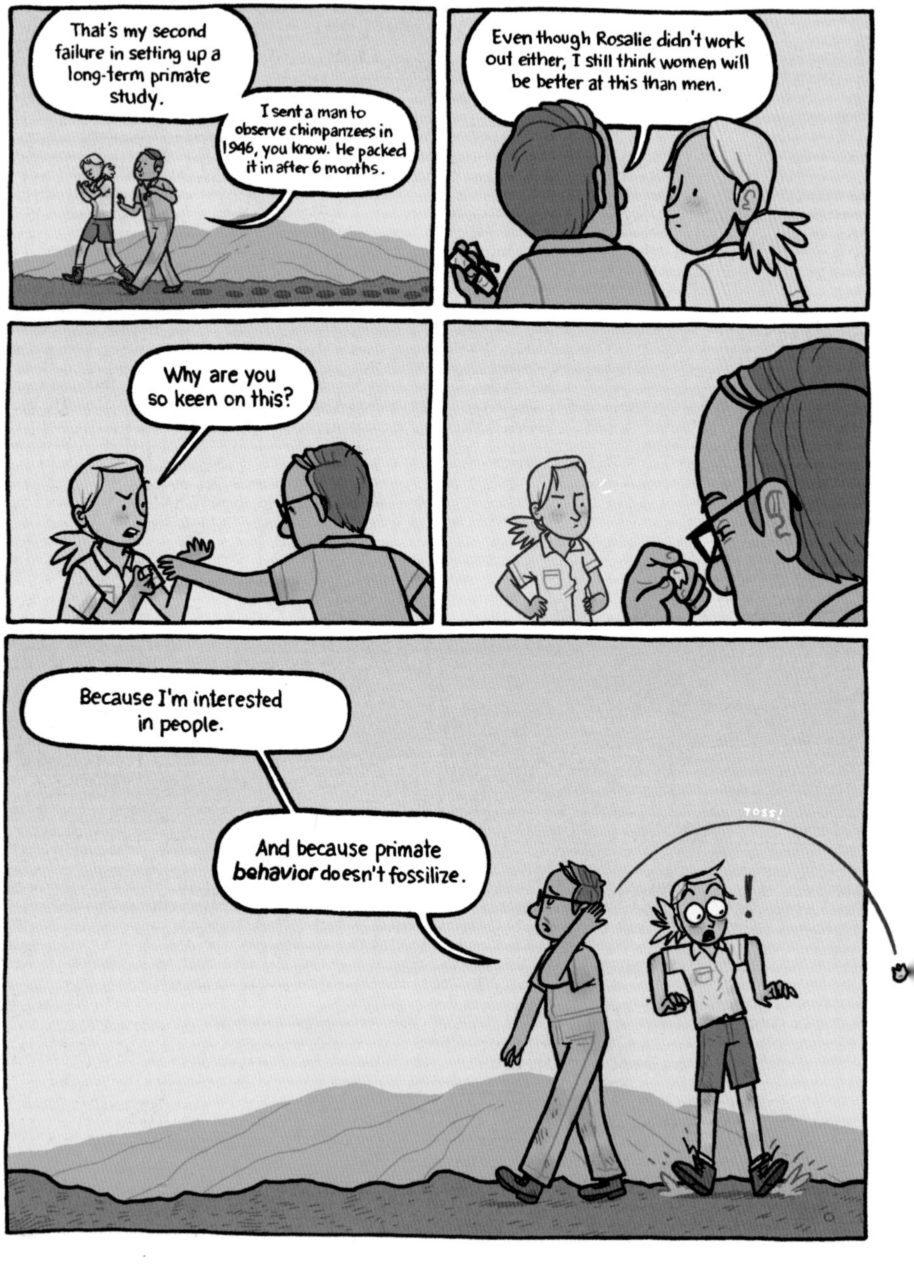
That's my second failure in setting up a long-term primate study.
I sent a man to observe chimpanzees in 1946, you know. He packed it in after 6 months.
Even though Rosalie didn't work out either, I still think women will be better at this than men.
Why are you so keen on this?
Because I'm interested in people.
And because primate ***behavior*** doesn't fossilize.
TOSS!
!

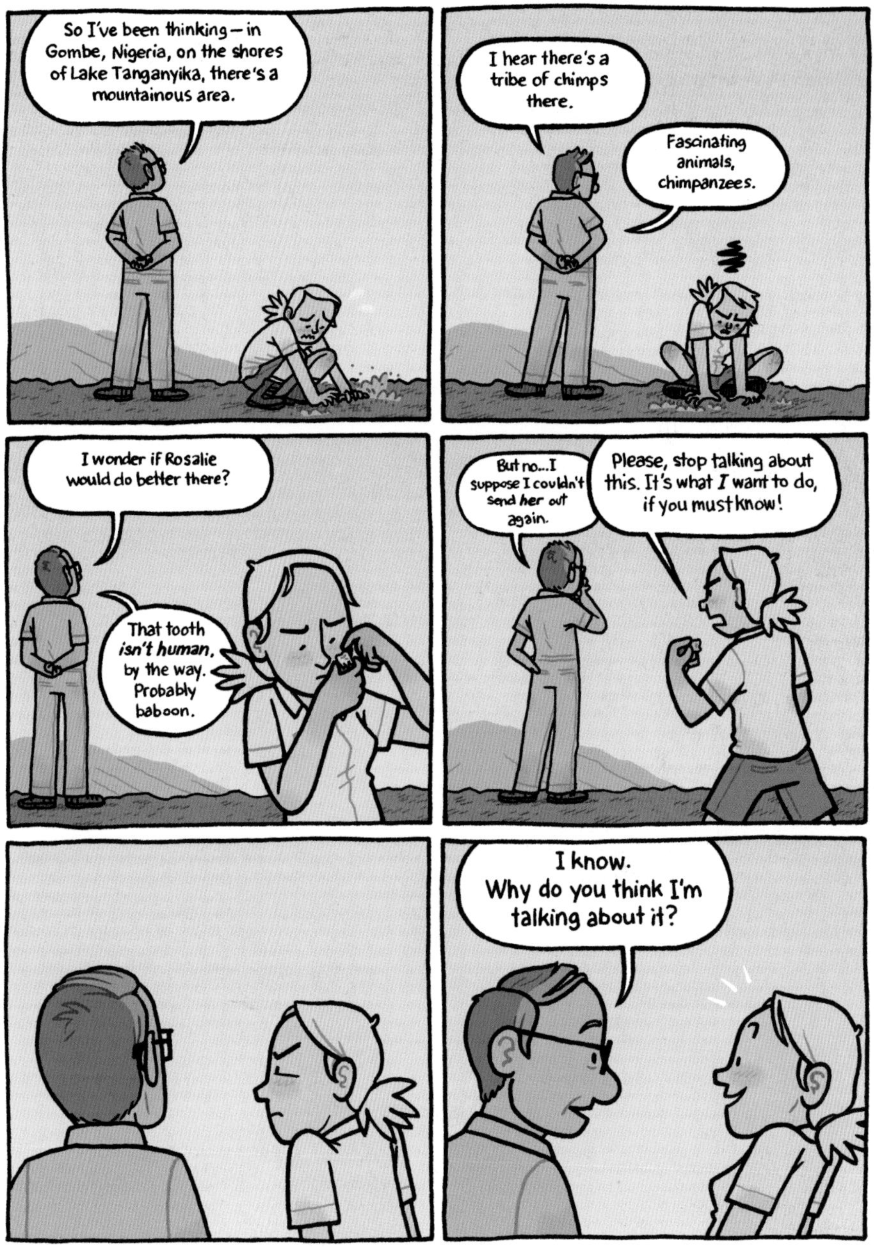
So I've been thinking—in Gombe, Nigeria, on the shores of Lake Tanganyika, there's a mountainous area.
I hear there's a tribe of chimps there.
Fascinating animals, chimpanzees.
I wonder if Rosalie would do better there?
That tooth *isn't human*, by the way. Probably baboon.
But no...I suppose I couldn't send *her* out again.
Please, stop talking about this. It's what *I* want to do, if you must know!
I know.
Why do you think I'm talking about it?

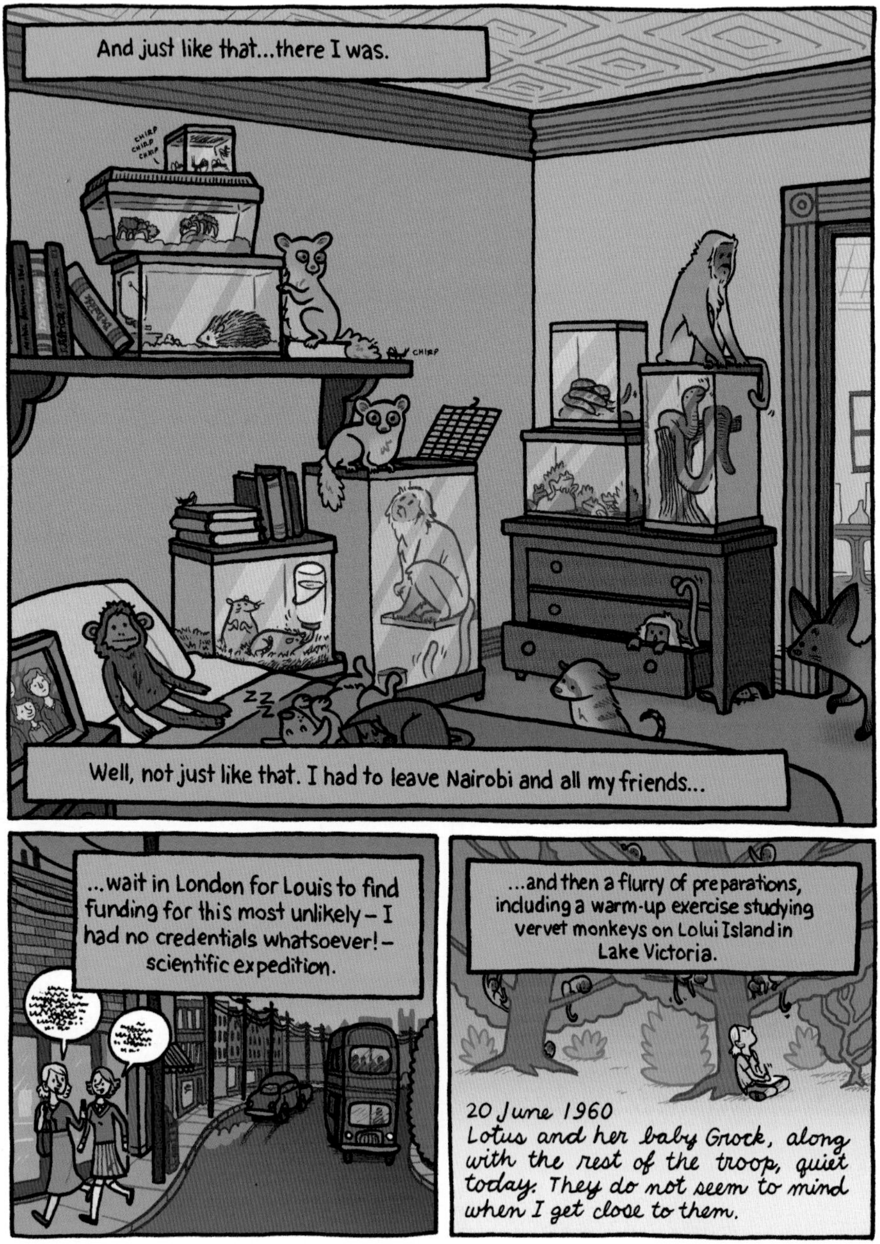
And just like that...there I was.
CHIRP CHIRP CHIRP
CHIRP
Well, not just like that. I had to leave Nairobi and all my friends...
...wait in London for Louis to find funding for this most unlikely – I had no credentials whatsoever! – scientific expedition.
...and then a flurry of preparations, including a warm-up exercise studying vervet monkeys on Lolui Island in Lake Victoria.
20 June 1960
Lotus and her baby Grock, along with the rest of the troop, quiet today. They do not seem to mind when I get close to them.

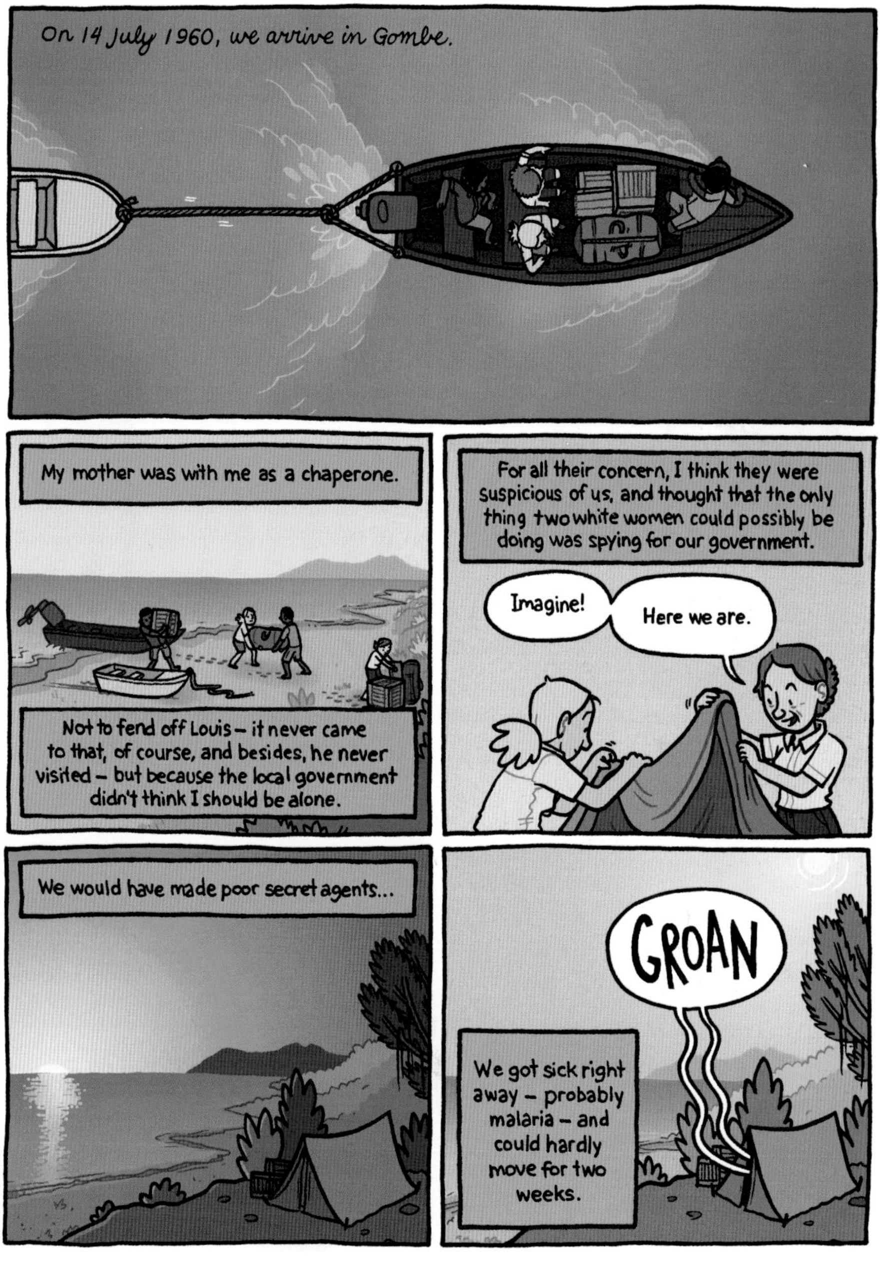
On 14 July 1960, we arrive in Gombe.
My mother was with me as a chaperone.
Not to fend off Louis – it never came to that, of course, and besides, he never visited – but because the local government didn't think I should be alone.
For all their concern, I think they were suspicious of us, and thought that the only thing two white women could possibly be doing was spying for our government.
Imagine!
Here we are.
We would have made poor secret agents...
GROAN
We got sick right away – probably malaria – and could hardly move for two weeks.

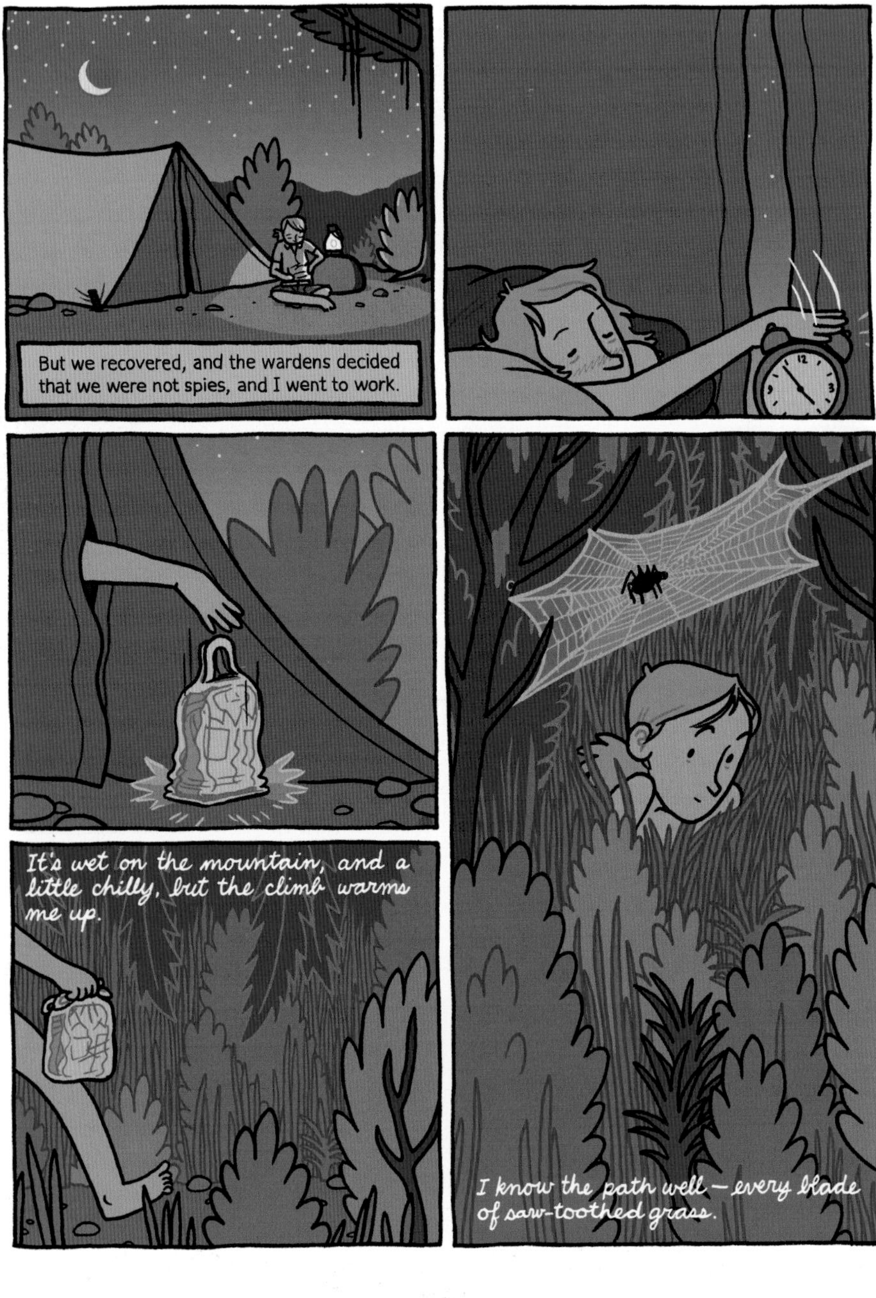
But we recovered, and the wardens decided that we were not spies, and I went to work.
12
3
9
It's wet on the mountain, and a little chilly, but the climb warms me up.
I know the path well — every blade of saw-toothed grass.

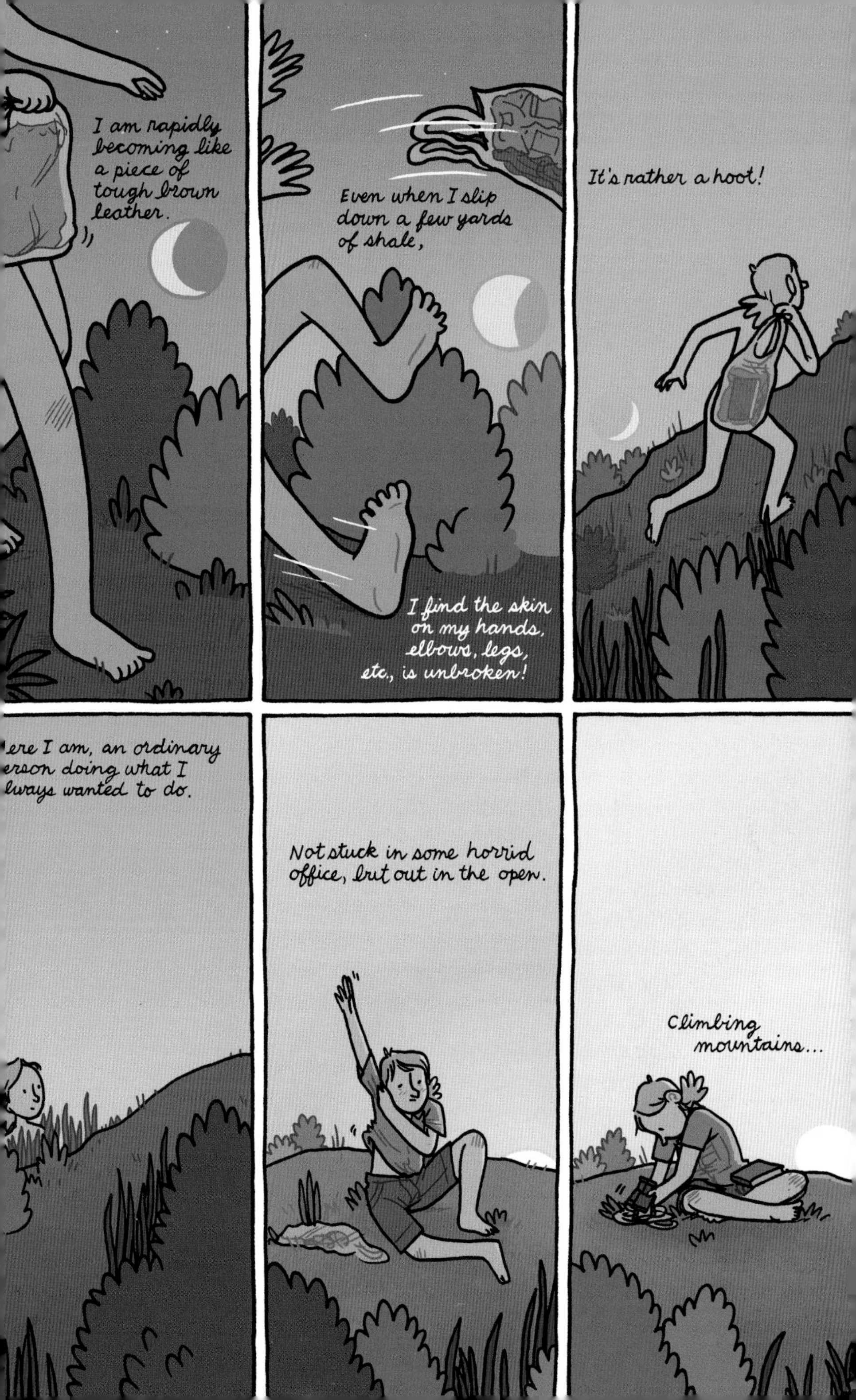
I am rapidly becoming like a piece of tough brown leather.
Even when I slip down a few yards of shale,
I find the skin on my hands, elbows, legs, etc., is unbroken!
It's rather a hoot!
ere I am, an ordinary erson doing what I lways wanted to do.
Not stuck in some horrid office, but out in the open.
Climbing mountains...

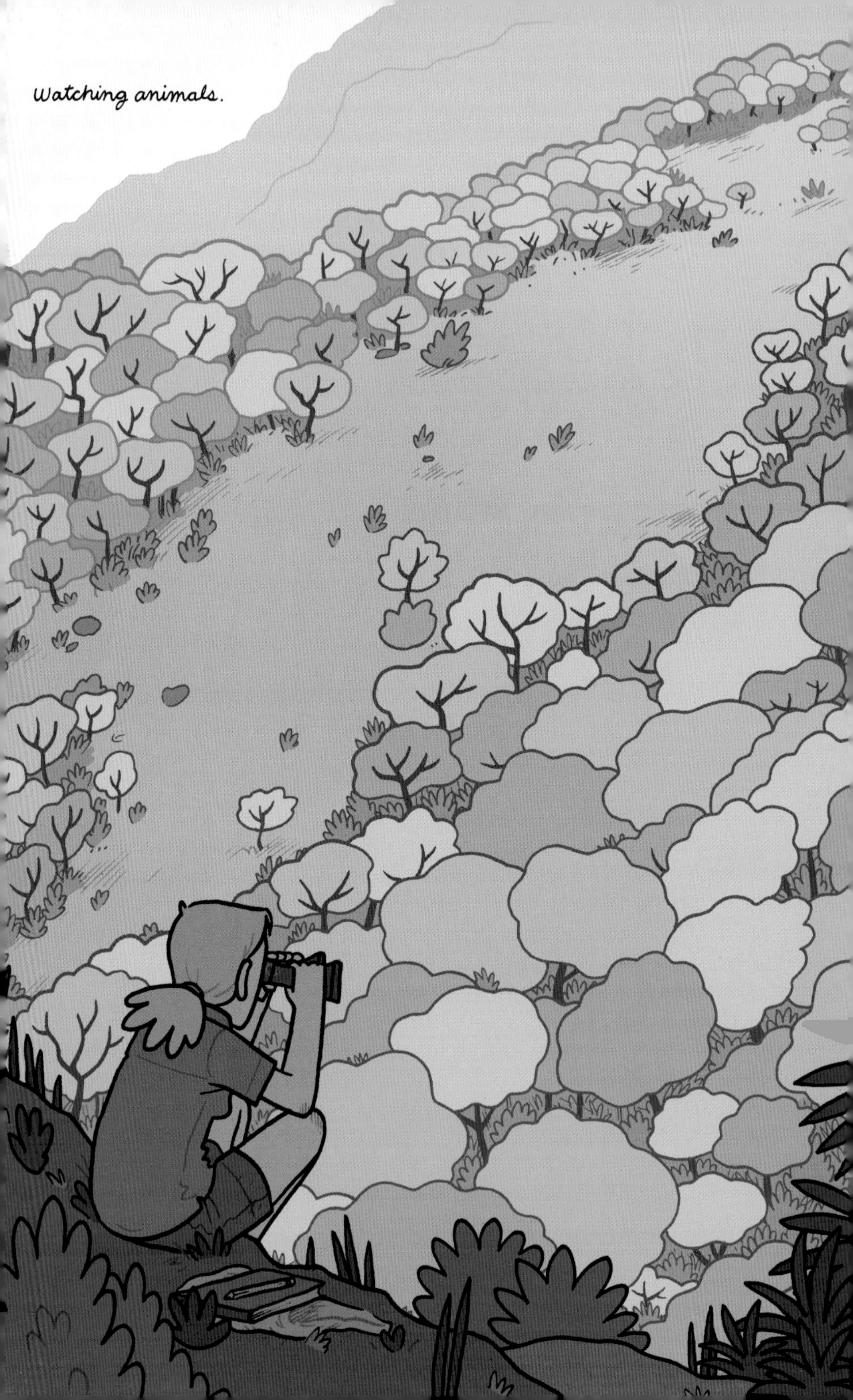
Watching animals.

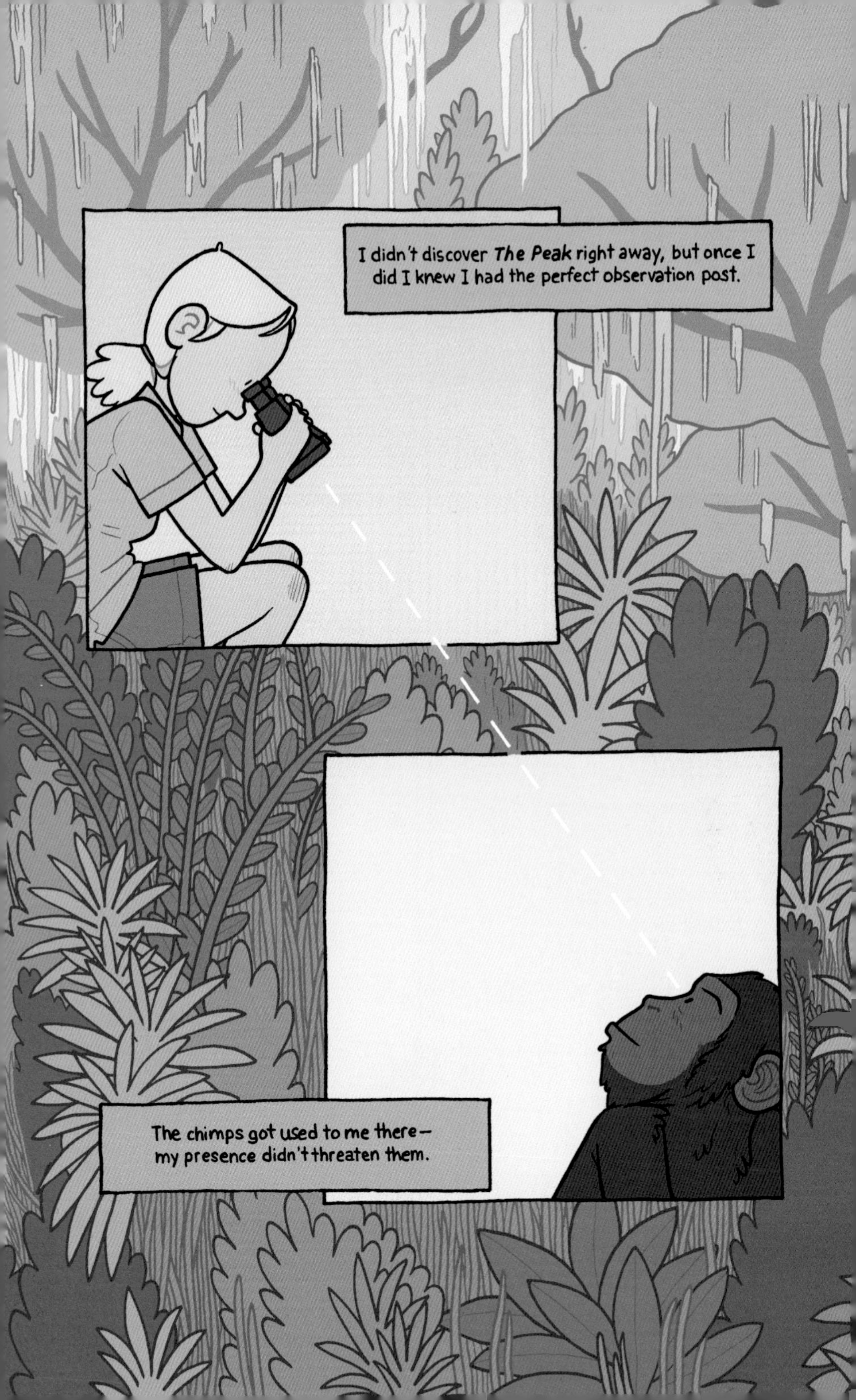
I didn't discover *The Peak* right away, but once I did I knew I had the perfect observation post.
The chimps got used to me there—my presence didn't threaten them.

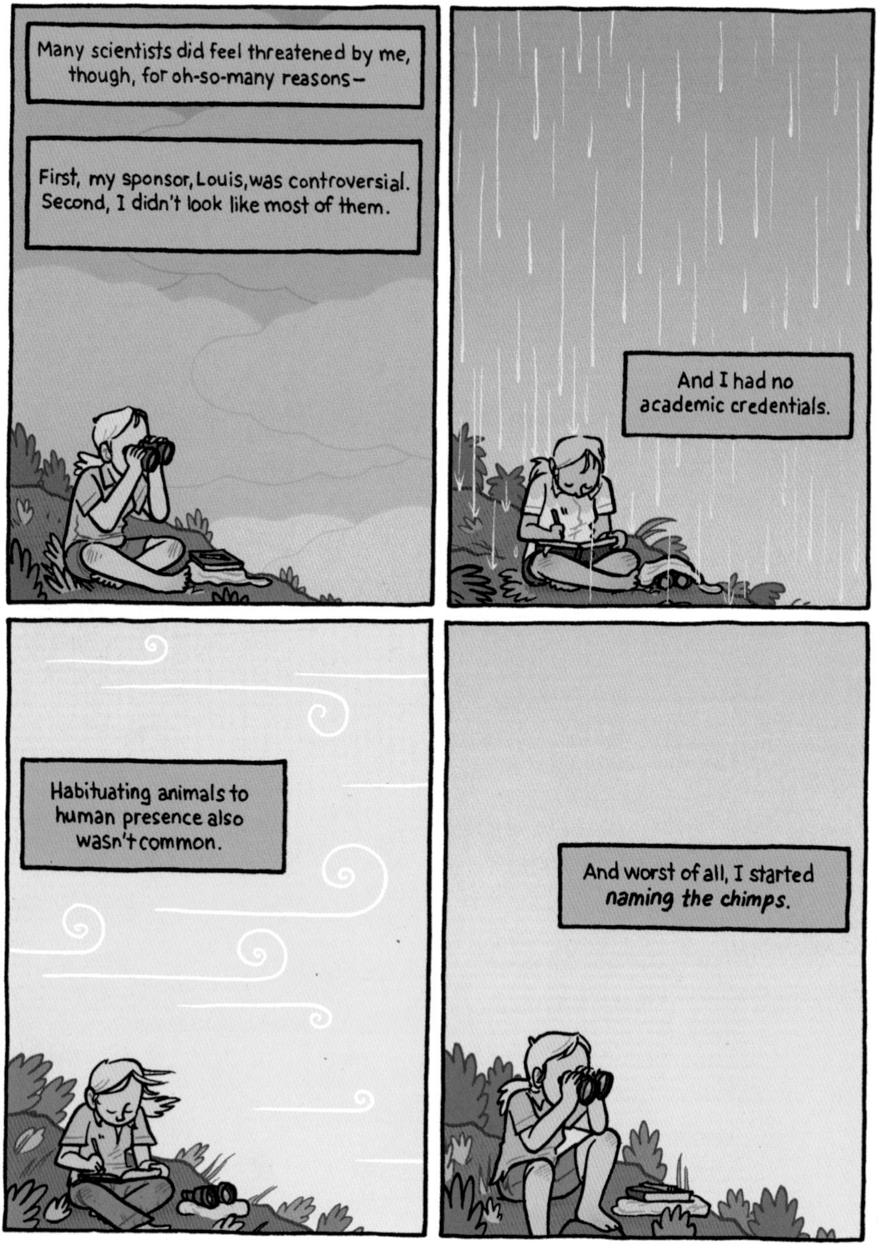

Many scientists did feel threatened by me, though, for oh-so-many reasons—
First, my sponsor, Louis, was controversial. Second, I didn't look like most of them.
And I had no academic credentials.
Habituating animals to human presence also wasn't common.
And worst of all, I started *naming the chimps*.

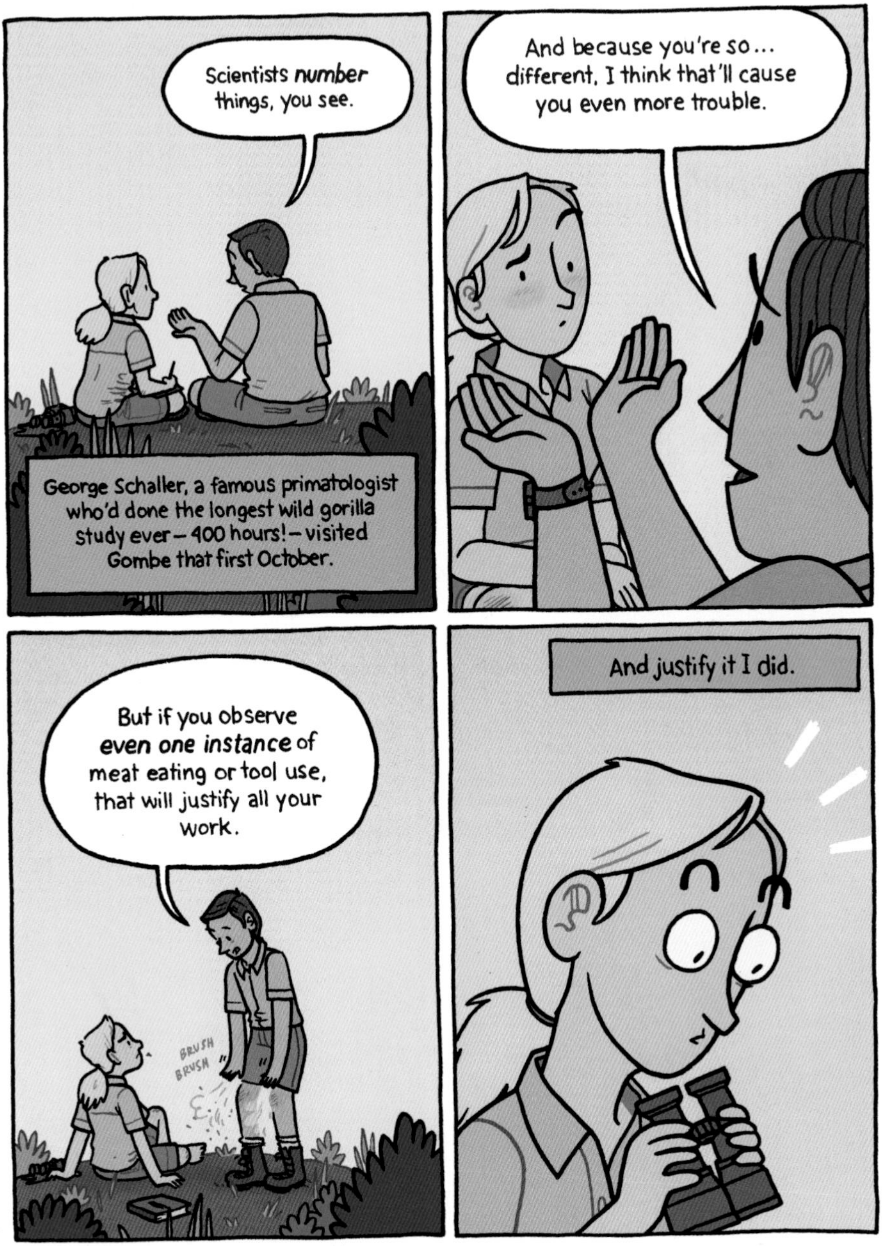
Scientists *number* things, you see.
George Schaller, a famous primatologist who'd done the longest wild gorilla study ever — 400 hours! — visited Gombe that first October.
And because you're so... different, I think that'll cause you even more trouble.
But if you observe **even one instance** of meat eating or tool use, that will justify all your work.
BRUSH BRUSH
And justify it I did.

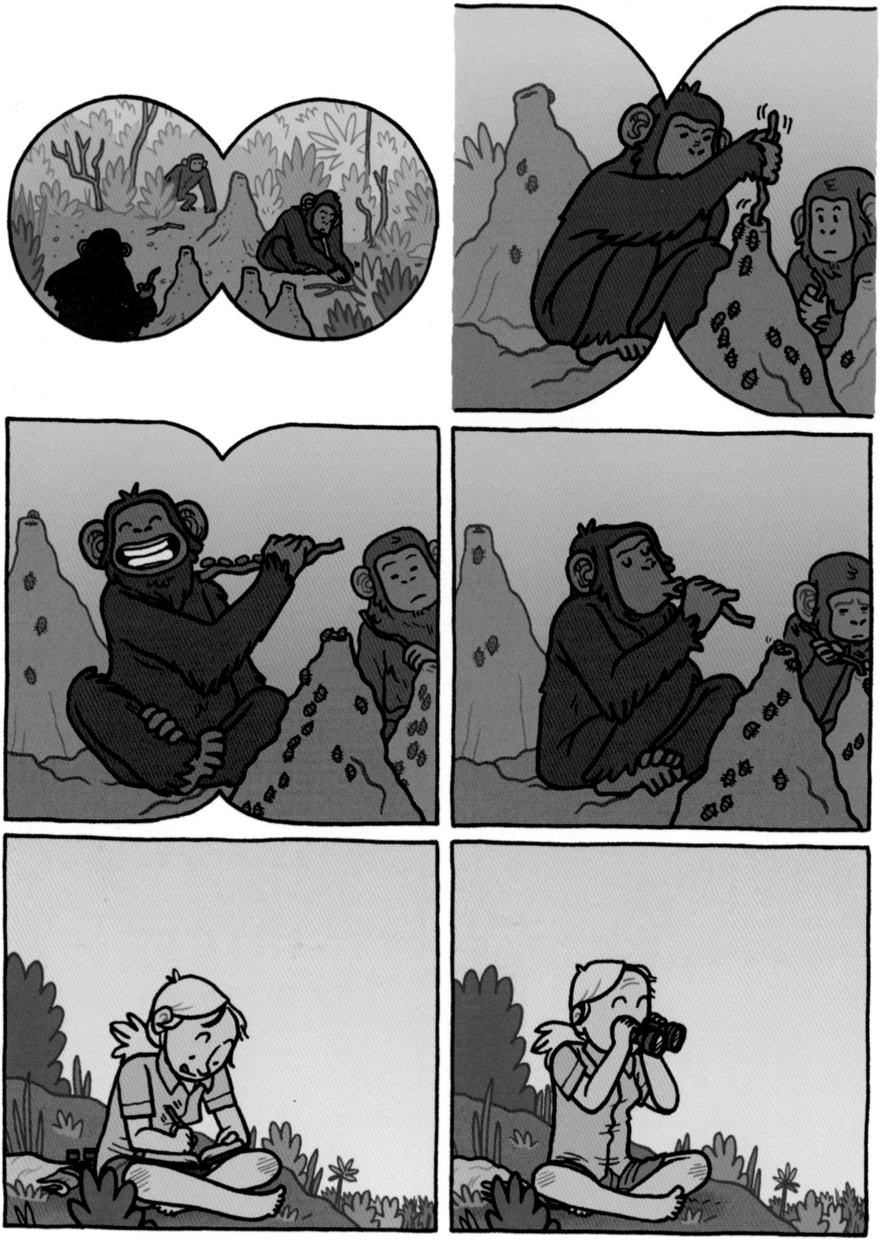

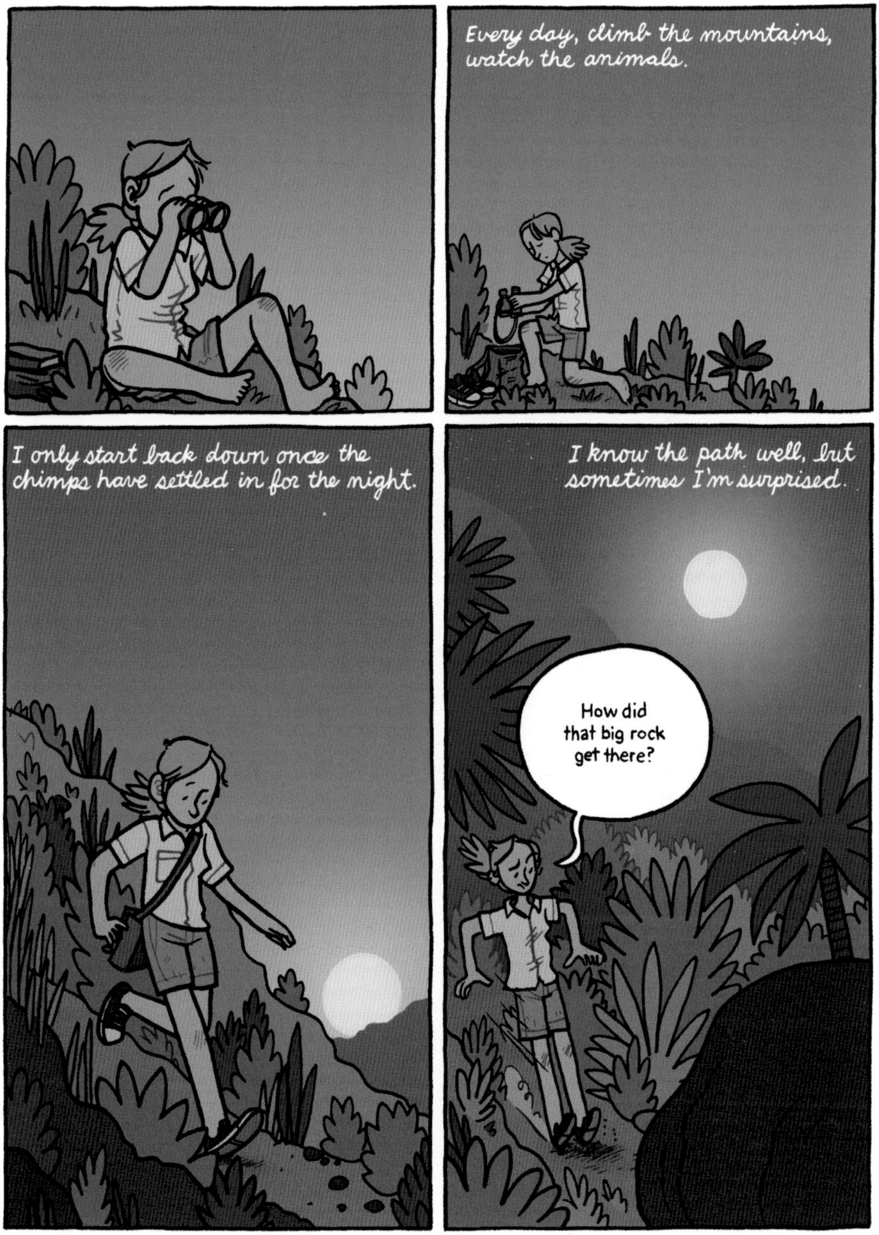
Every day, climb the mountains, watch the animals.
I only start back down once the chimps have settled in for the night.
I know the path well, but sometimes I'm surprised.
How did that big rock get there?

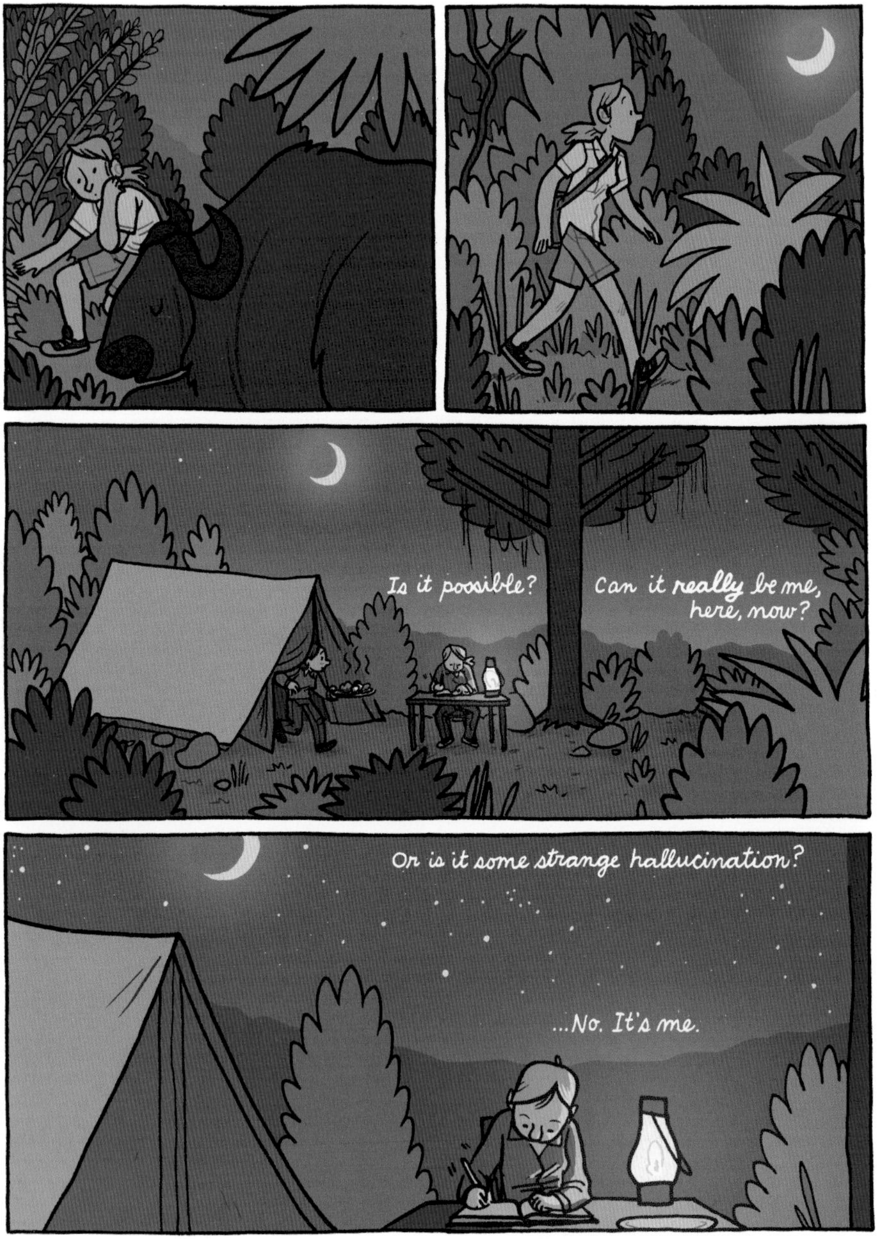
Is it possible?
Can it really be me, here, now?
Or is it some strange hallucination?
...No. It's me.

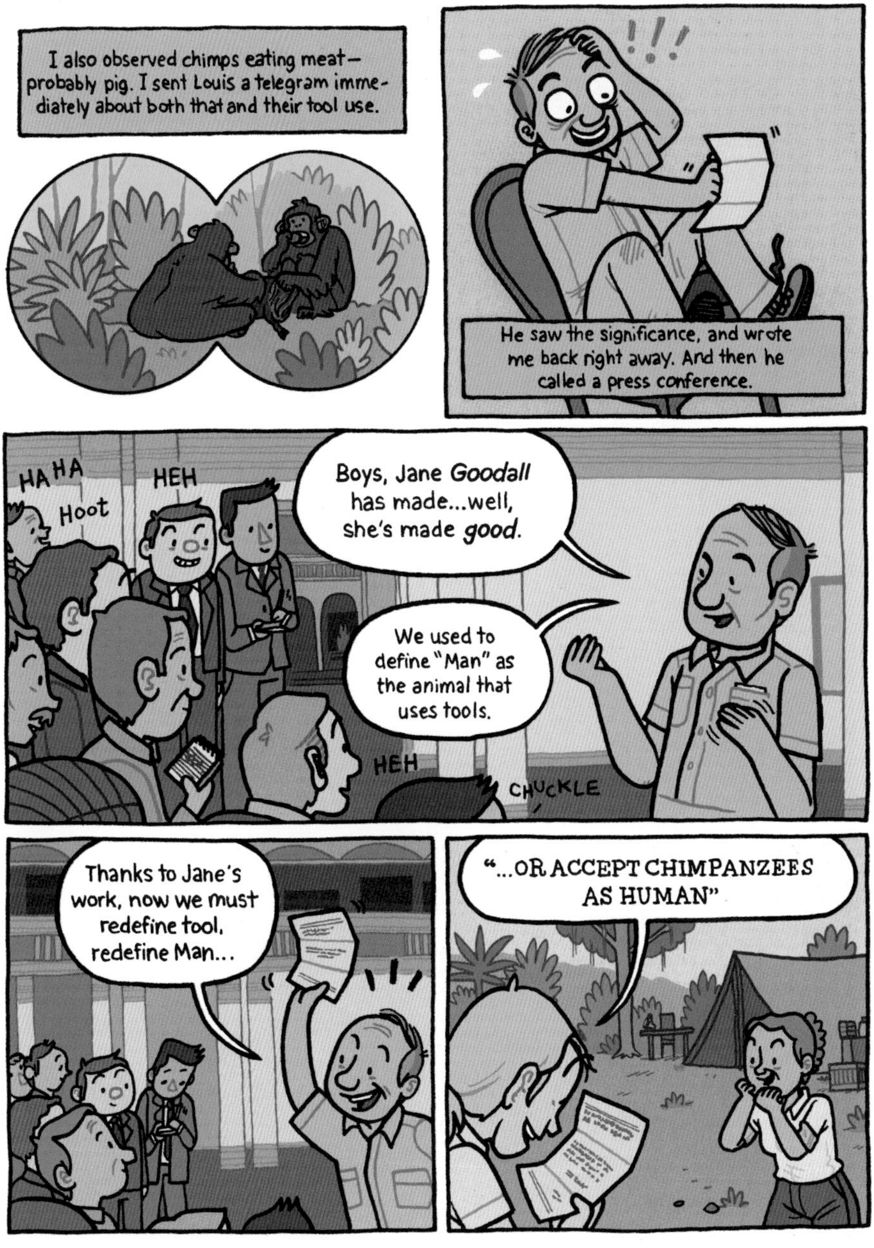
I also observed chimps eating meat—probably pig. I sent Louis a telegram immediately about both that and their tool use.
!!!
He saw the significance, and wrote me back right away. And then he called a press conference.
HAHA
HEH
Hoot
Boys, Jane *Goodall* has made...well, she's made *good*.
We used to define "Man" as the animal that uses tools.
HEH
CHUCKLE
Thanks to Jane's work, now we must redefine tool, redefine Man...
"...OR ACCEPT CHIMPANZEES AS HUMAN"

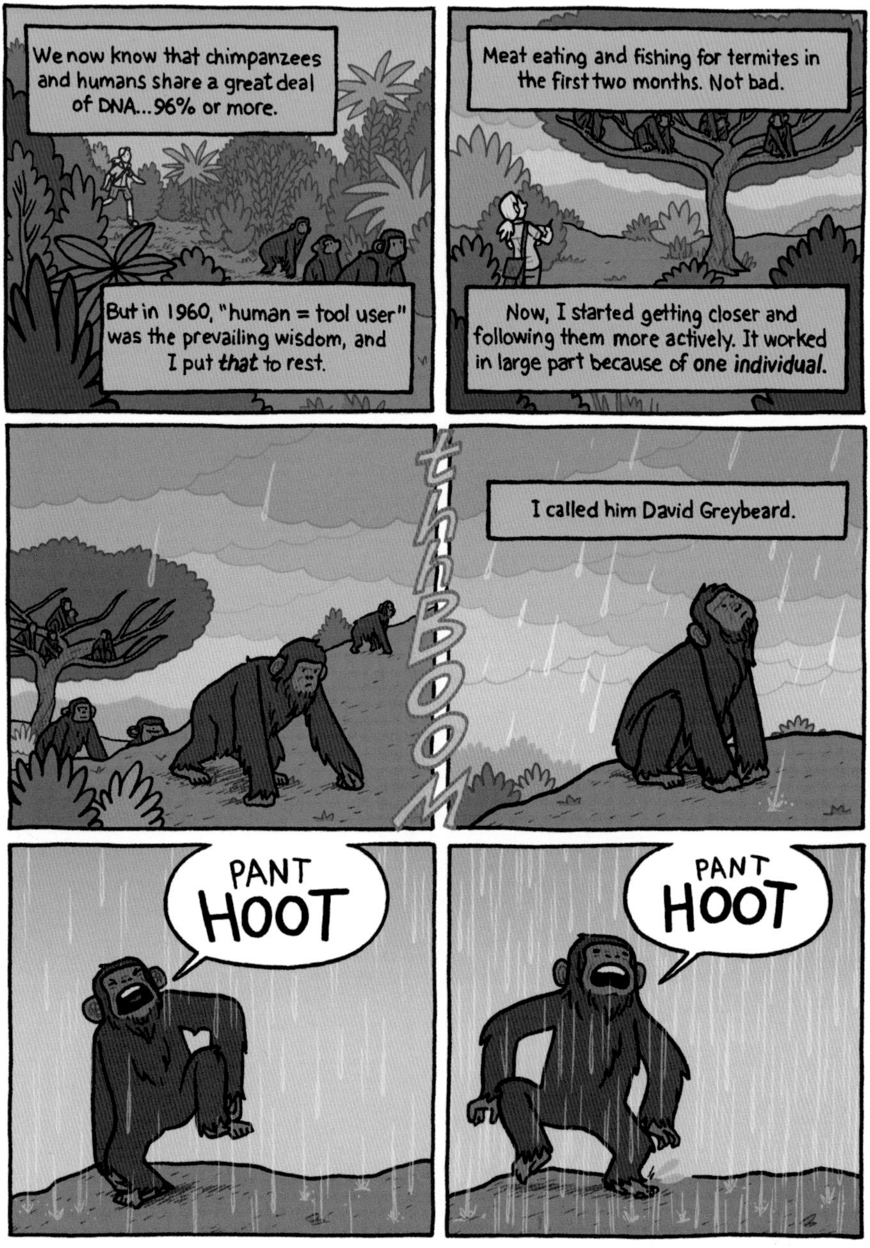
We now know that chimpanzees and humans share a great deal of DNA...96% or more.
But in 1960, "human = tool user" was the prevailing wisdom, and I put *that* to rest.
Meat eating and fishing for termites in the first two months. Not bad.
Now, I started getting closer and following them more actively. It worked in large part because of one *individual*.
thhBOOM
I called him David Greybeard.
PANT HOOT
PANT HOOT

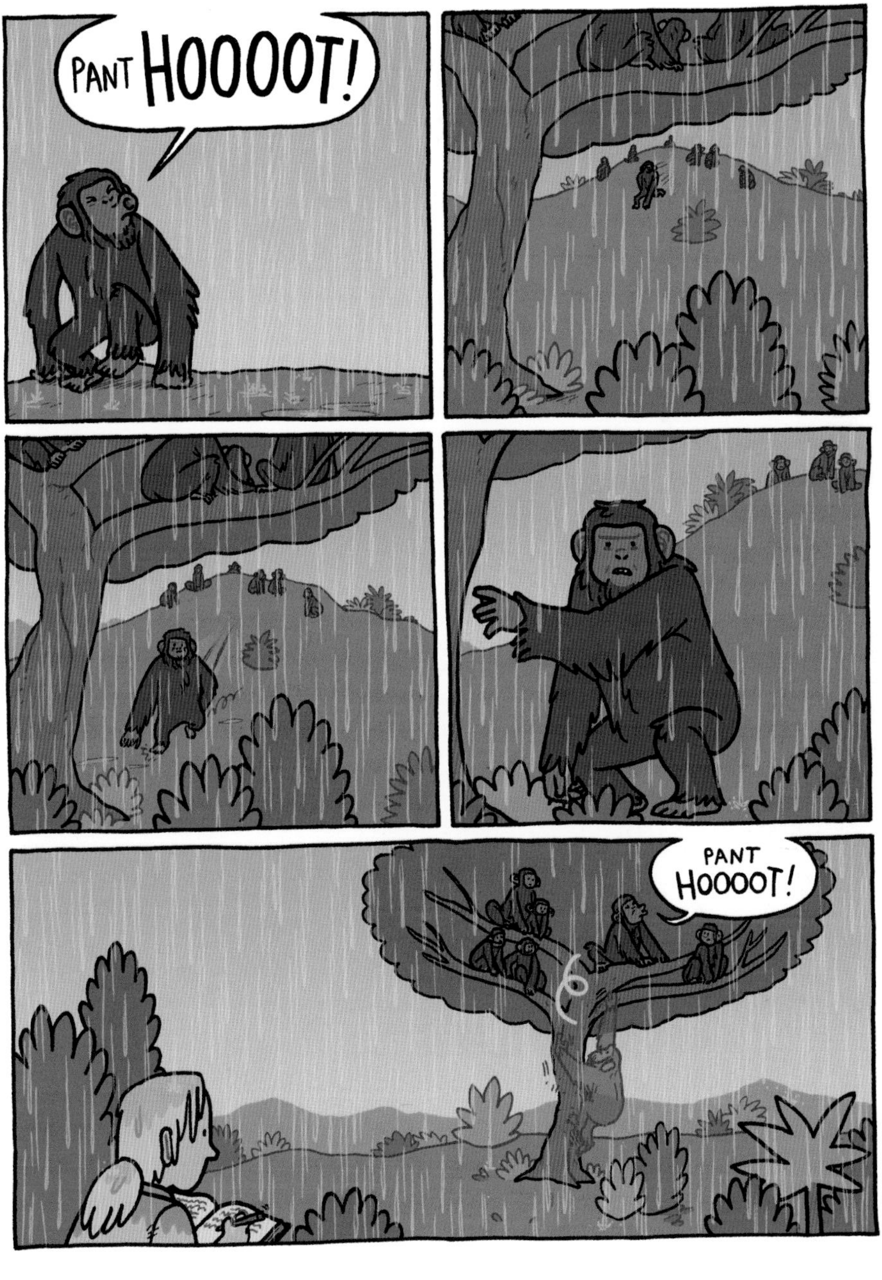
PANT HOOOOT!
PANT HOOOOT!

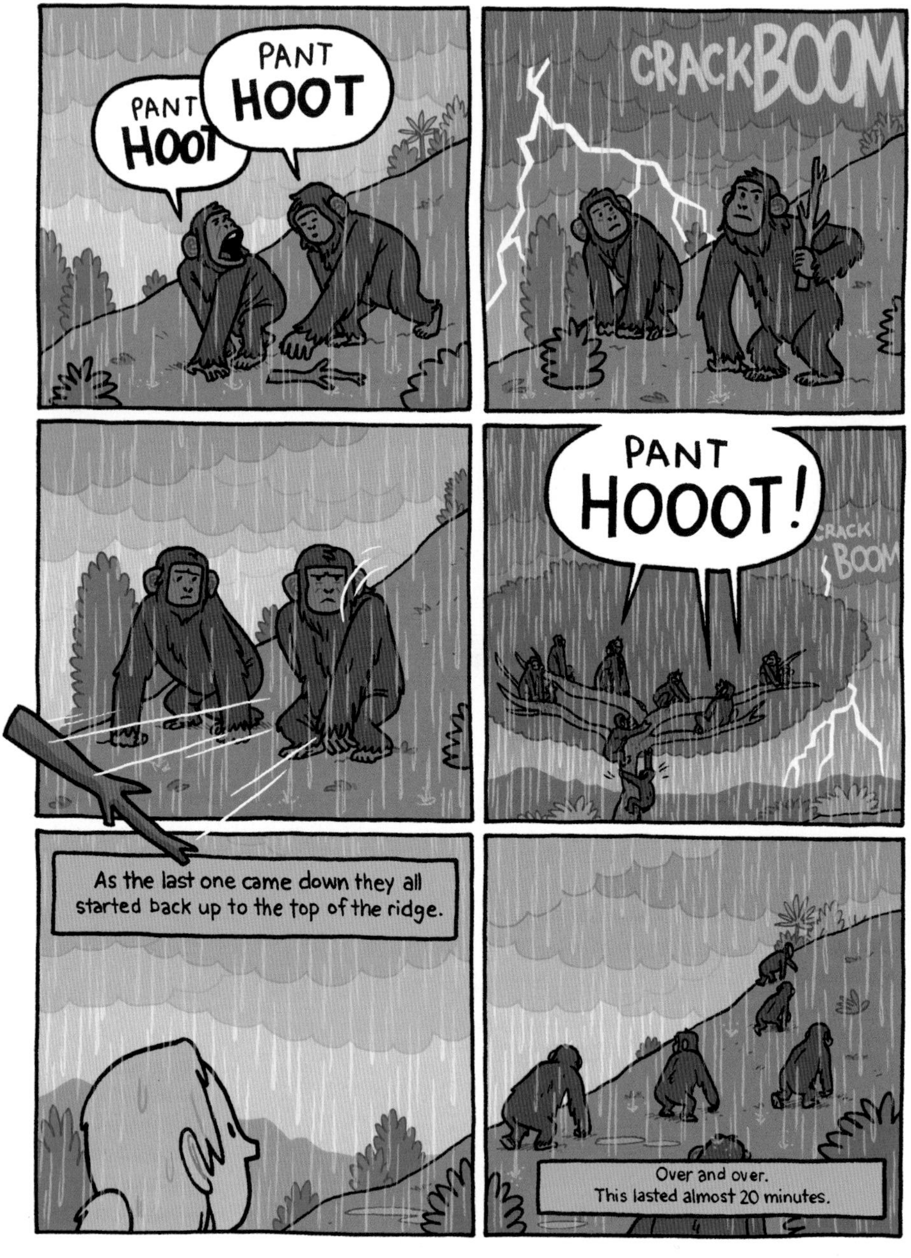
PANT HOOT
PANT HOOT
CRACK BOOM
PANT HOOOT!
CRACK BOOM
As the last one came down they all started back up to the top of the ridge.
Over and over.
This lasted almost 20 minutes.

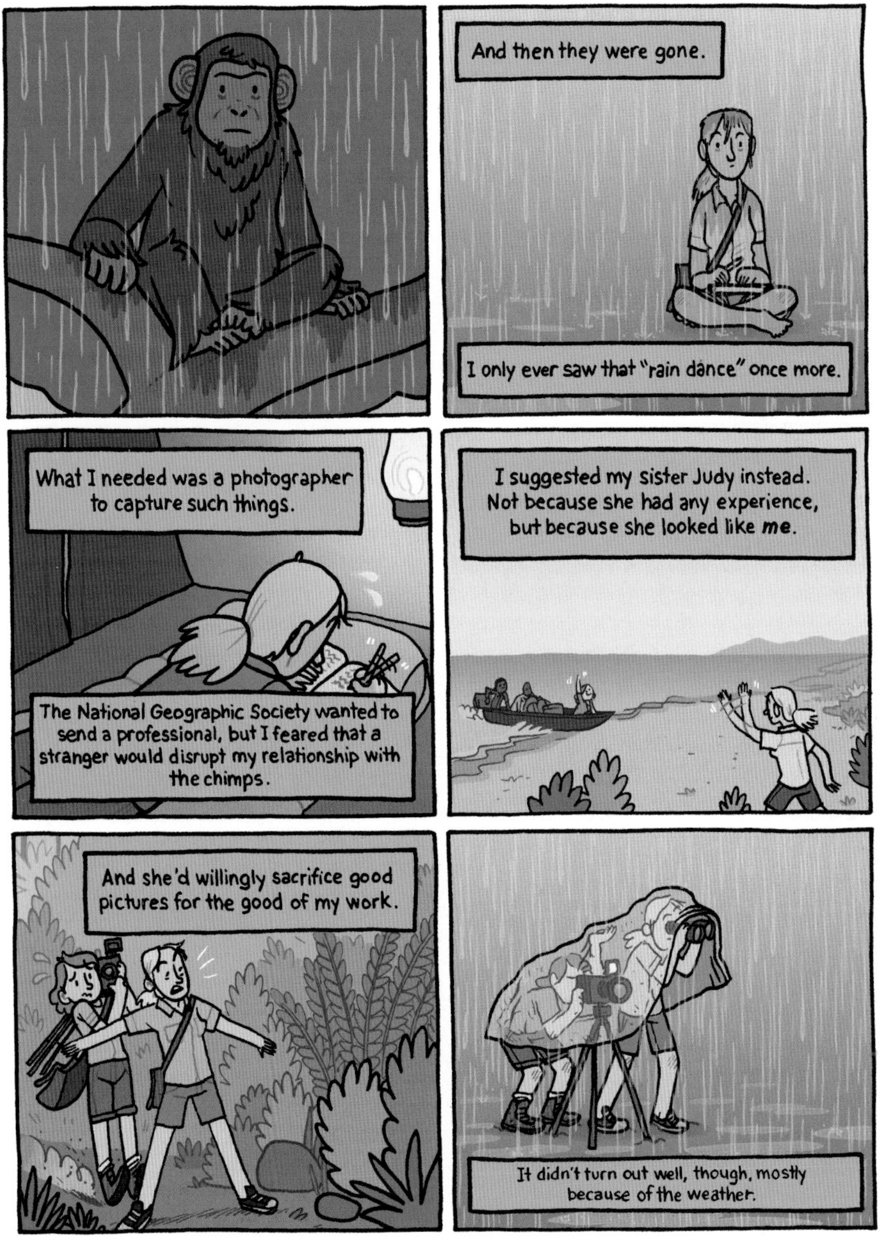
And then they were gone.
I only ever saw that "rain dance" once more.
What I needed was a photographer to capture such things.
The National Geographic Society wanted to send a professional, but I feared that a stranger would disrupt my relationship with the chimps.
I suggested my sister Judy instead. Not because she had any experience, but because she looked like *me*.
And she'd willingly sacrifice good pictures for the good of my work.
It didn't turn out well, though, mostly because of the weather.

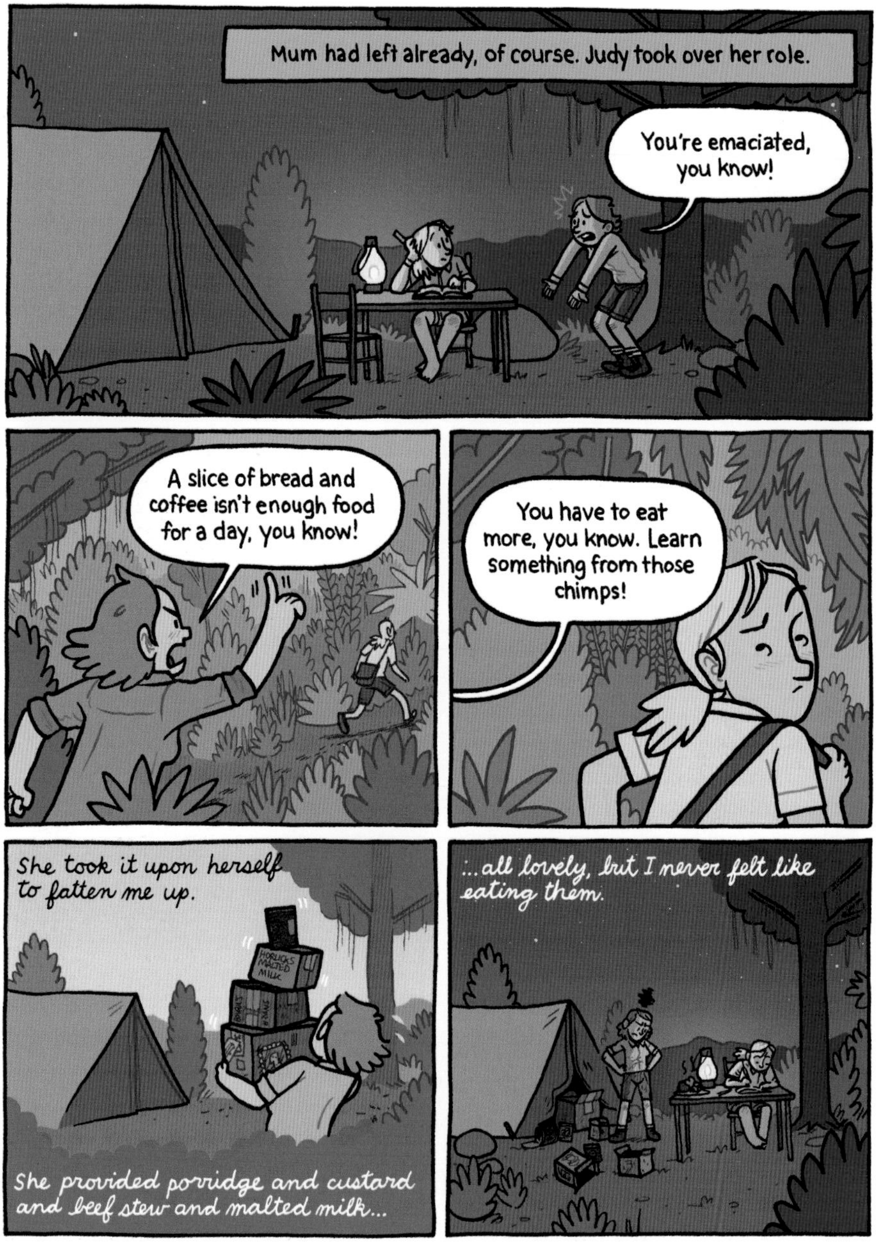
Mum had left already, of course. Judy took over her role.
You're emaciated, you know!
A slice of bread and coffee isn't enough food for a day, you know!
You have to eat more, you know. Learn something from those chimps!
She took it upon herself to fatten me up.
HORLICKS MALTED MILK
She provided porridge and custard and beef stew and malted milk...
...all lovely, but I never felt like eating them.

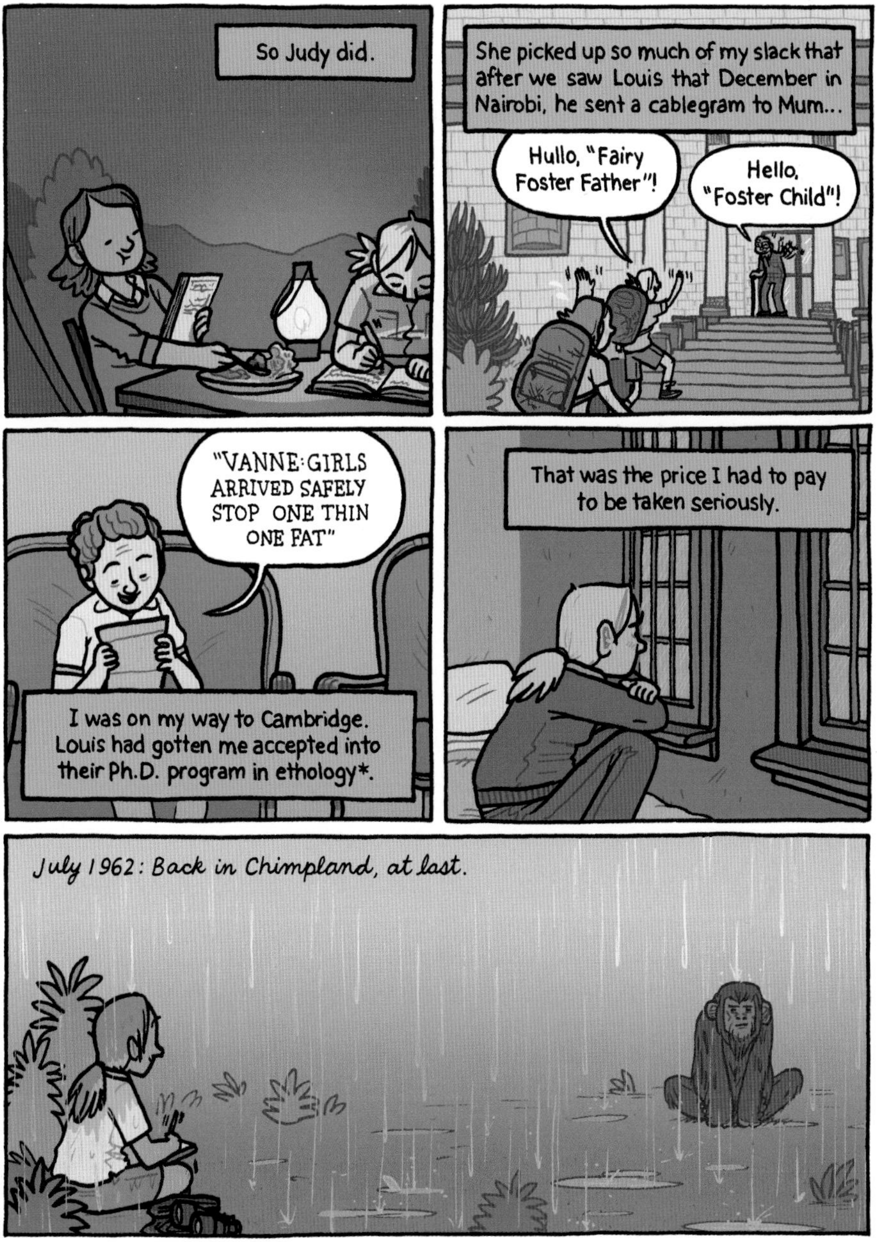
So Judy did.
She picked up so much of my slack that after we saw Louis that December in Nairobi, he sent a cablegram to Mum...
Hullo, "Fairy Foster Father"!
Hello, "Foster Child"!
"VANNE: GIRLS ARRIVED SAFELY STOP ONE THIN ONE FAT"
I was on my way to Cambridge. Louis had gotten me accepted into their Ph.D. program in ethology*.
That was the price I had to pay to be taken seriously.
July 1962: Back in Chimpland, at last.

* Ethology: the study of animal behavior

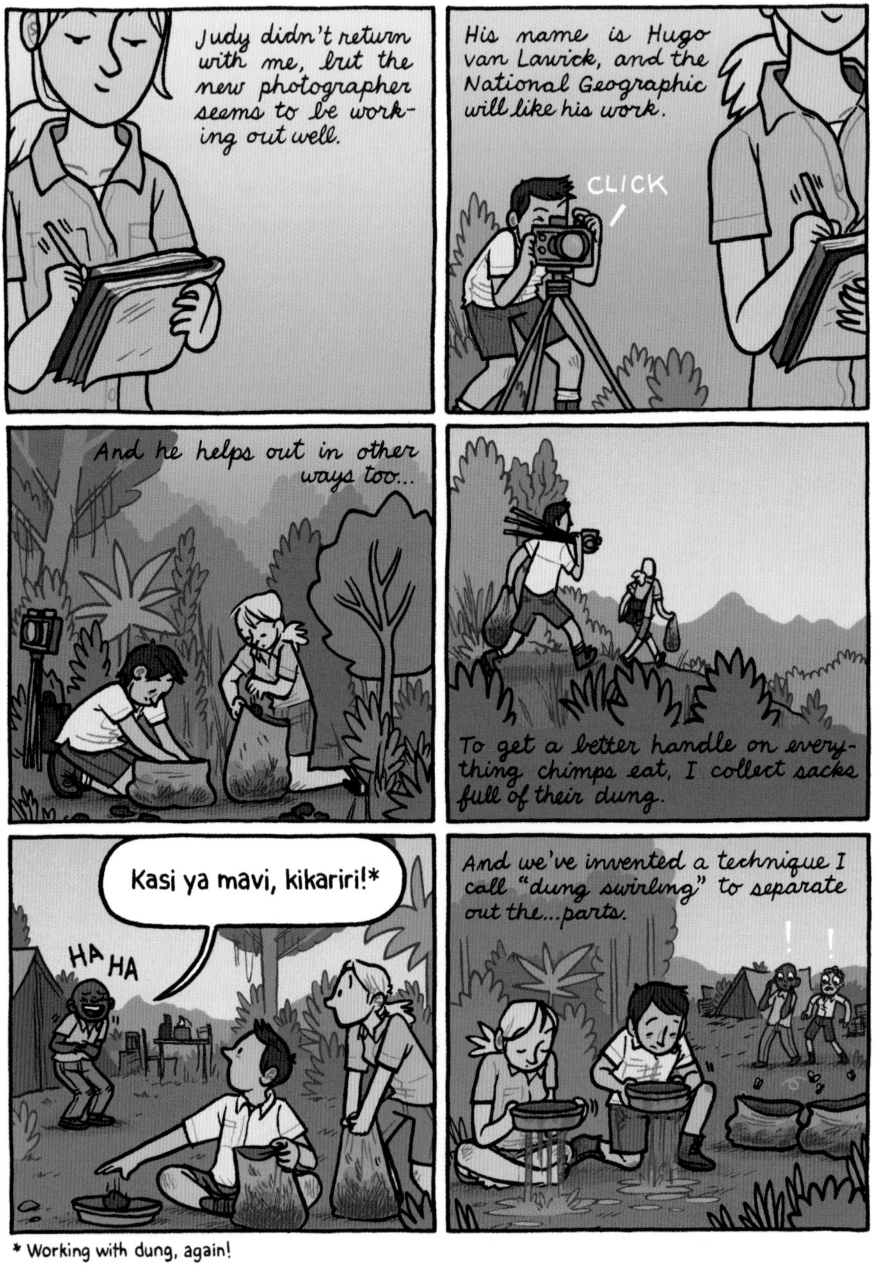
Judy didn't return with me, but the new photographer seems to be working out well.
His name is Hugo van Lawick, and the National Geographic will like his work.
CLICK
And he helps out in other ways too...
To get a better handle on everything chimps eat, I collect sacks full of their dung.
Kasi ya mavi, kikariri!*
HA HA
And we've invented a technique I call "dung swirling" to separate out the...parts.
! !

* Working with dung, again!

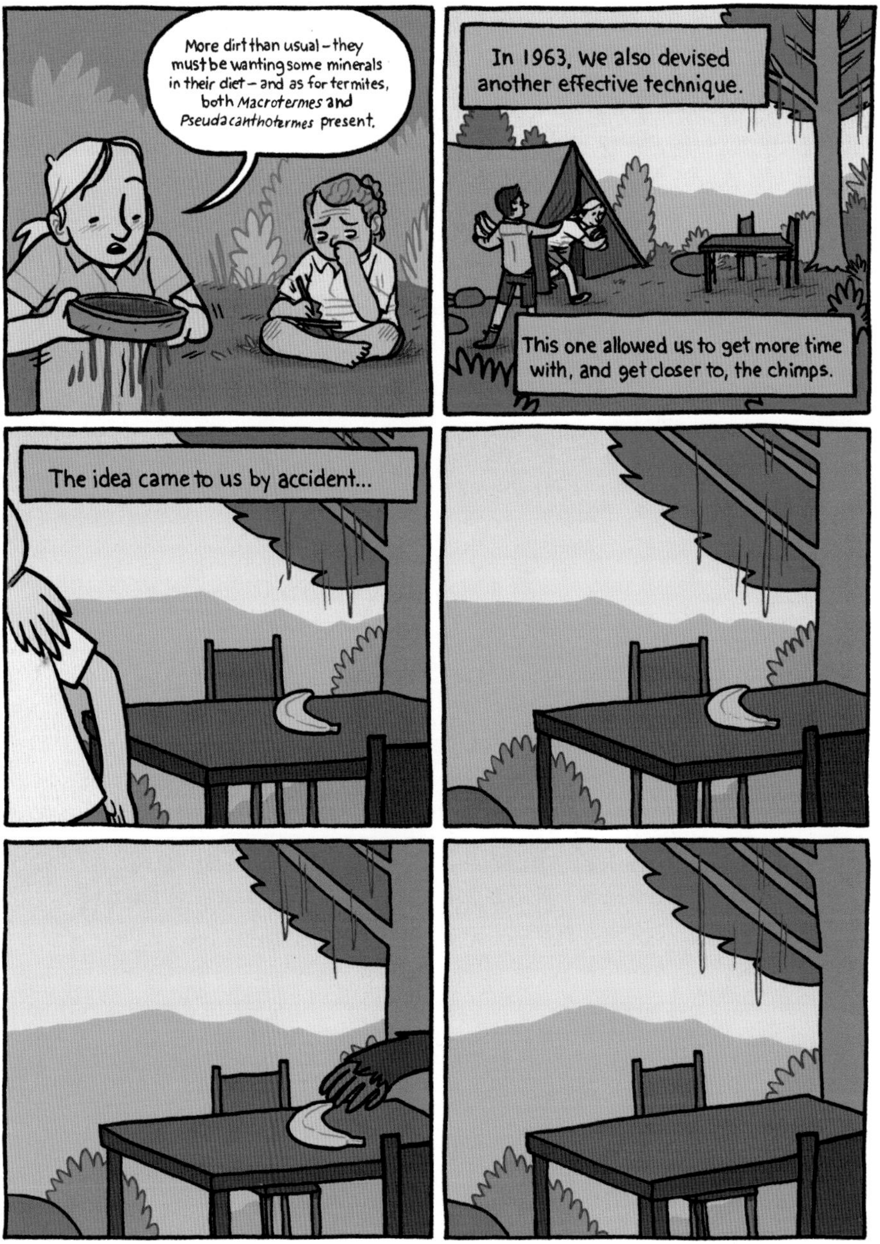
More dirt than usual – they must be wanting some minerals in their diet – and as for termites, both *Macrotermes* and *Pseudacanthotermes* present.
In 1963, we also devised another effective technique.
This one allowed us to get more time with, and get closer to, the chimps.
The idea came to us by accident...

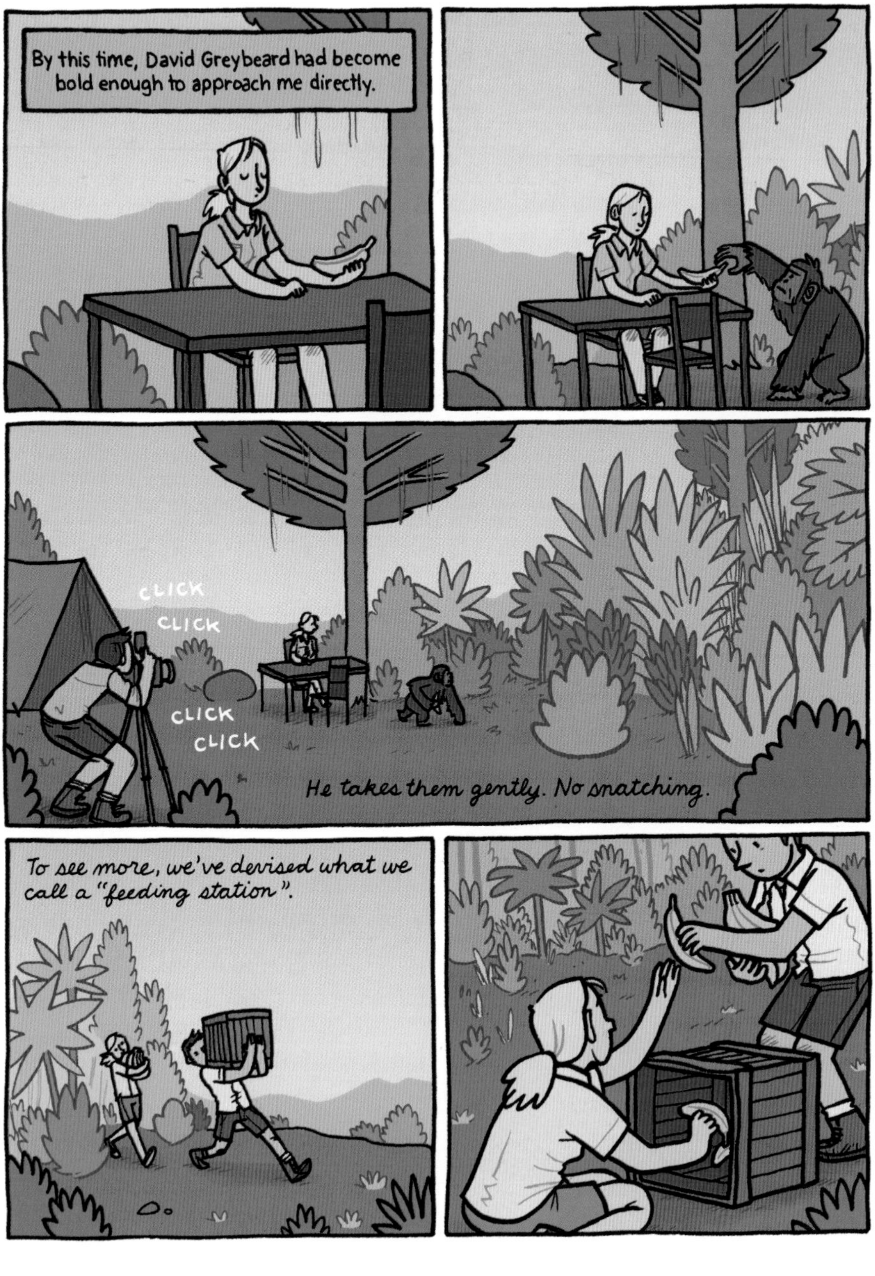
By this time, David Greybeard had become bold enough to approach me directly.
CLICK
CLICK
CLICK
CLICK
He takes them gently. No snatching.
To see more, we've devised what we call a "feeding station".

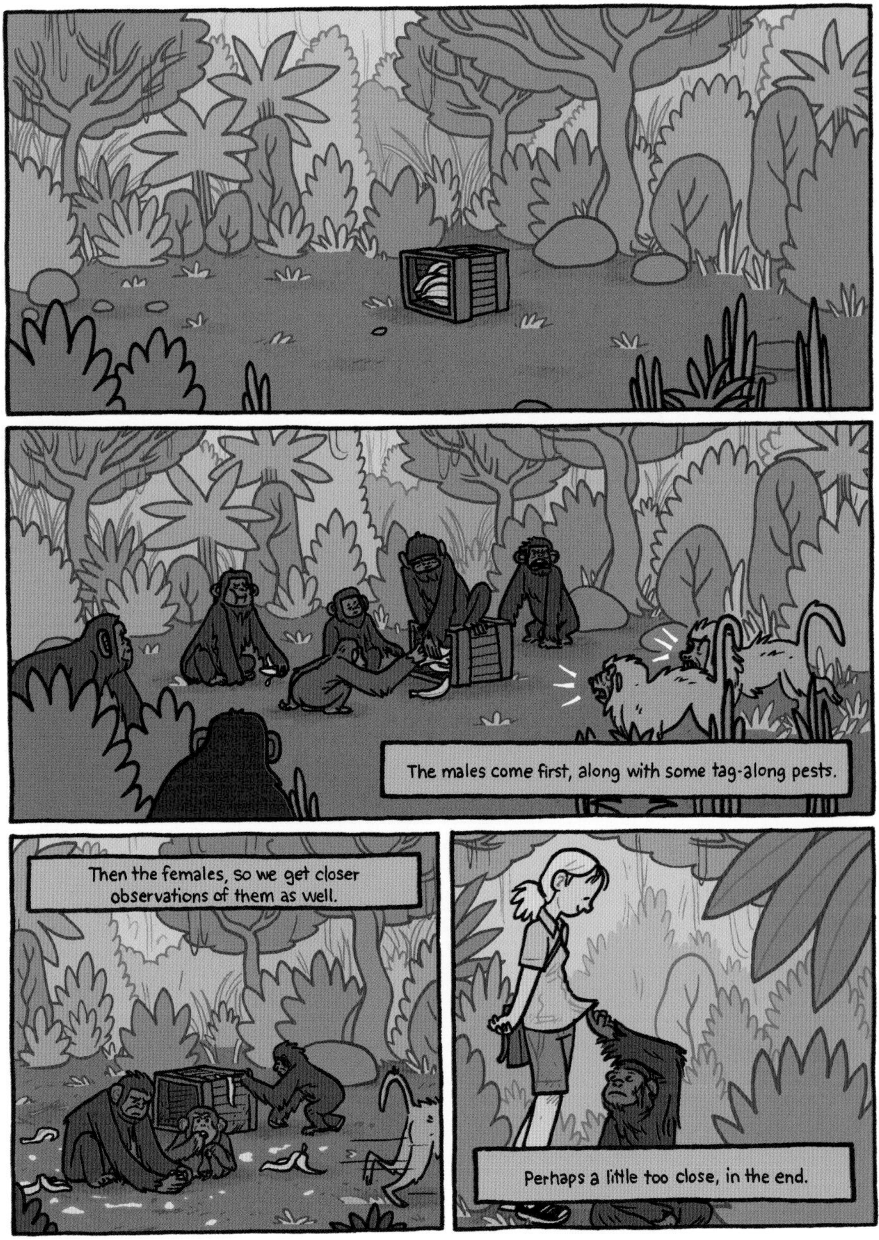
The males come first, along with some tag-along pests.
Then the females, so we get closer observations of them as well.
Perhaps a little too close, in the end.

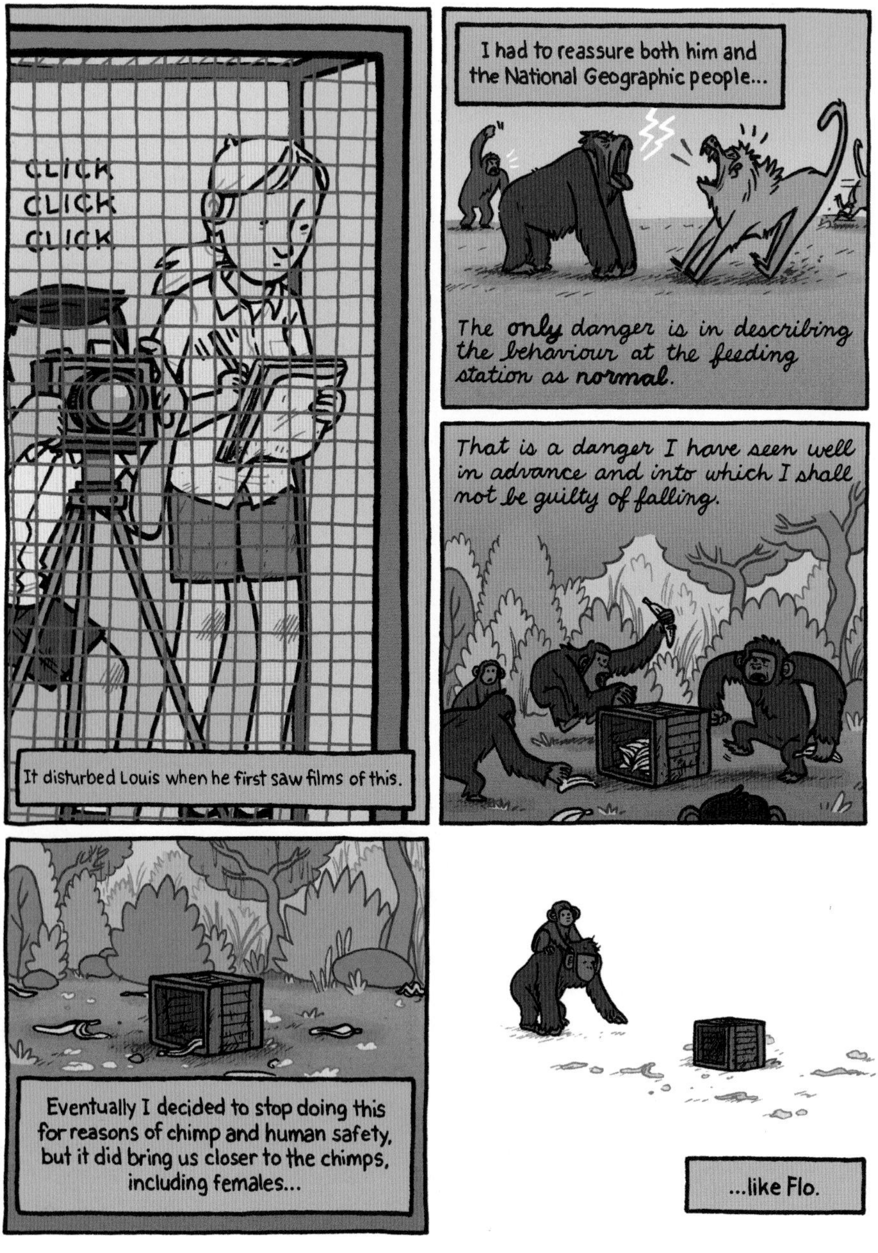
CLICK
CLICK
CLICK
It disturbed Louis when he first saw films of this.
I had to reassure both him and the National Geographic people...
The only danger is in describing the behaviour at the feeding station as normal.
That is a danger I have seen well in advance and into which I shall not be guilty of falling.
Eventually I decided to stop doing this for reasons of chimp and human safety, but it did bring us closer to the chimps, including females...
...like Flo.

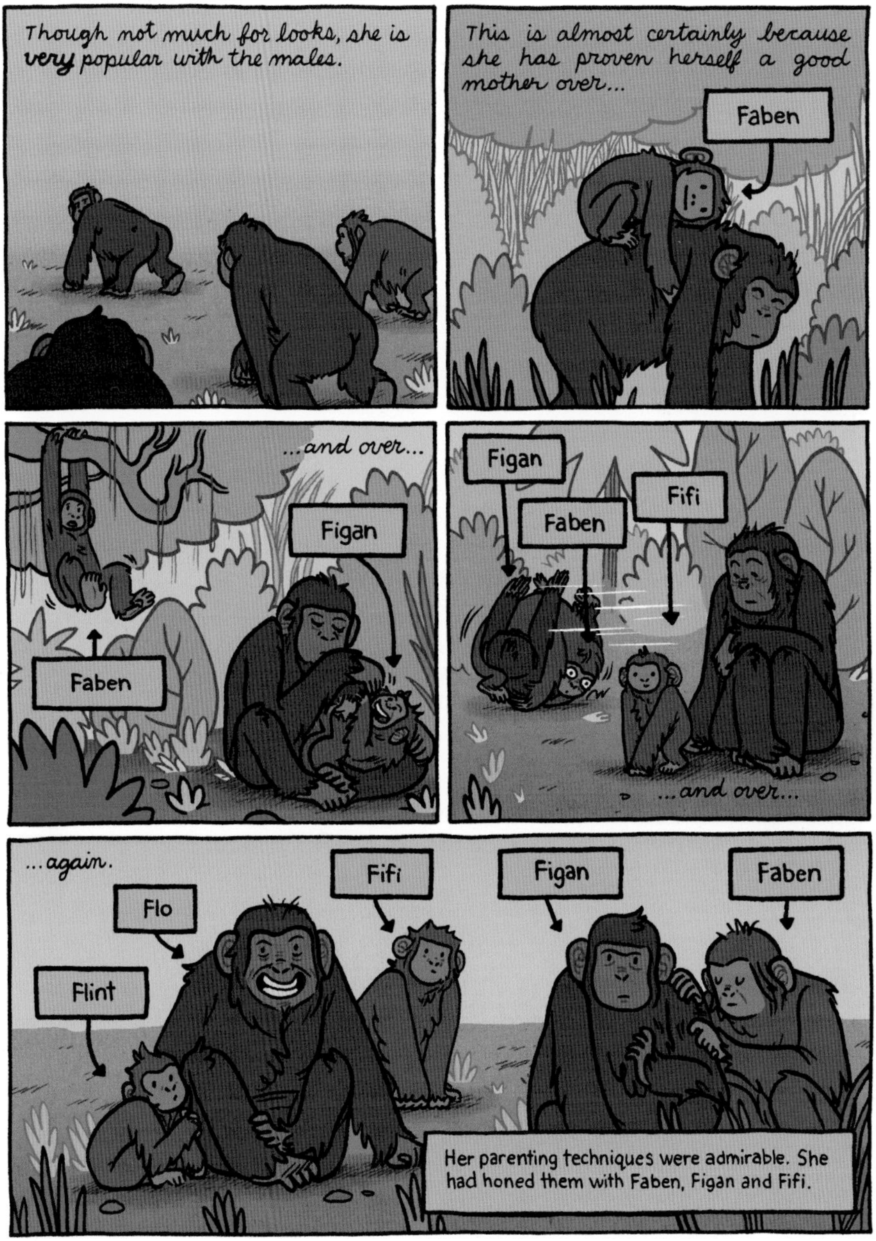
Though not much for looks, she is **very** popular with the males.
This is almost certainly because she has proven herself a good mother over...
Faben
...and over...
Figan
Faben
Figan
Faben
Fifi
...and over...
...again.
Flo
Fifi
Figan
Faben
Flint
Her parenting techniques were admirable. She had honed them with Faben, Figan and Fifi.

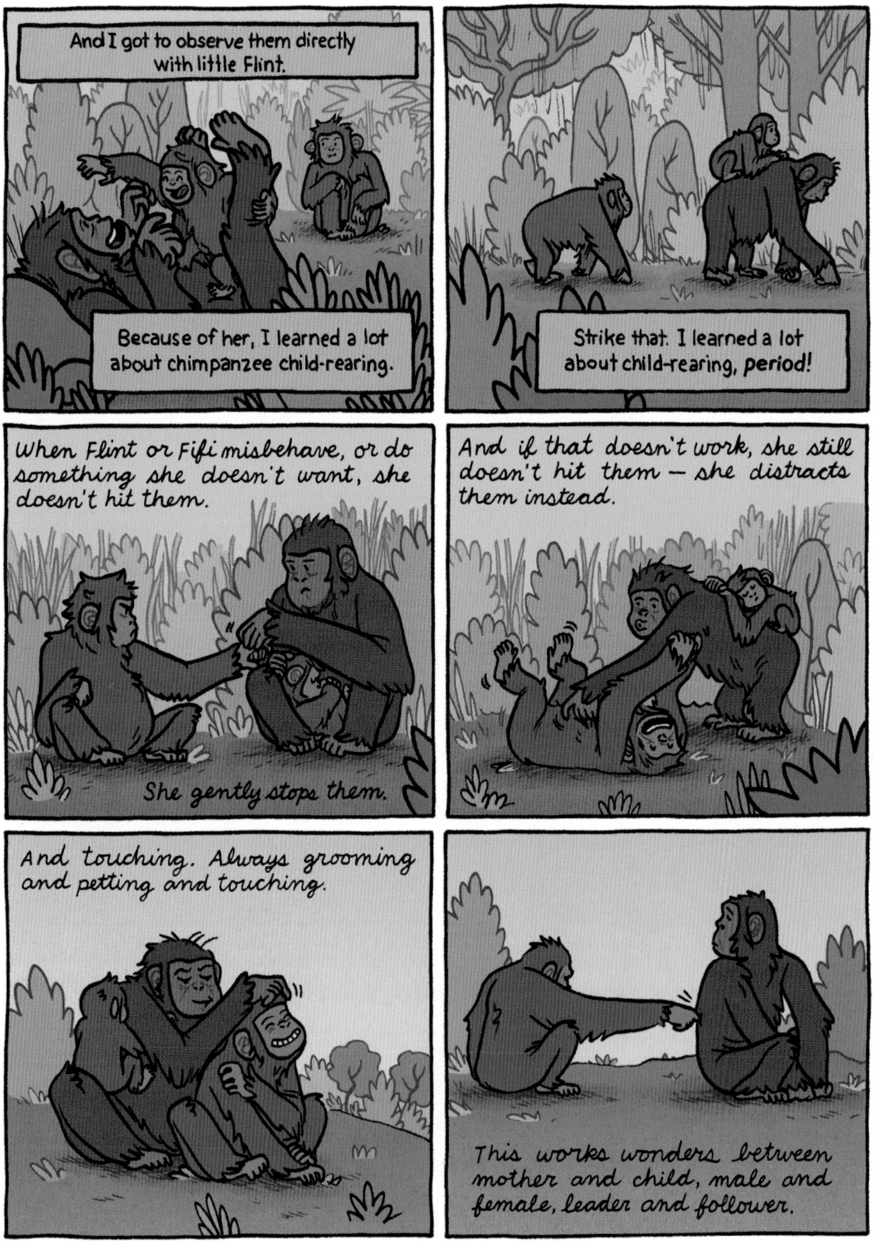
And I got to observe them directly with little Flint.
Because of her, I learned a lot about chimpanzee child-rearing.
Strike that. I learned a lot about child-rearing, period!
When Flint or Fifi misbehave, or do something she doesn't want, she doesn't hit them.
She gently stops them.
And if that doesn't work, she still doesn't hit them — she distracts them instead.
And touching. Always grooming and petting and touching.
This works wonders between mother and child, male and female, leader and follower.

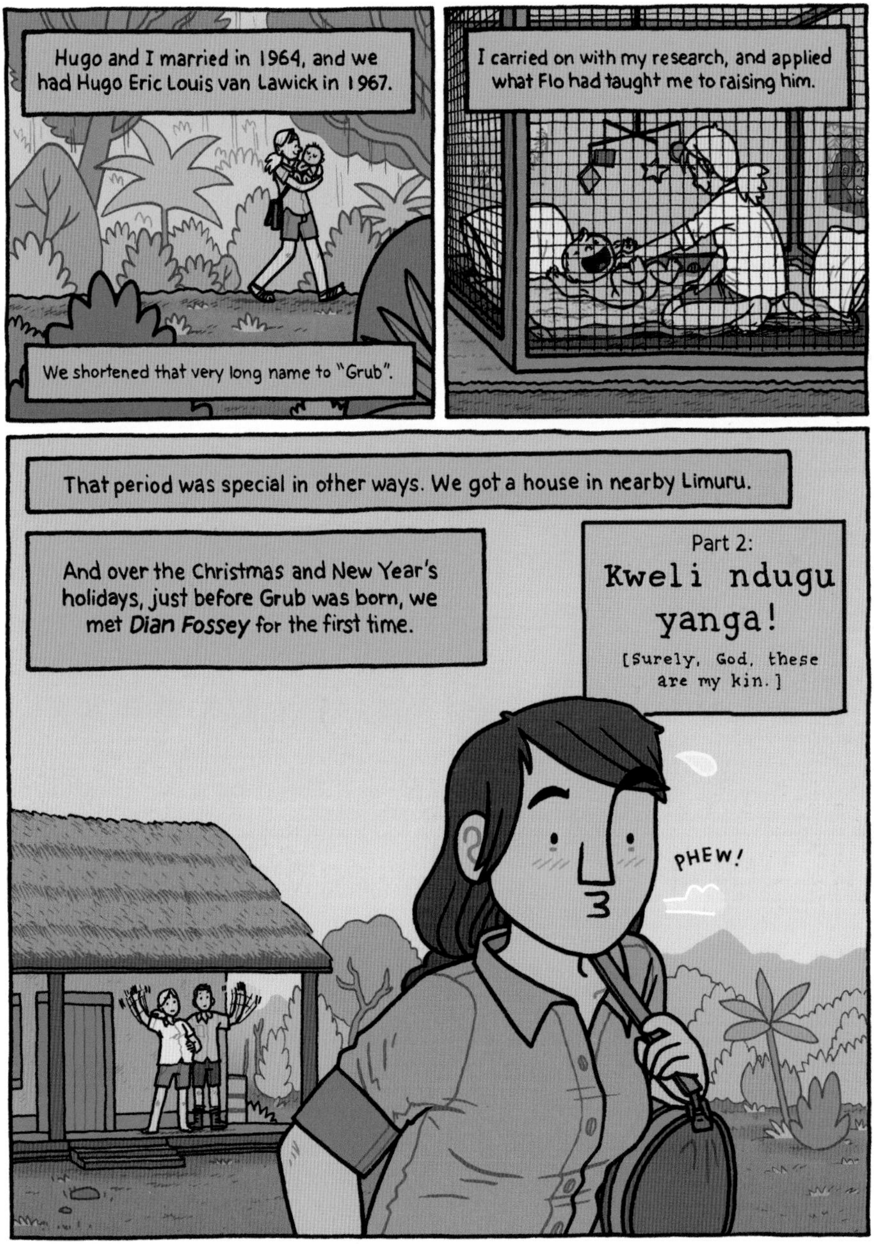
Hugo and I married in 1964, and we had Hugo Eric Louis van Lawick in 1967.
We shortened that very long name to "Grub".
I carried on with my research, and applied what Flo had taught me to raising him.
That period was special in other ways. We got a house in nearby Limuru.
And over the Christmas and New Year's holidays, just before Grub was born, we met *Dian Fossey* for the first time.
Part 2:
Kweli ndugu yanga!
[Surely, God, these are my kin.]
PHEW!

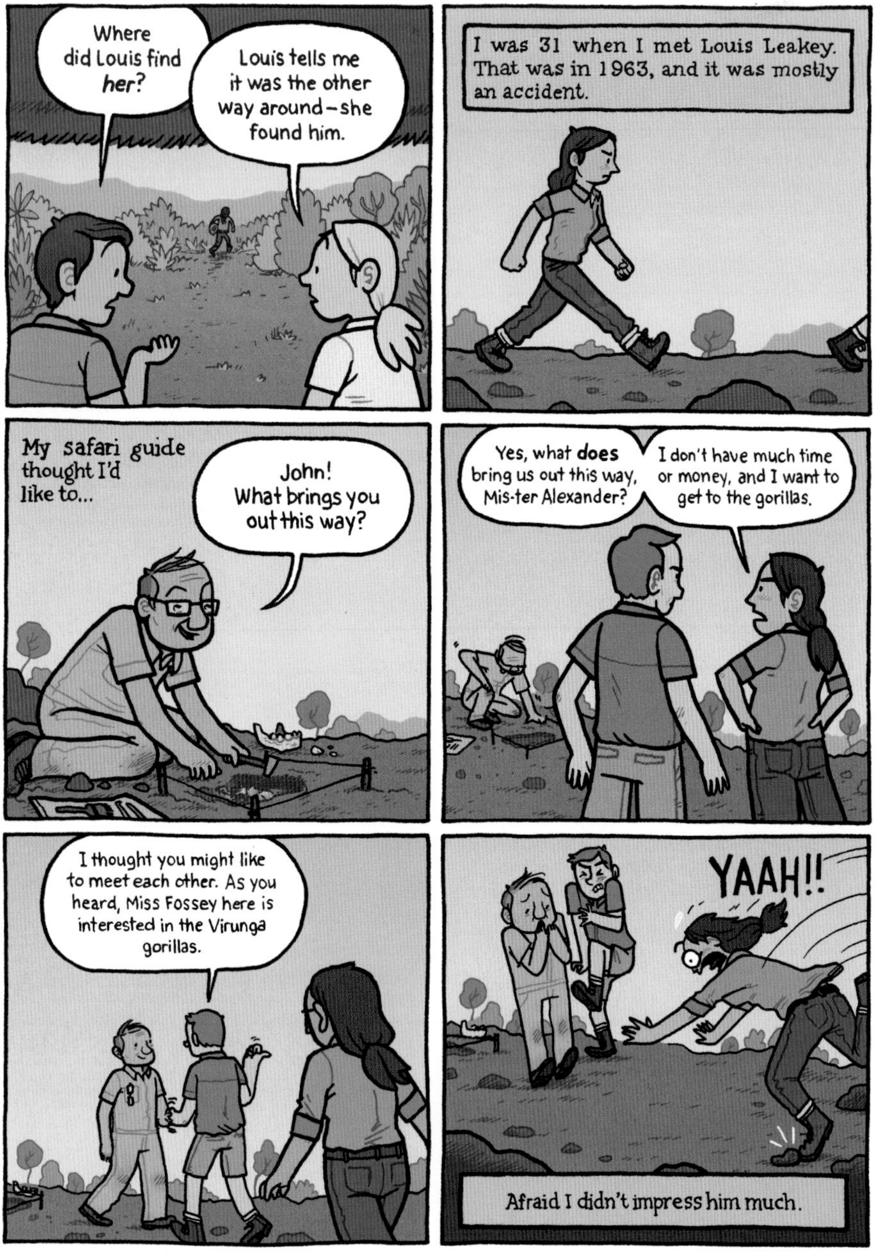
Where did Louis find *her*?
Louis tells me it was the other way around–she found him.
I was 31 when I met Louis Leakey. That was in 1963, and it was mostly an accident.
My safari guide thought I'd like to...
John! What brings you out this way?
Yes, what **does** bring us out this way, Mis-ter Alexander?
I don't have much time or money, and I want to get to the gorillas.
I thought you might like to meet each other. As you heard, Miss Fossey here is interested in the Virunga gorillas.
YAAH!!
Afraid I didn't impress him much.

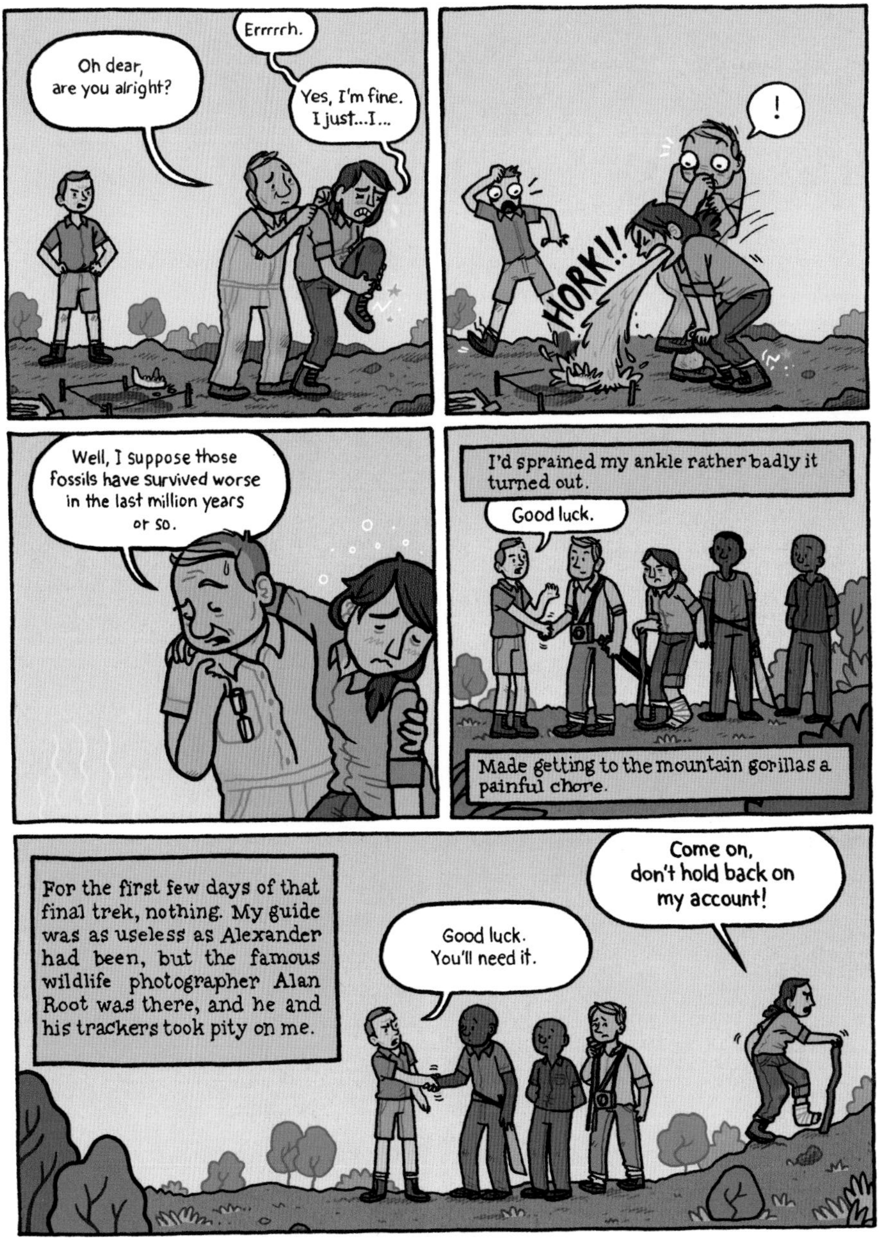
Oh dear,
are you alright?
Errrrh.
Yes, I'm fine.
I just...I...
!
HORK!!
Well, I suppose those fossils have survived worse in the last million years or so.
I'd sprained my ankle rather badly it turned out.
Good luck.
Made getting to the mountain gorillas a painful chore.
For the first few days of that final trek, nothing. My guide was as useless as Alexander had been, but the famous wildlife photographer Alan Root was there, and he and his trackers took pity on me.
Good luck.
You'll need it.
Come on,
don't hold back on
my account!

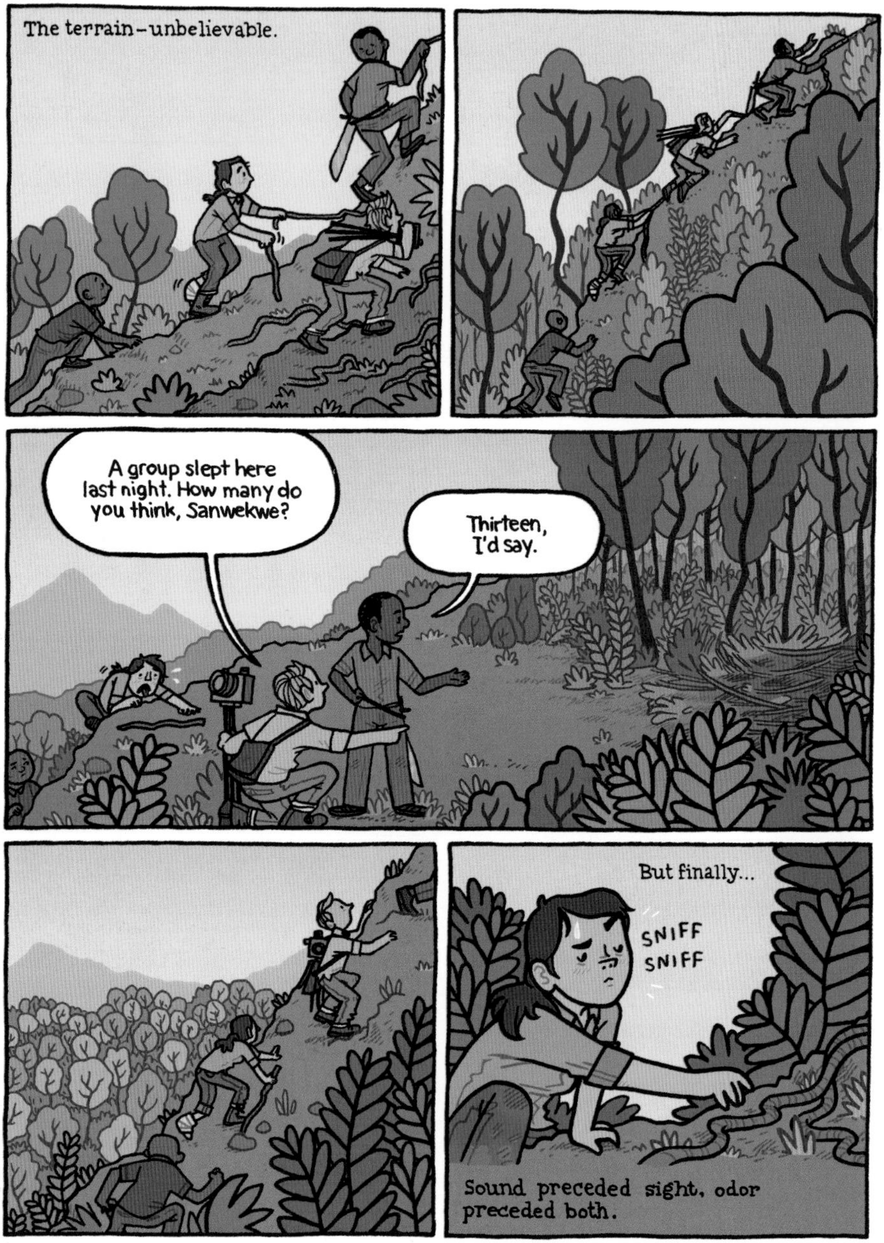
The terrain—unbelievable.
A group slept here last night. How many do you think, Sanwekwe?
Thirteen, I'd say.
But finally...
SNIFF SNIFF
Sound preceded sight, odor preceded both.

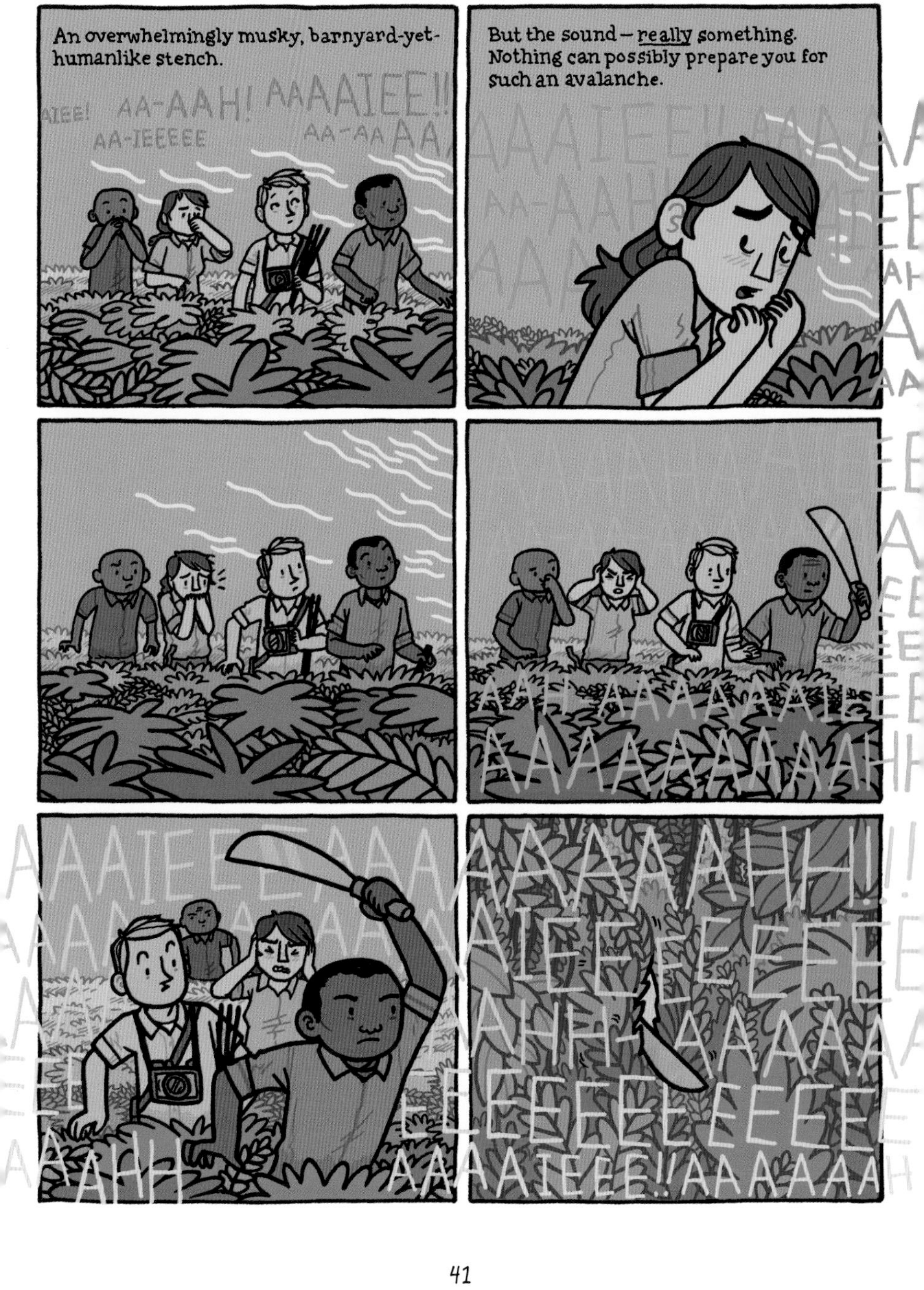
An overwhelmingly musky, barnyard-yet-humanlike stench.
AIEE! AA-AAH! AAAAIEE!!
AA-IEEEEE
AA-AA AA
But the sound — really something. Nothing can possibly prepare you for such an avalanche.
AAAIEE!! AAAAA
AA-AAH!
AAAAAAAAAAAAH
AAAAAAAAAAAAH!!
AAAAIEEE!AAAAAAA

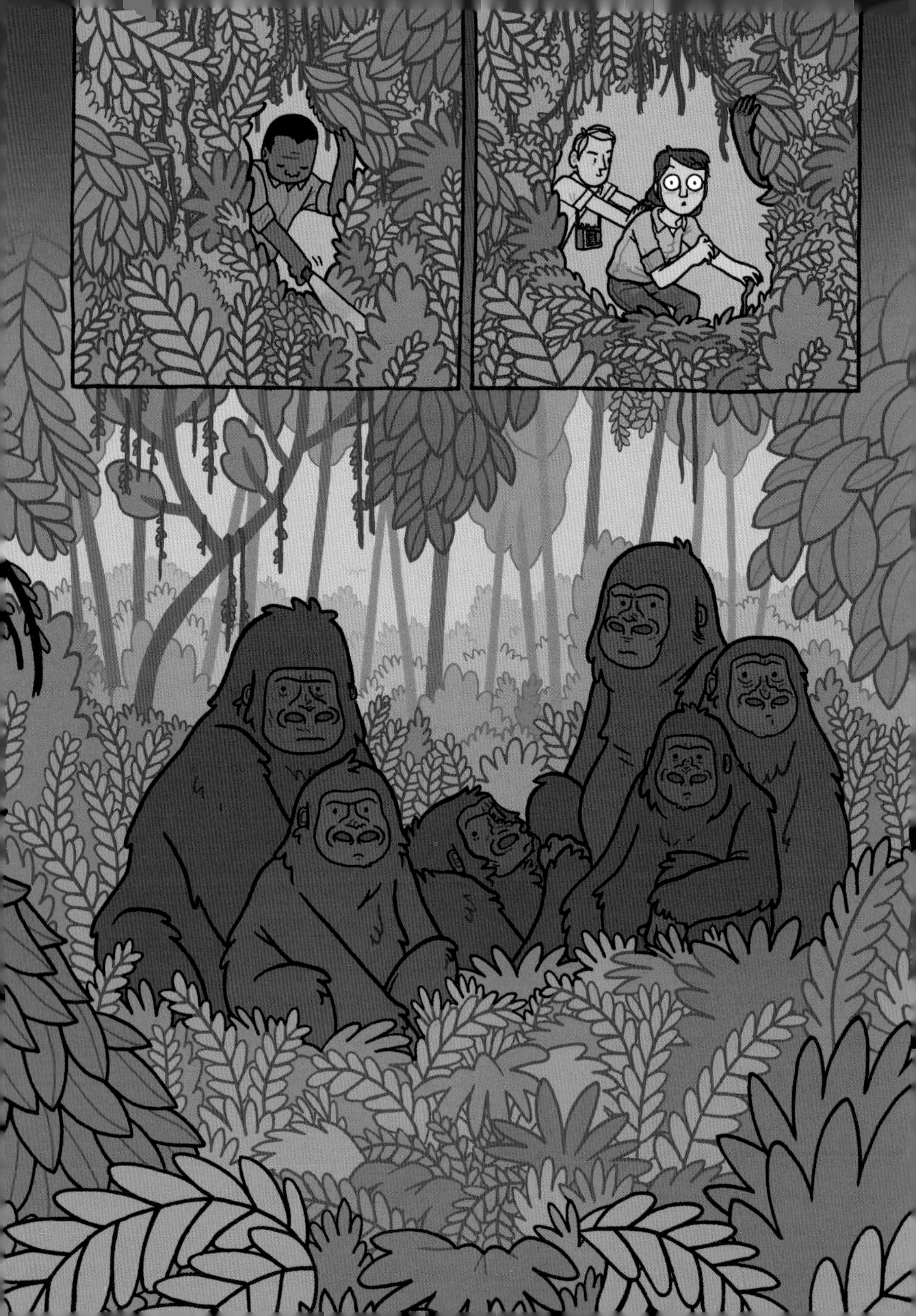

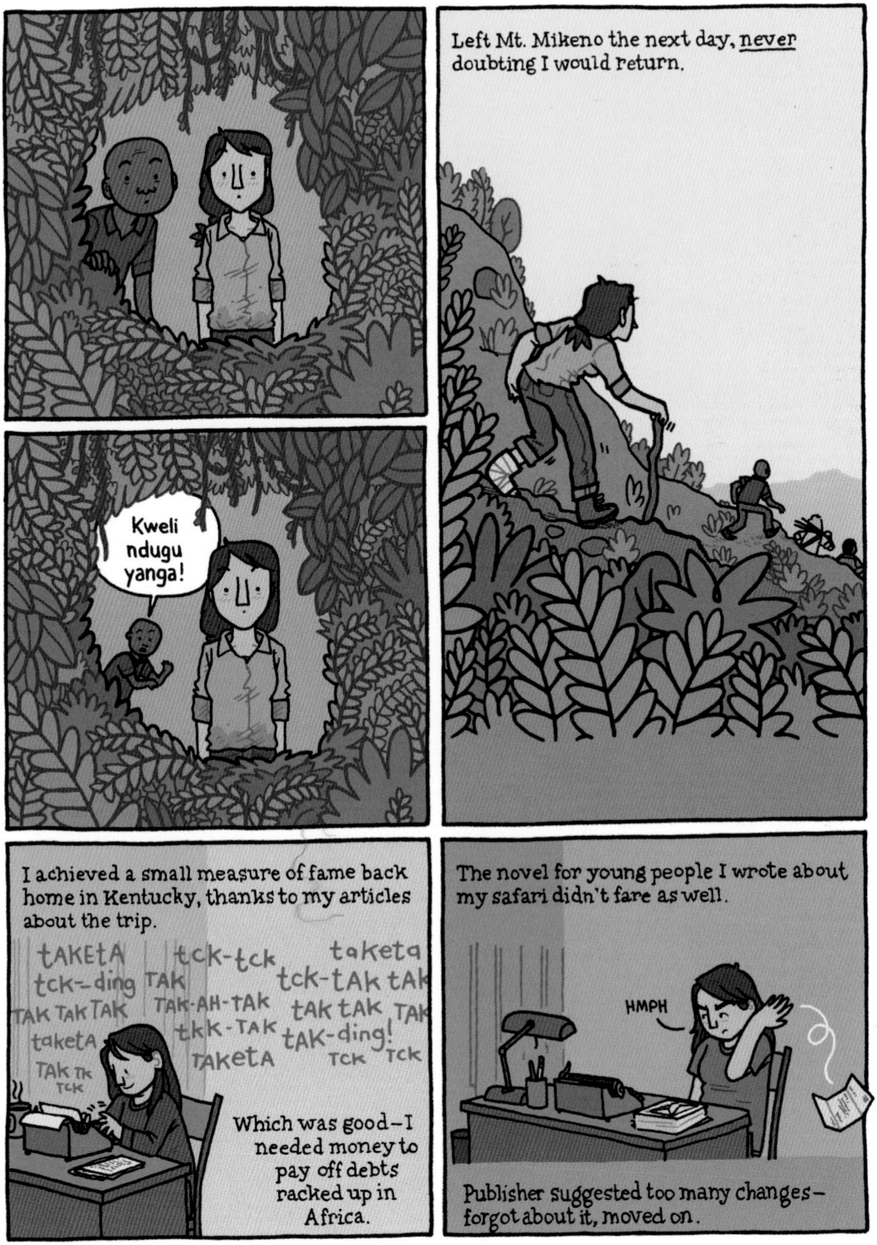
Kweli ndugu yanga!
Left Mt. Mikeno the next day, never doubting I would return.
I achieved a small measure of fame back home in Kentucky, thanks to my articles about the trip.
tAKEtA tck-tck taketa tck-ding TAK tck-tAK tAK TAK TAK TAK TAK-AH-TAK tAK tAK TAK taketA tkk-TAK tAK-ding! TAK TK TCK TAKetA TCK TCK
Which was good–I needed money to pay off debts racked up in Africa.
The novel for young people I wrote about my safari didn't fare as well.
HMPH
Publisher suggested too many changes–forgot about it, moved on.

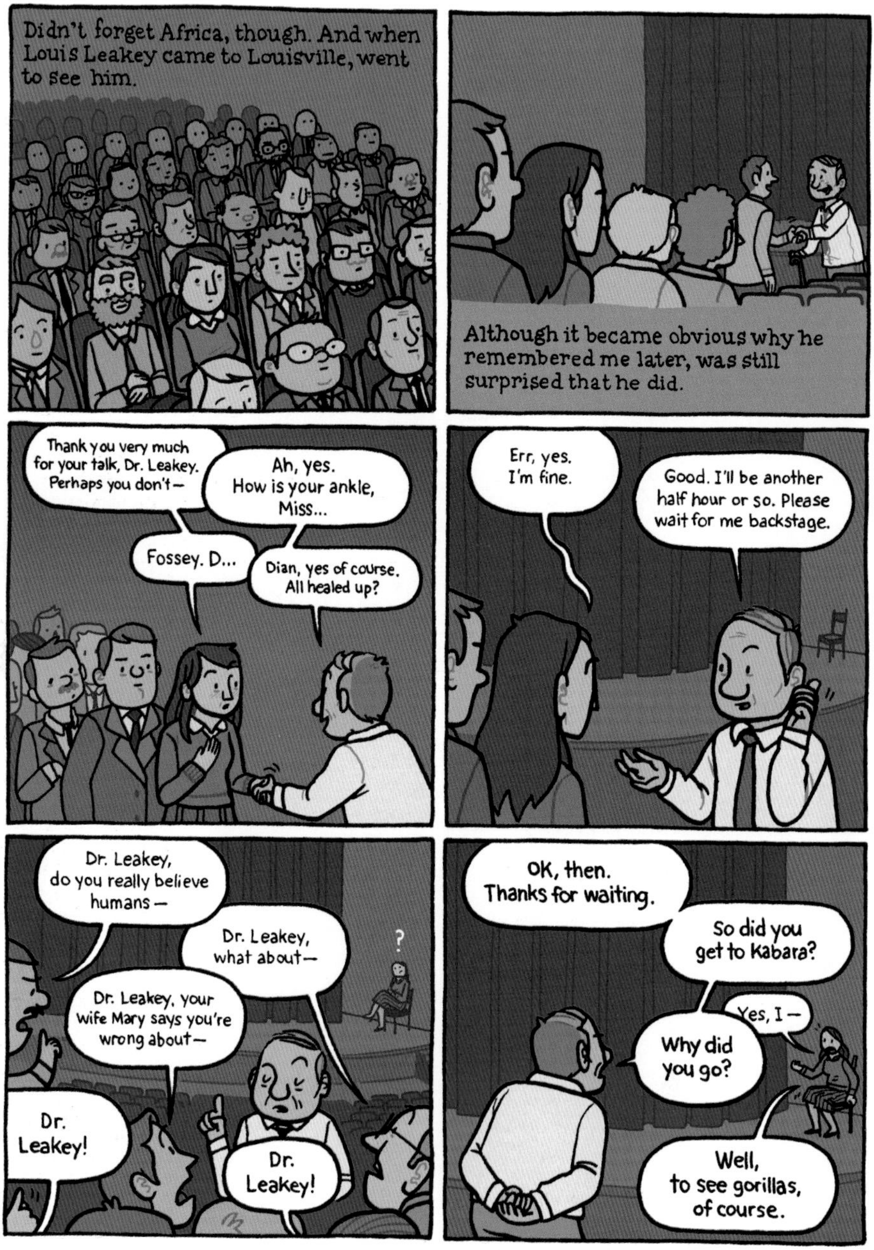
Didn't forget Africa, though. And when Louis Leakey came to Louisville, went to see him.
Although it became obvious why he remembered me later, was still surprised that he did.
Thank you very much for your talk, Dr. Leakey. Perhaps you don't—
Ah, yes. How is your ankle, Miss...
Fossey. D...
Dian, yes of course. All healed up?
Err, yes. I'm fine.
Good. I'll be another half hour or so. Please wait for me backstage.
Dr. Leakey, do you really believe humans—
Dr. Leakey, what about—
?
Dr. Leakey, your wife Mary says you're wrong about—
Dr. Leakey!
Dr. Leakey!
OK, then. Thanks for waiting.
So did you get to Kabara?
Yes, I—
Why did you go?
Well, to see gorillas, of course.

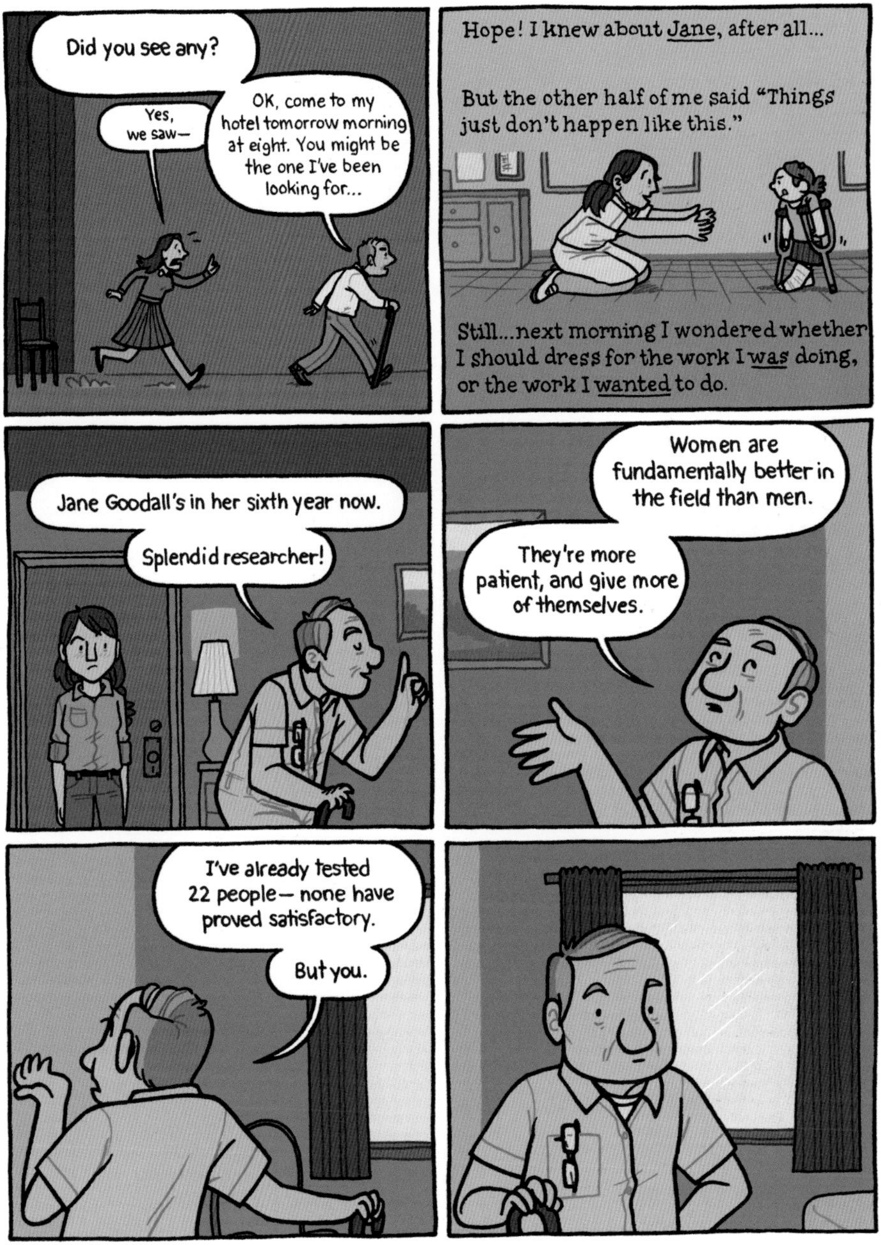
Did you see any?
Yes, we saw—
OK, come to my hotel tomorrow morning at eight. You might be the one I've been looking for...
Hope! I knew about Jane, after all...
But the other half of me said "Things just don't happen like this."
Still...next morning I wondered whether I should dress for the work I was doing, or the work I wanted to do.
Jane Goodall's in her sixth year now.
Splendid researcher!
Women are fundamentally better in the field than men.
They're more patient, and give more of themselves.
I've already tested 22 people— none have proved satisfactory.
But you.

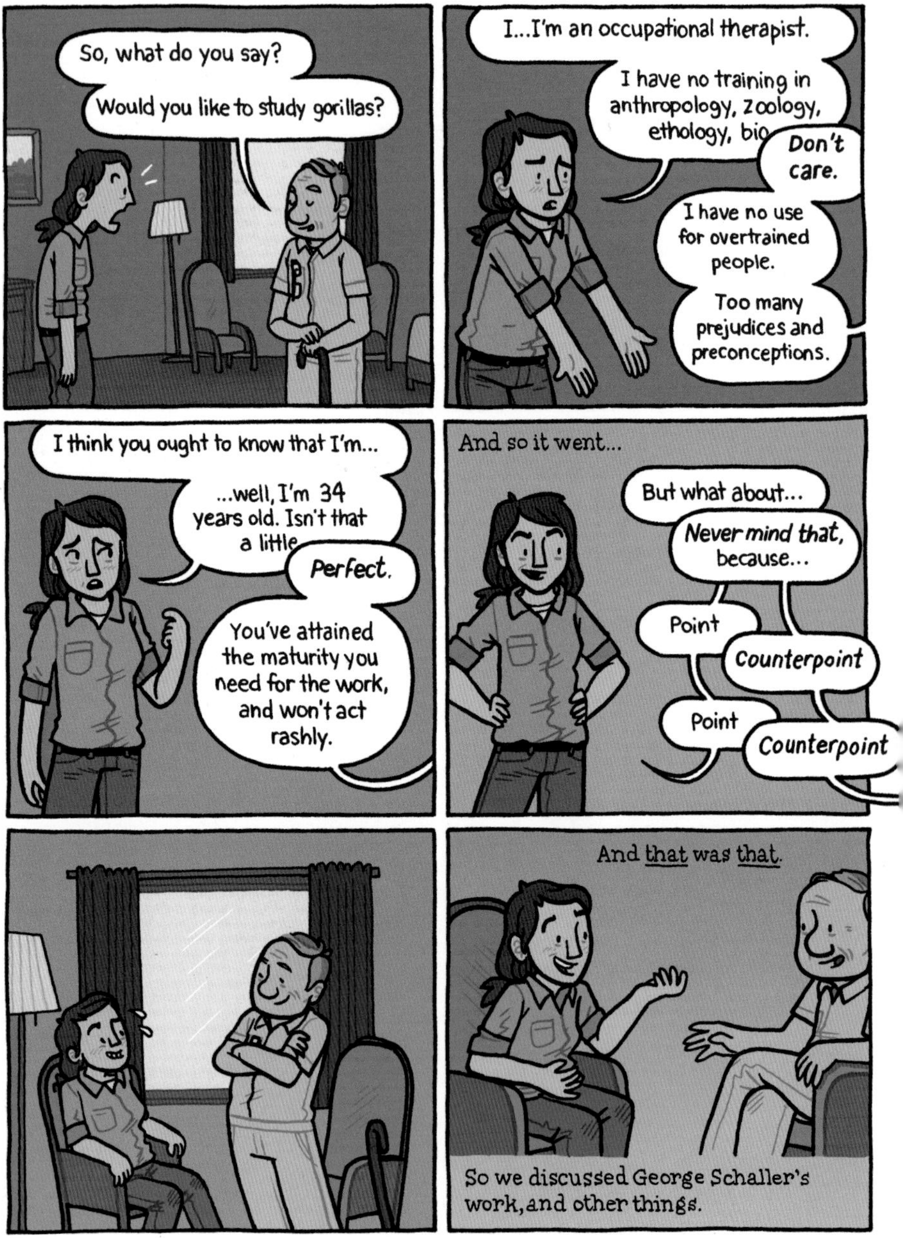

So, what do you say?
Would you like to study gorillas?
I...I'm an occupational therapist.
I have no training in anthropology, zoology, ethology, bio
Don't care.
I have no use for overtrained people.
Too many prejudices and preconceptions.
I think you ought to know that I'm...
...well, I'm 34 years old. Isn't that a little
Perfect.
You've attained the maturity you need for the work, and won't act rashly.
And so it went...
But what about...
Never mind that, because...
Point
Counterpoint
Point
Counterpoint
And that was that.
So we discussed George Schaller's work, and other things.

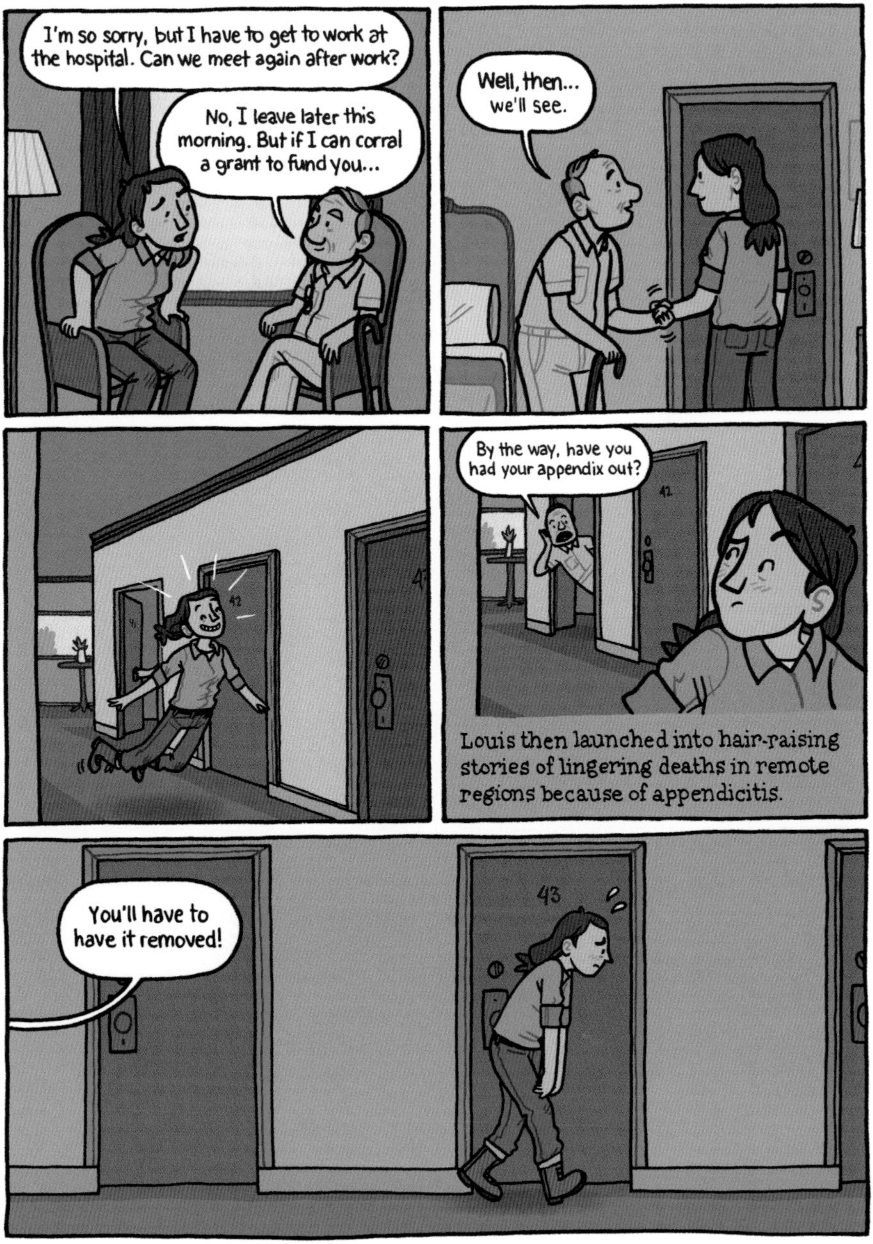
I'm so sorry, but I have to get to work at the hospital. Can we meet again after work?
No, I leave later this morning. But if I can corral a grant to fund you...
Well, then... we'll see.
By the way, have you had your appendix out?
Louis then launched into hair-raising stories of lingering deaths in remote regions because of appendicitis.
You'll have to have it removed!

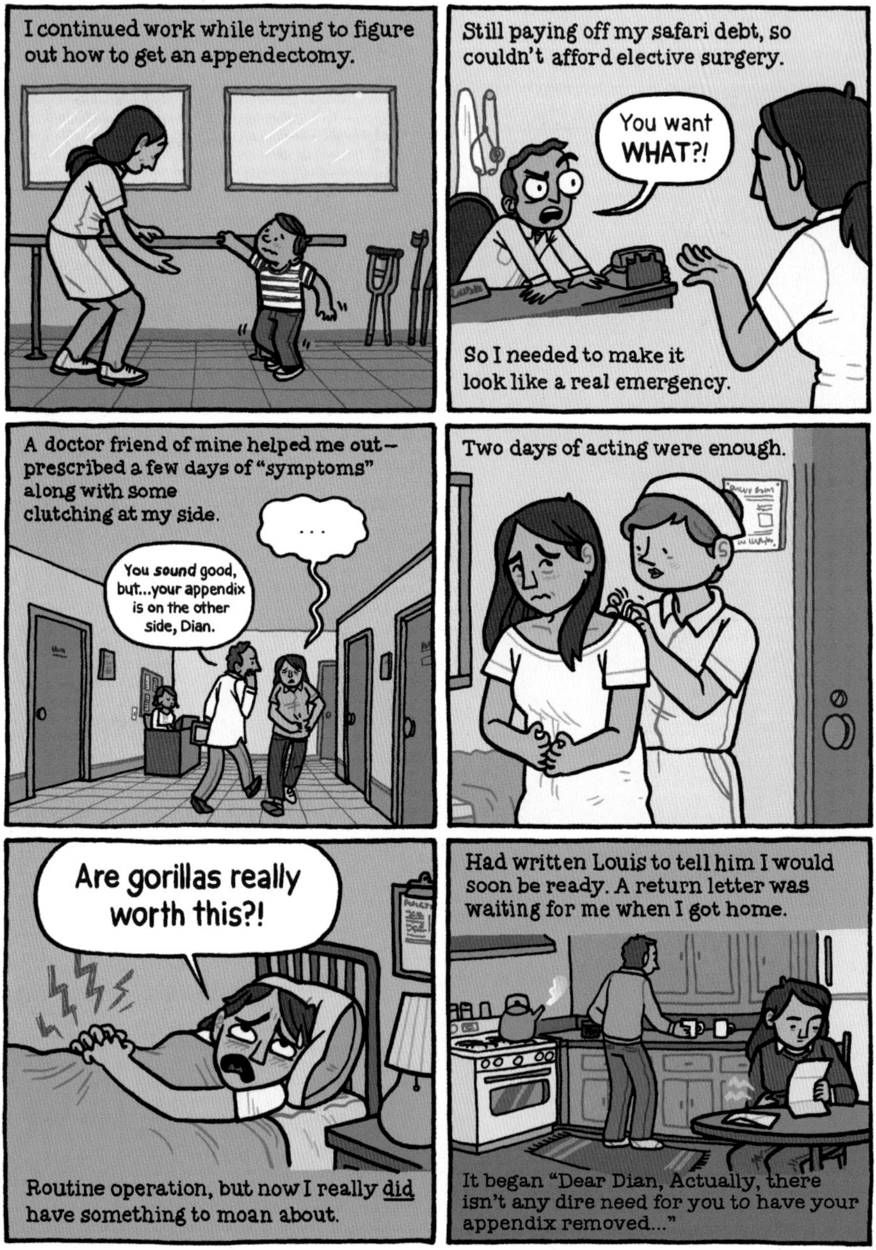
I continued work while trying to figure out how to get an appendectomy.
Still paying off my safari debt, so couldn't afford elective surgery.
You want WHAT?!
So I needed to make it look like a real emergency.
A doctor friend of mine helped me out—prescribed a few days of "symptoms" along with some clutching at my side.
You *sound* good, but...your appendix is on the other side, Dian.
. . .
Two days of acting were enough.
Are gorillas really worth this?!
Routine operation, but now I really did have something to moan about.
Had written Louis to tell him I would soon be ready. A return letter was waiting for me when I got home.
It began "Dear Dian, Actually, there isn't any dire need for you to have your appendix removed..."

hey

Hey

HEY!

You'll burst your stitches!

AHHH!!

But I read on and saw that Louis was formally offering me the job.

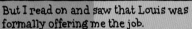

So when he got the grant to pay for travel and equipment and African helpers and food and photographic supplies and...

...well, I left immediately.

On December 15, 1966 I was off to Africa. Just like that.

Louis had arranged for me to stop over with Jane Goodall on the way to the Congo.

Not an appreciative guest, I'm afraid— was <u>desperately</u> keen to reach Kabara and the mountain gorillas.

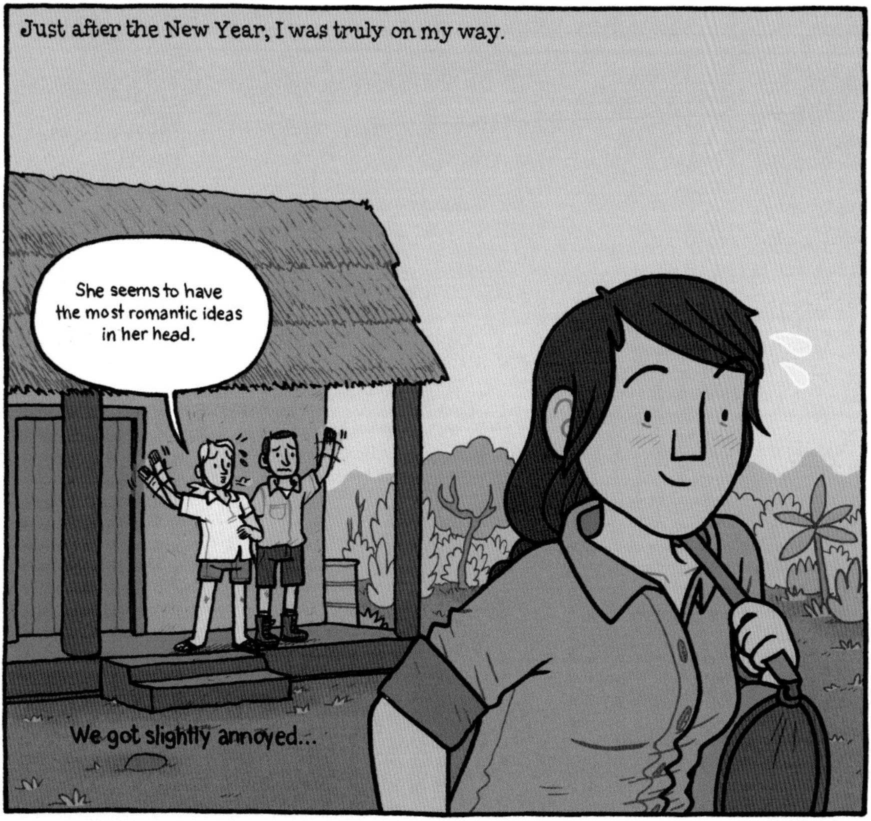
Just after the New Year, I was truly on my way.
She seems to have the most romantic ideas in her head.
We got slightly annoyed...

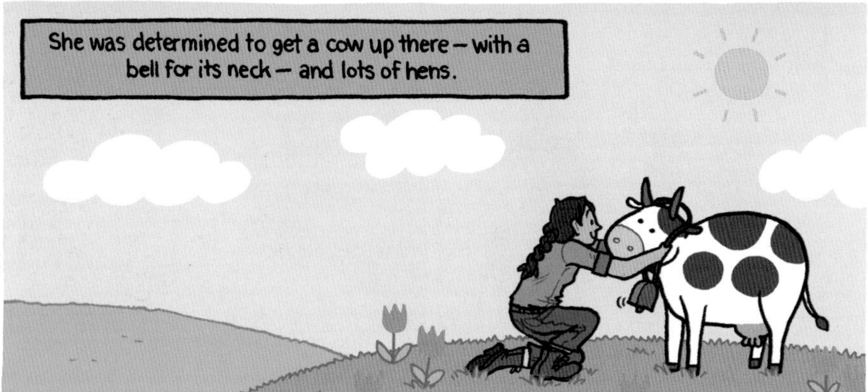
She was determined to get a cow up there — with a bell for its neck — and lots of hens.

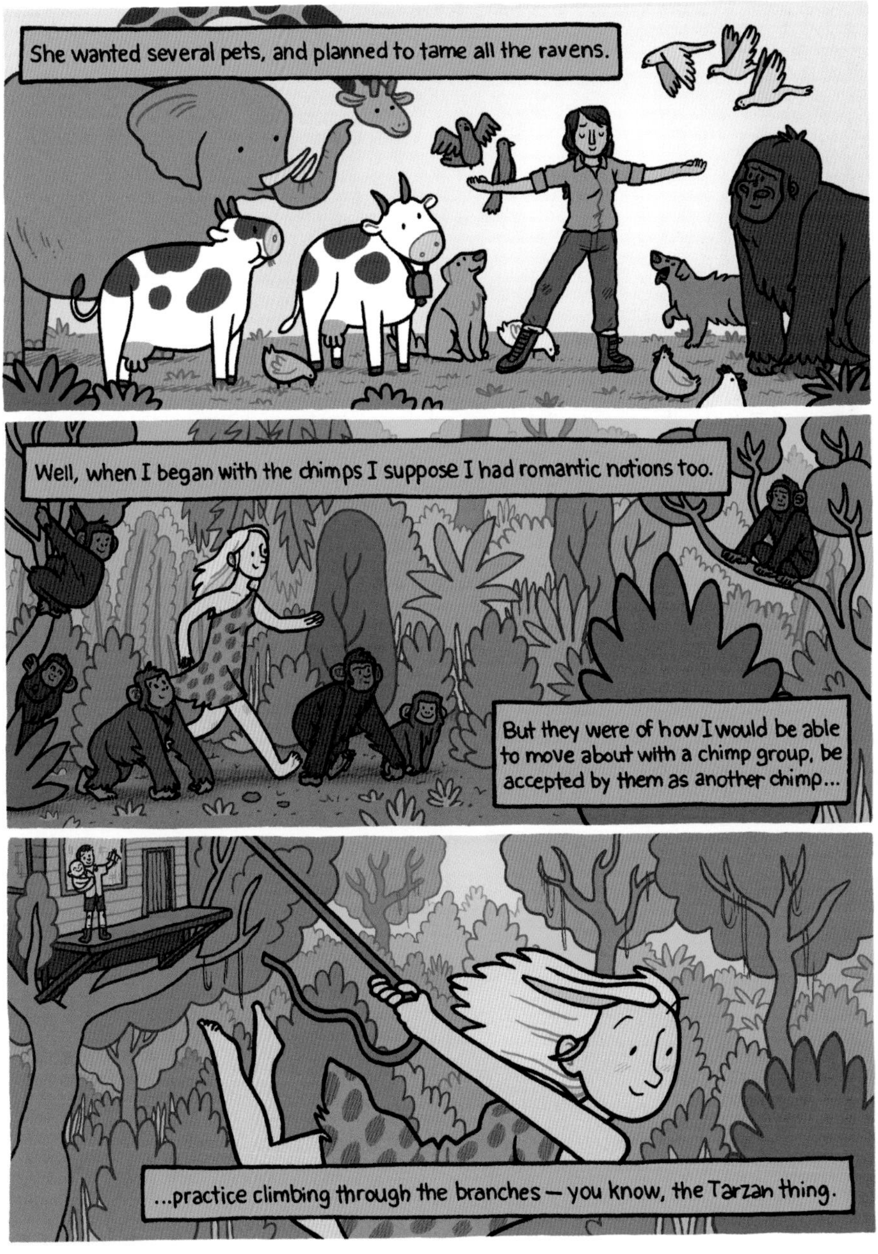

She wanted several pets, and planned to tame all the ravens.
Well, when I began with the chimps I suppose I had romantic notions too.
But they were of how I would be able to move about with a chimp group, be accepted by them as another chimp...
...practice climbing through the branches — you know, the Tarzan thing.

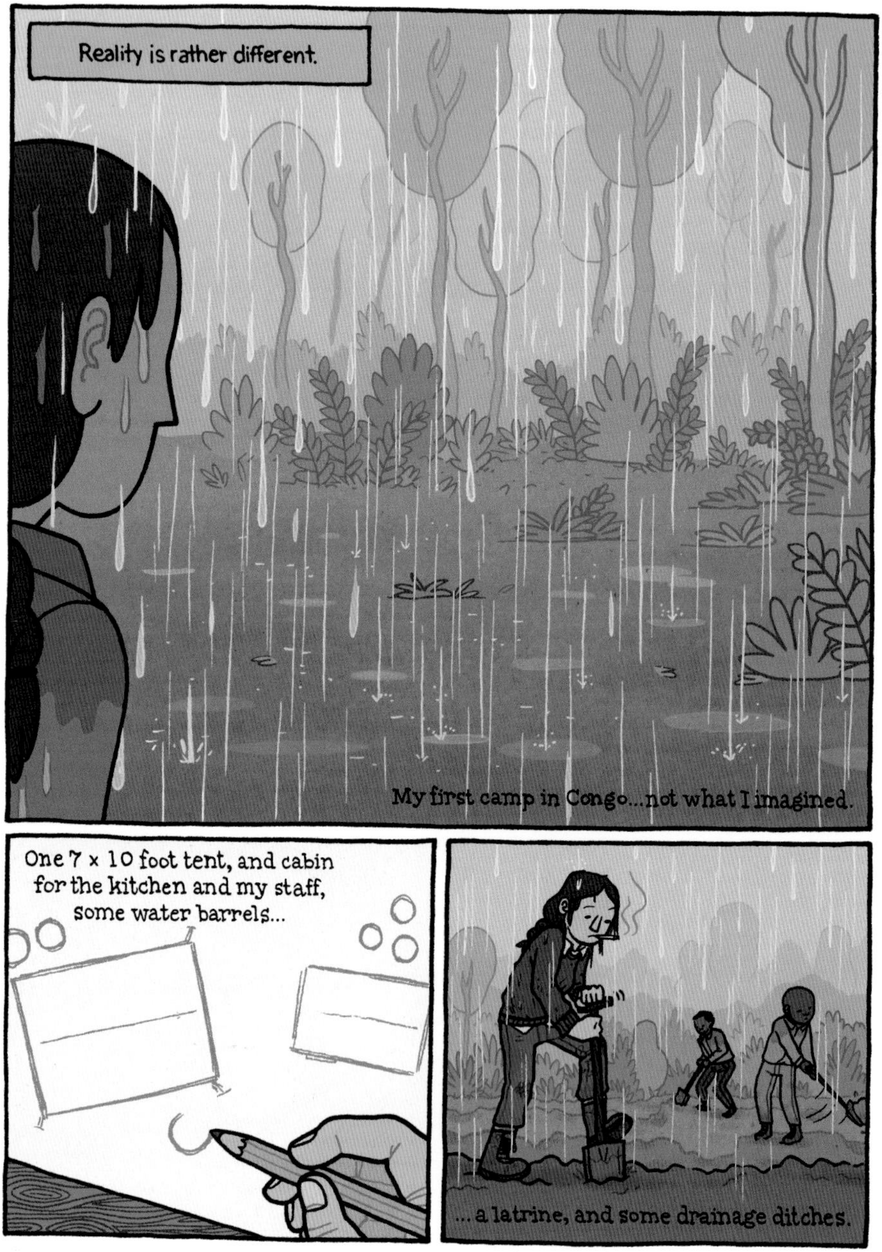
Reality is rather different.
My first camp in Congo... not what I imagined.
One 7 x 10 foot tent, and cabin for the kitchen and my staff, some water barrels...
... a latrine, and some drainage ditches.

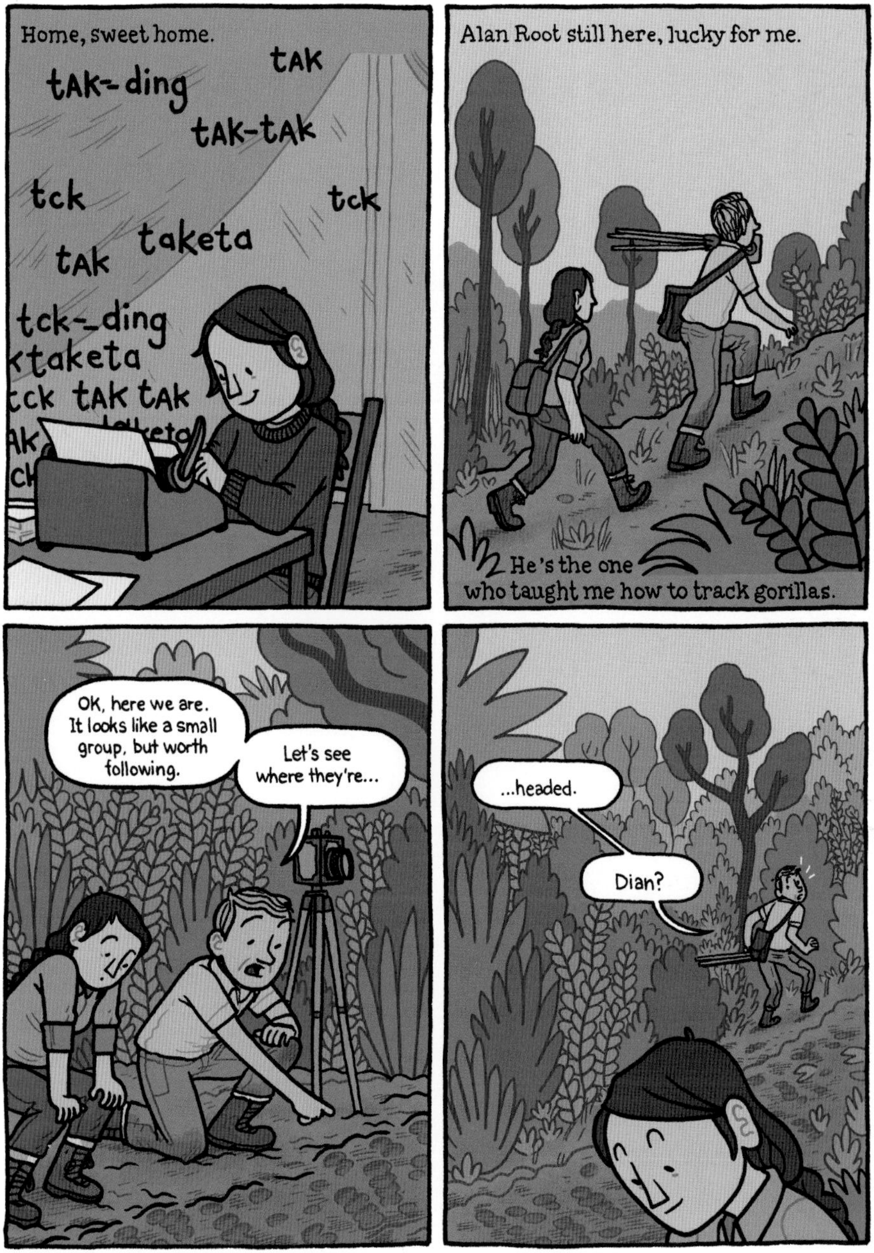
Home, sweet home.
TAK
TAK-ding
TAK-TAK
tck
tck
taketa
TAK
tck-ding
taketa
tck TAK TAK
Alan Root still here, lucky for me.
He's the one who taught me how to track gorillas.
OK, here we are. It looks like a small group, but worth following.
Let's see where they're...
...headed.
Dian?

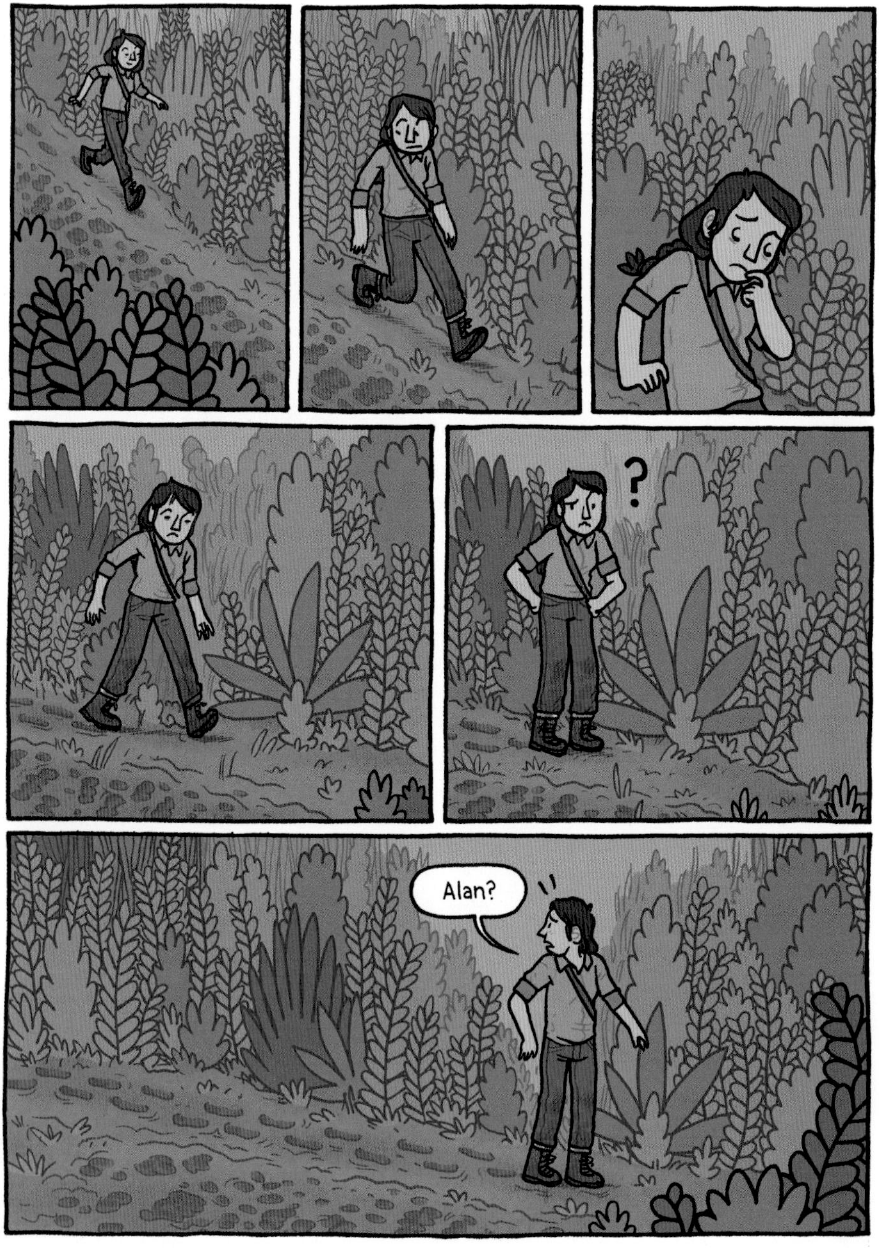
?
Alan?

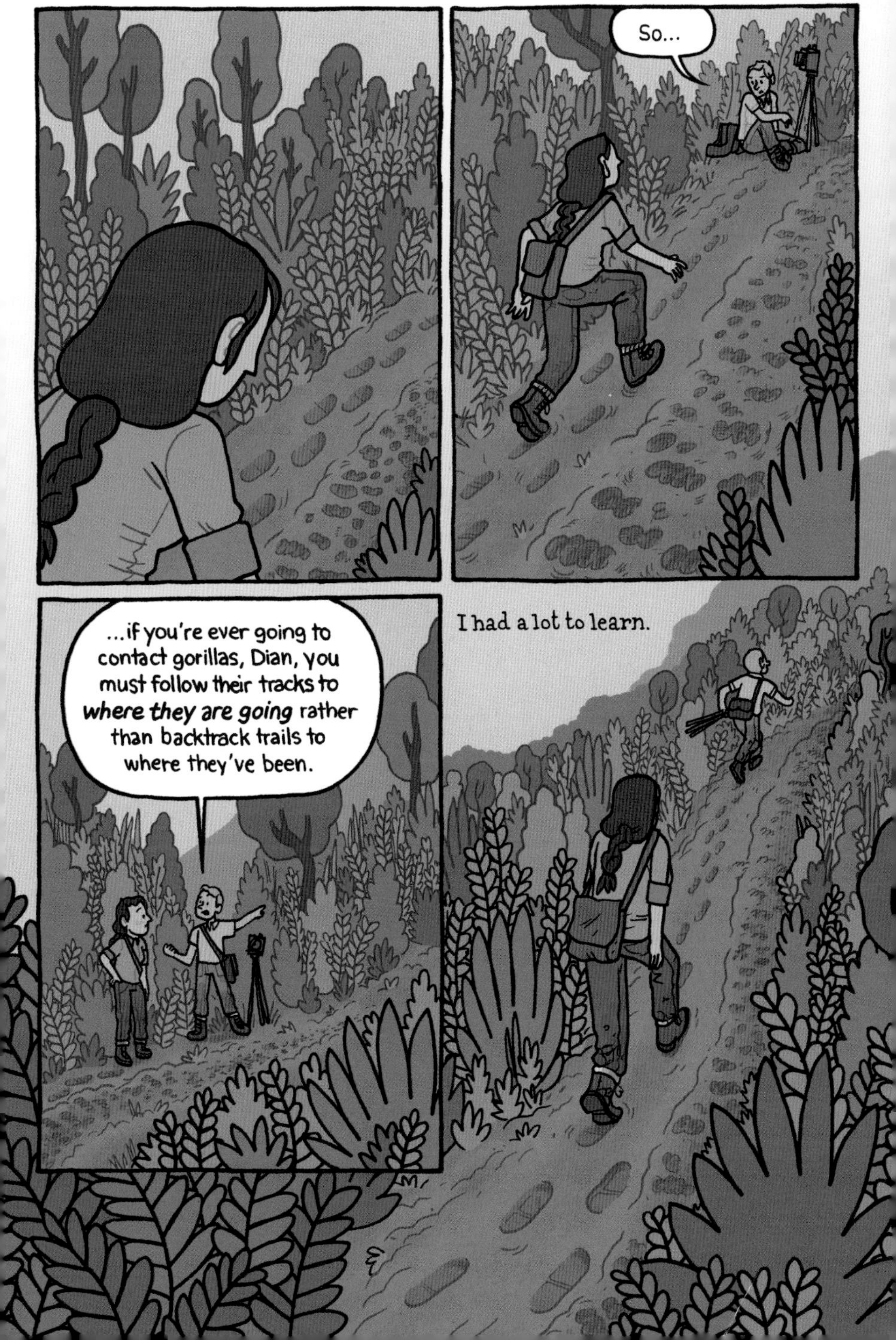
So...
...if you're ever going to contact gorillas, Dian, you must follow their tracks to *where they are going* rather than backtrack trails to where they've been.
I had a lot to learn.

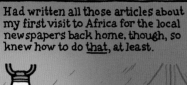

Had written all those articles about my first visit to Africa for the local newspapers back home, though, so knew how to do that, at least.

tck
taketa
tck tak tck
tak tck tak

CLICK

And that served me well. The National Geographic, when they saw I was here to stay, asked me to write for them.

But field notes? As new to me as tracking.

AA-AAAIEEEEEEEEE
AAH
SNIFF AAH!!
SNIFF
EEEEE!
EEEE
AAIE
EEE!!AAH
AA

And harder — even though scent still precedes sound, sound doesn't always precede sight.

?

Harder still, quickly learning I wasn't the only one looking. The jungle isn't peaceful.

Kanyaragana, what is this?

Cheese sandwich, with gelatin.

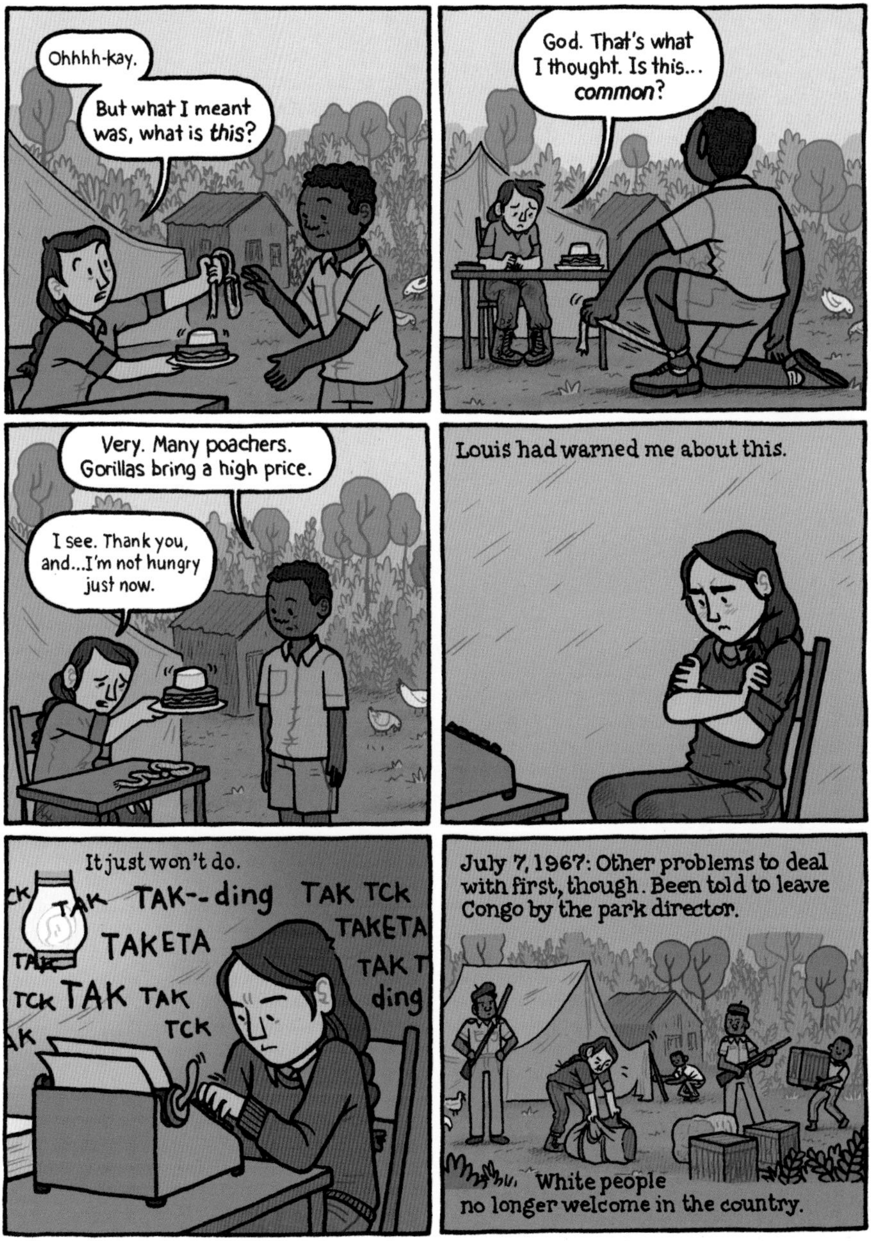
Ohhhh-kay.
But what I meant was, what is *this*?
God. That's what I thought. Is this... *common*?
Very. Many poachers. Gorillas bring a high price.
I see. Thank you, and...I'm not hungry just now.
Louis had warned me about this.
It just won't do.
TAK TAK-- ding TAK TCK TAKETA TAKETA TAK TAK TCK TAK TAK TCK ding
July 7, 1967: Other problems to deal with first, though. Been told to leave Congo by the park director.
White people no longer welcome in the country.

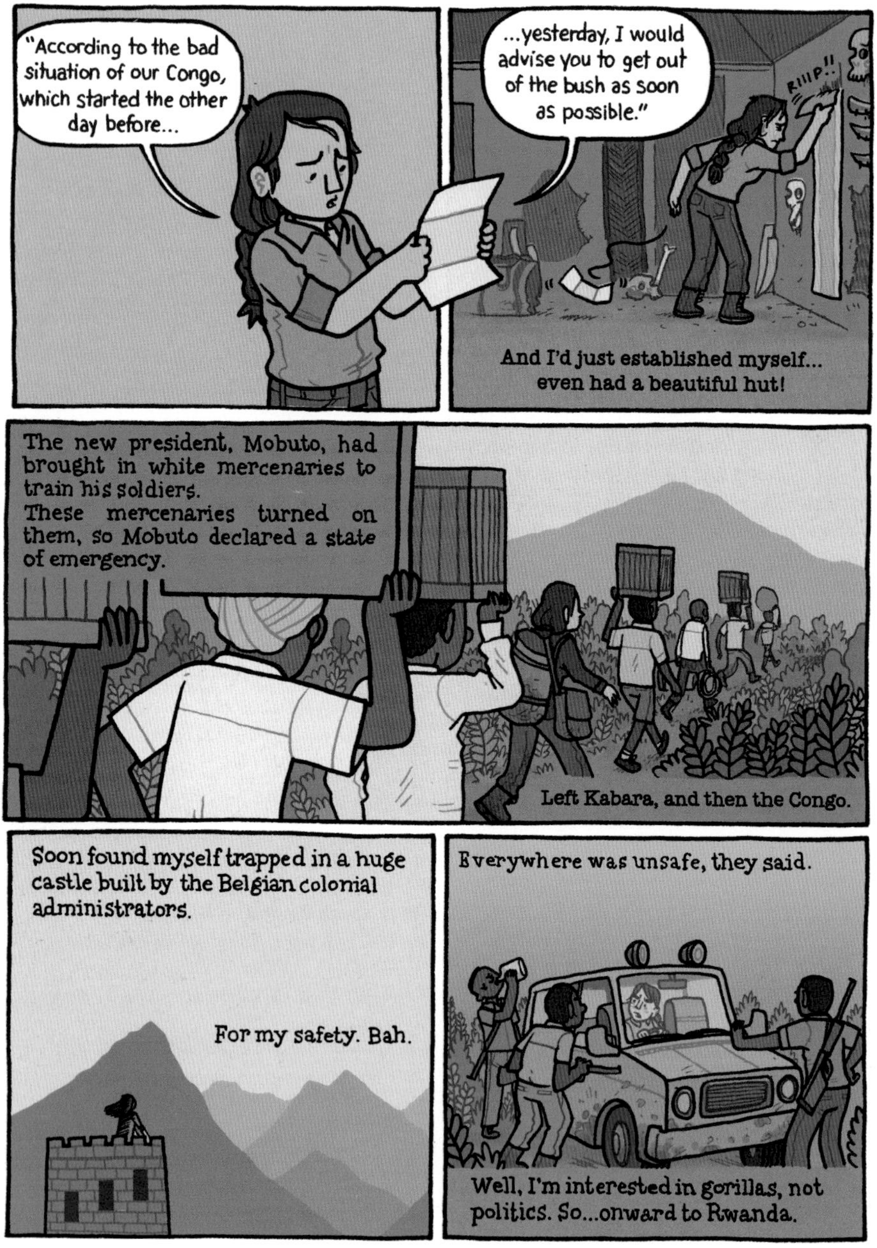
"According to the bad situation of our Congo, which started the other day before...
...yesterday, I would advise you to get out of the bush as soon as possible."
RIIIP!!
And I'd just established myself... even had a beautiful hut!
The new president, Mobuto, had brought in white mercenaries to train his soldiers.
These mercenaries turned on them, so Mobuto declared a state of emergency.
Left Kabara, and then the Congo.
Soon found myself trapped in a huge castle built by the Belgian colonial administrators.
For my safety. Bah.
Everywhere was unsafe, they said.
Well, I'm interested in gorillas, not politics. So...onward to Rwanda.

September, 1967:
Set up camp between
Mt. Karisimbi and
Mt. Visoke.

Calling it the
Karisoke Research Center.

Just a few kilometers away from my
original site — the conditions are much
the same.

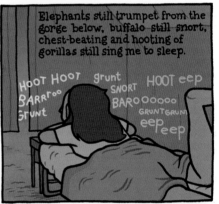

Elephants still trumpet from the
gorge below, buffalo still snort,
chest-beating and hooting of
gorillas still sing me to sleep.

HOOT HOOT grunt HOOT eep
BARRroo SNORT
Grunt BAROOooooo
GRUNT GRUN
eep eep

The nights are beautiful.

oot BARrooooo... eep
eep HOOT HOOT oot
eep eep oot
HOOT oot
GRUNT oot GRUNT
HOOT

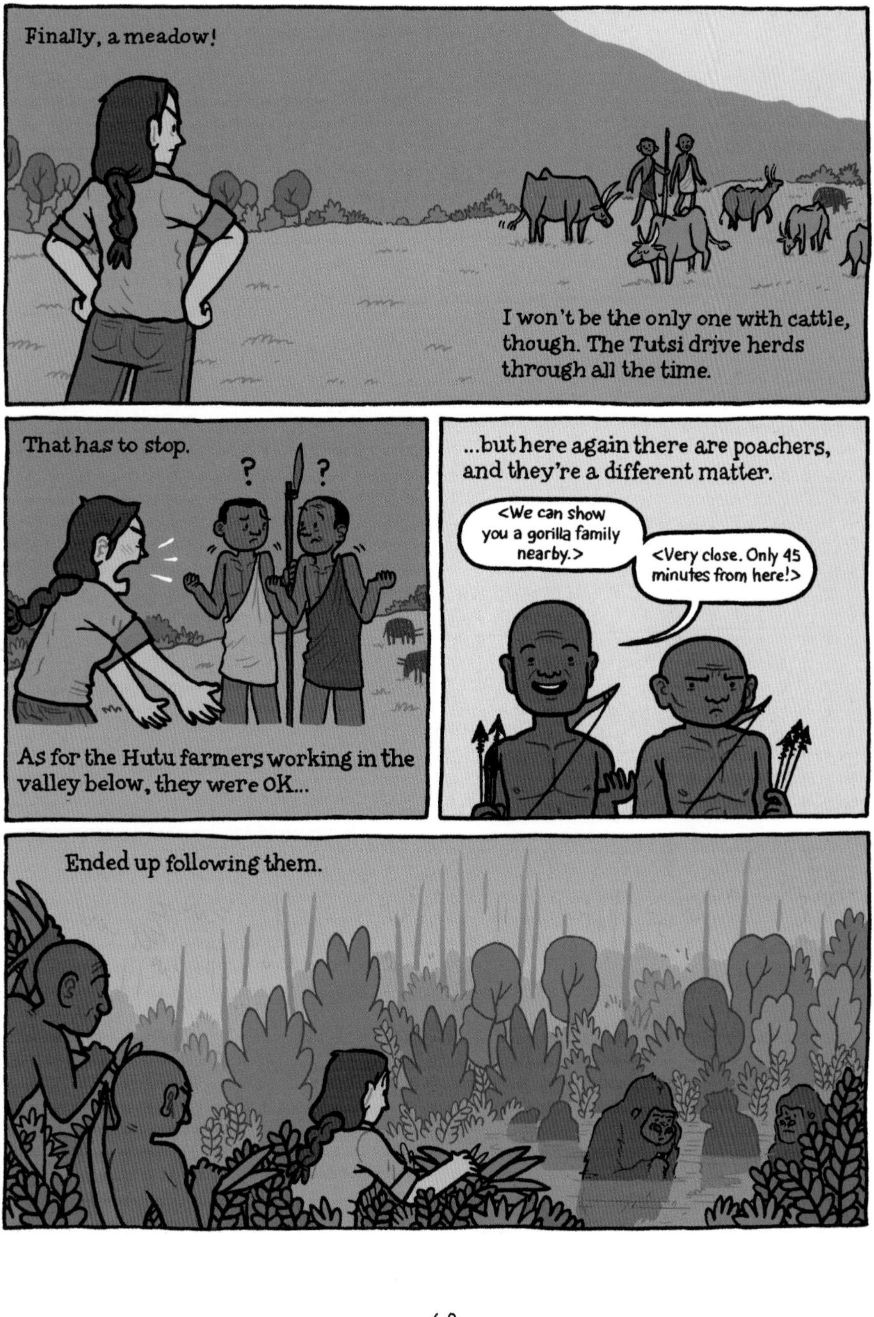
Finally, a meadow!
I won't be the only one with cattle, though. The Tutsi drive herds through all the time.
That has to stop.
? ?
As for the Hutu farmers working in the valley below, they were OK...
...but here again there are poachers, and they're a different matter.
<We can show you a gorilla family nearby.>
<Very close. Only 45 minutes from here!>
Ended up following them.

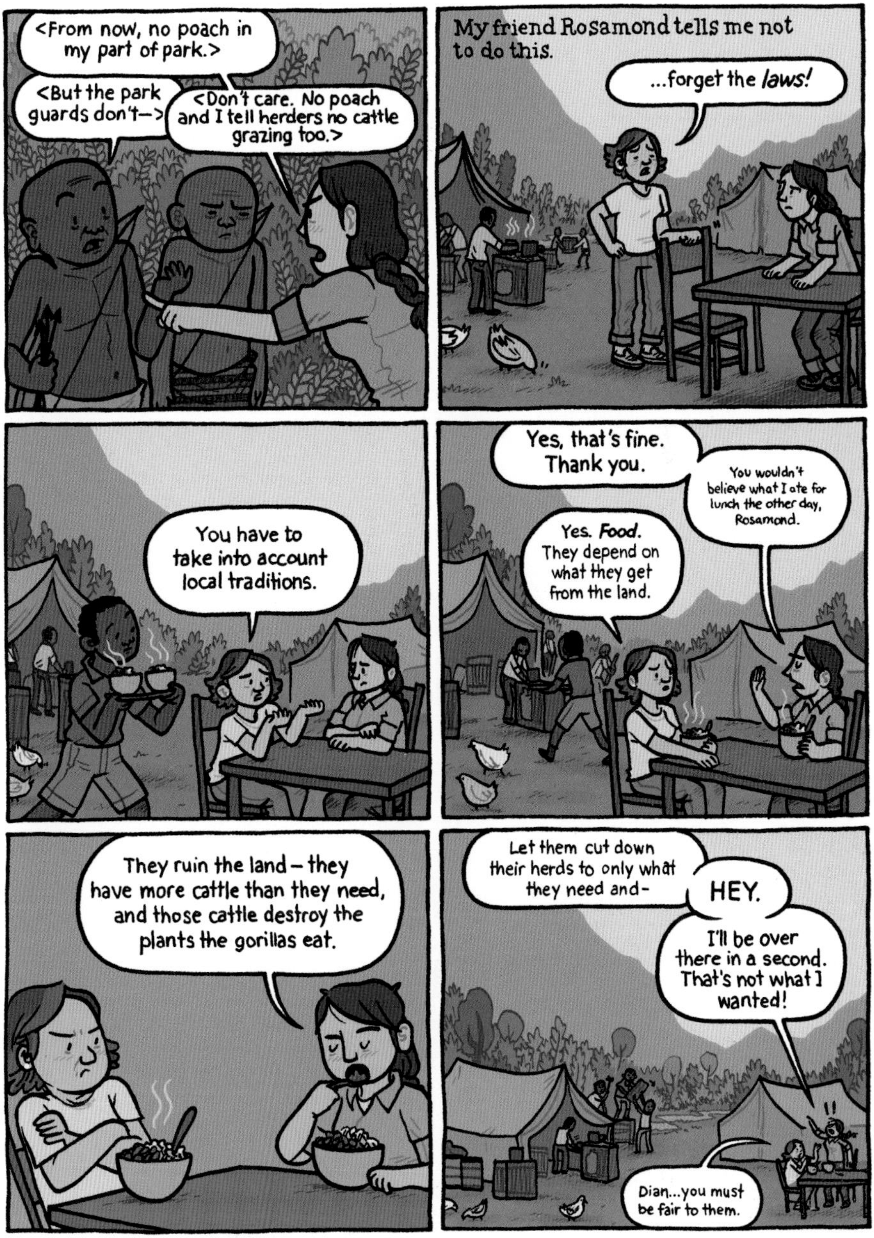

<From now, no poach in my part of park.>
<But the park guards don't—>
<Don't care. No poach and I tell herders no cattle grazing too.>
My friend Rosamond tells me not to do this.
...forget the *laws!*
You have to take into account local traditions.
Yes, that's fine. Thank you.
You wouldn't believe what I ate for lunch the other day, Rosamond.
Yes. *Food.* They depend on what they get from the land.
They ruin the land – they have more cattle than they need, and those cattle destroy the plants the gorillas eat.
Let them cut down their herds to only what they need and-
HEY.
I'll be over there in a second. That's not what I wanted!
Dian...you must be fair to them.

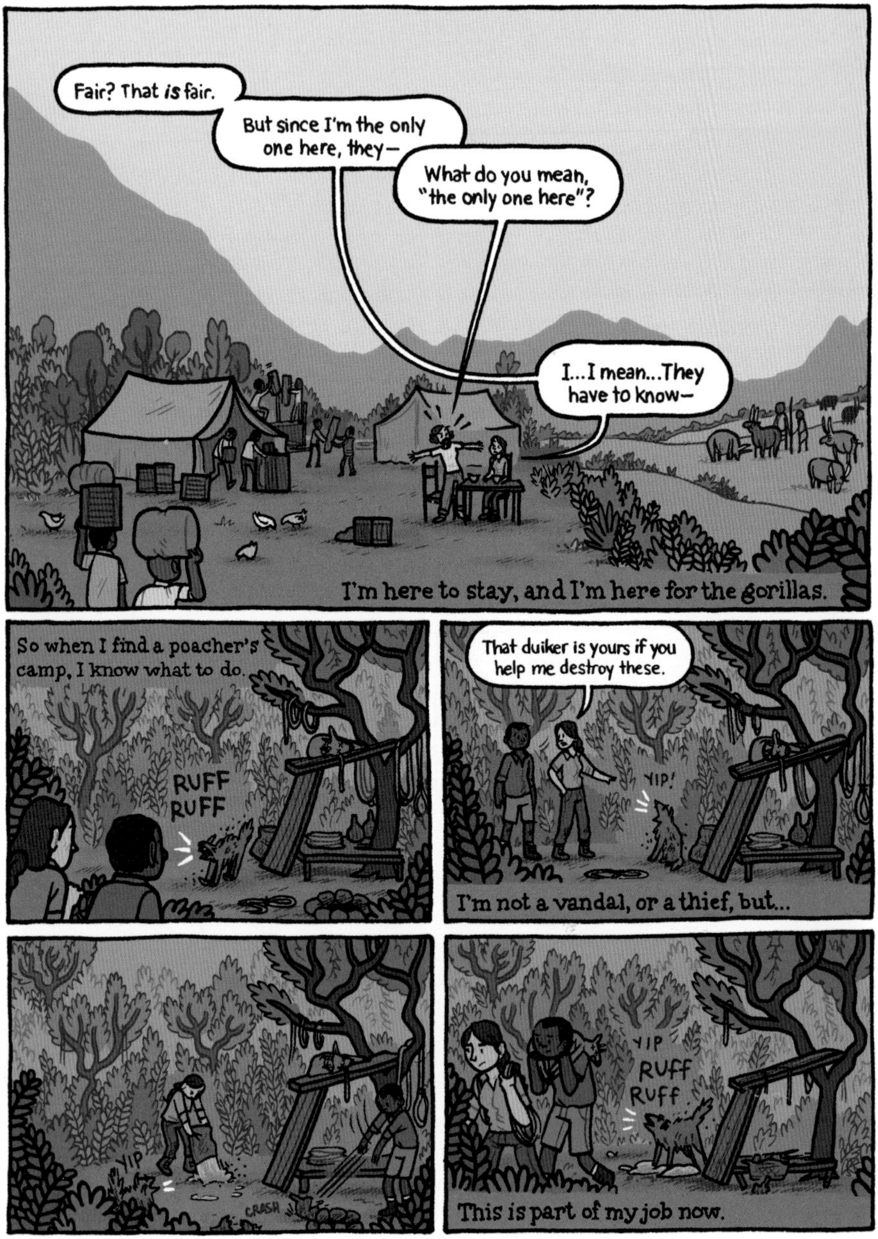
Fair? That *is* fair.
But since I'm the only one here, they—
What do you mean, "the only one here"?
I...I mean...They have to know—
I'm here to stay, and I'm here for the gorillas.
So when I find a poacher's camp, I know what to do.
RUFF RUFF
That duiker is yours if you help me destroy these.
YIP!
I'm not a vandal, or a thief, but...
YIP
CRASH
YIP
RUFF
RUFF
This is part of my job now.

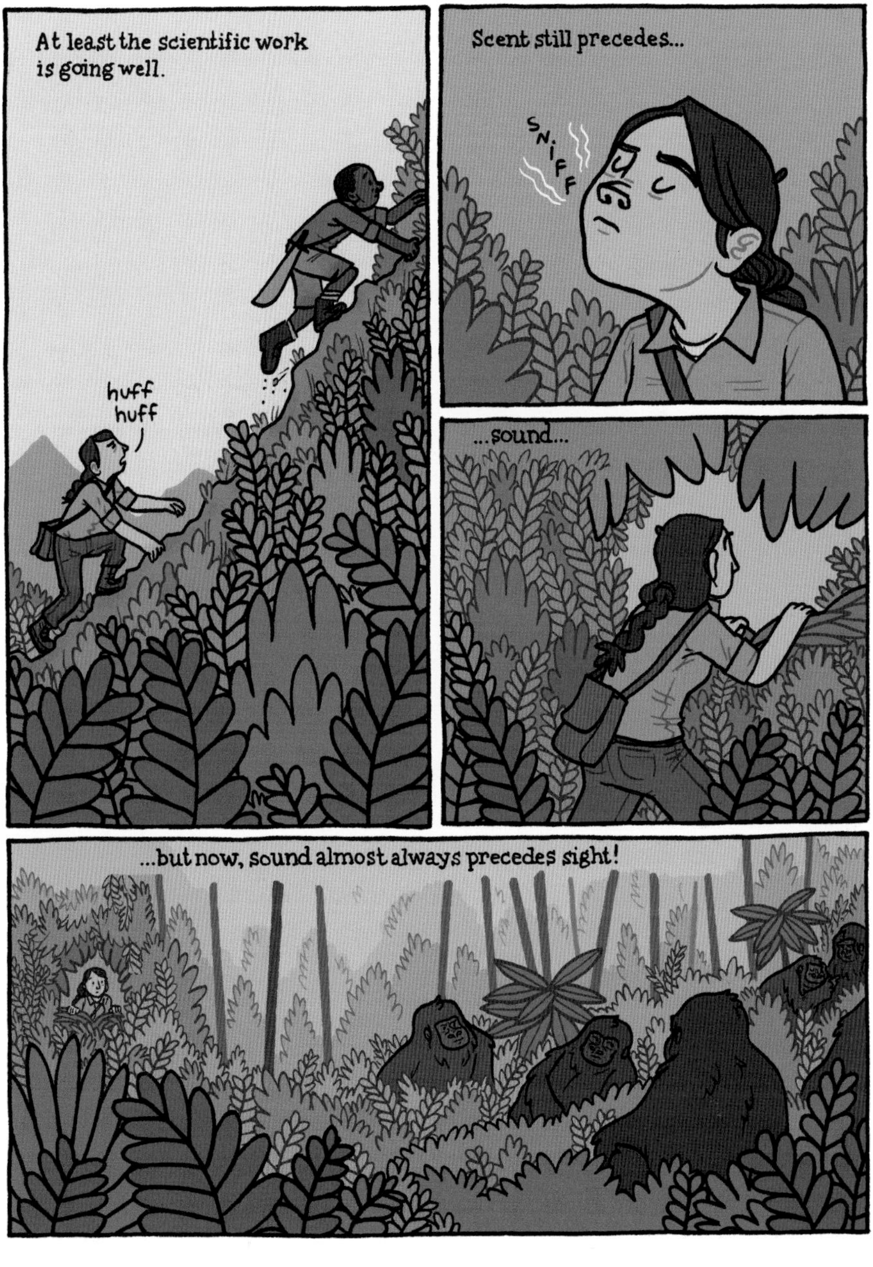
At least the scientific work is going well.
huff huff
Scent still precedes...
SNIFF
...sound...
...but now, sound almost always precedes sight!

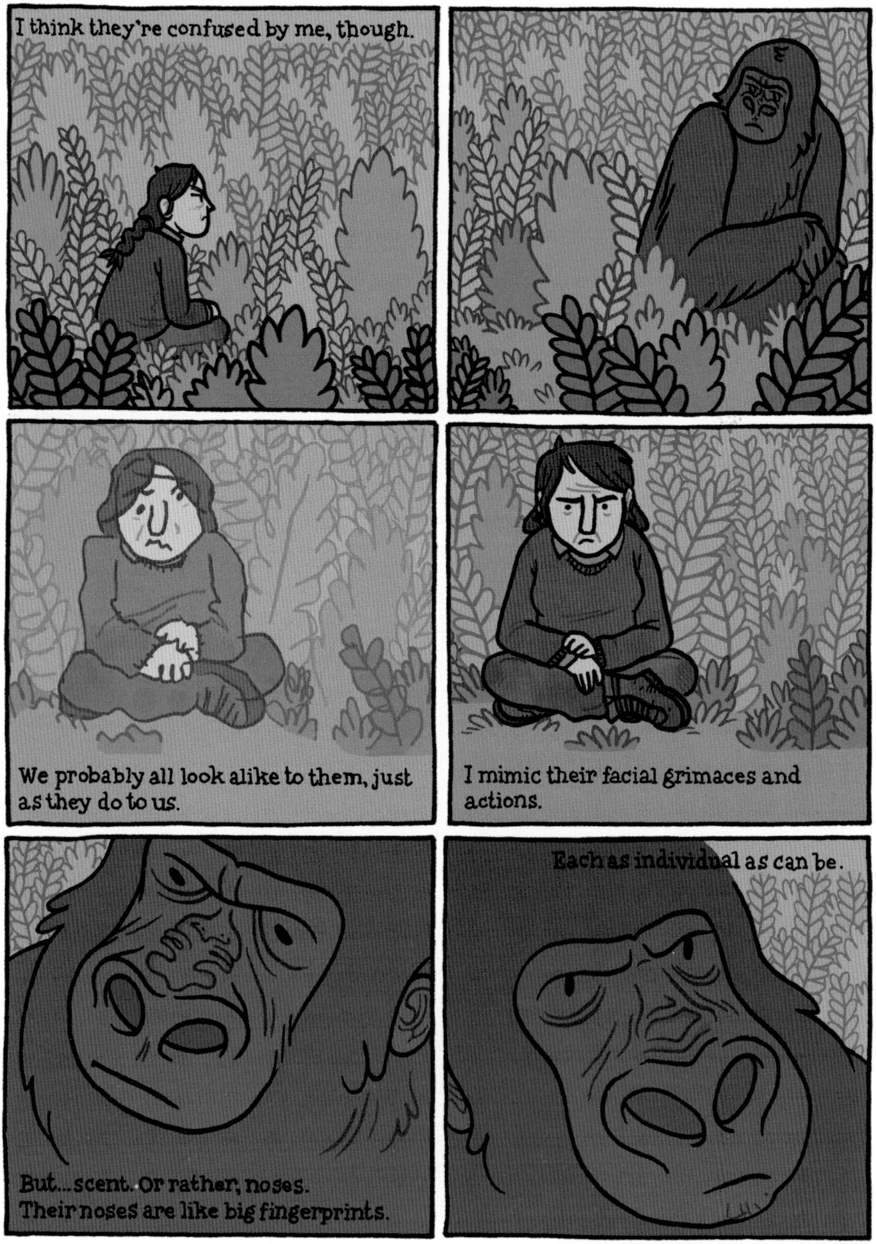
I think they're confused by me, though.
We probably all look alike to them, just as they do to us.
I mimic their facial grimaces and actions.
But...scent. Or rather, noses.
Their noses are like big fingerprints.
Each as individual as can be.

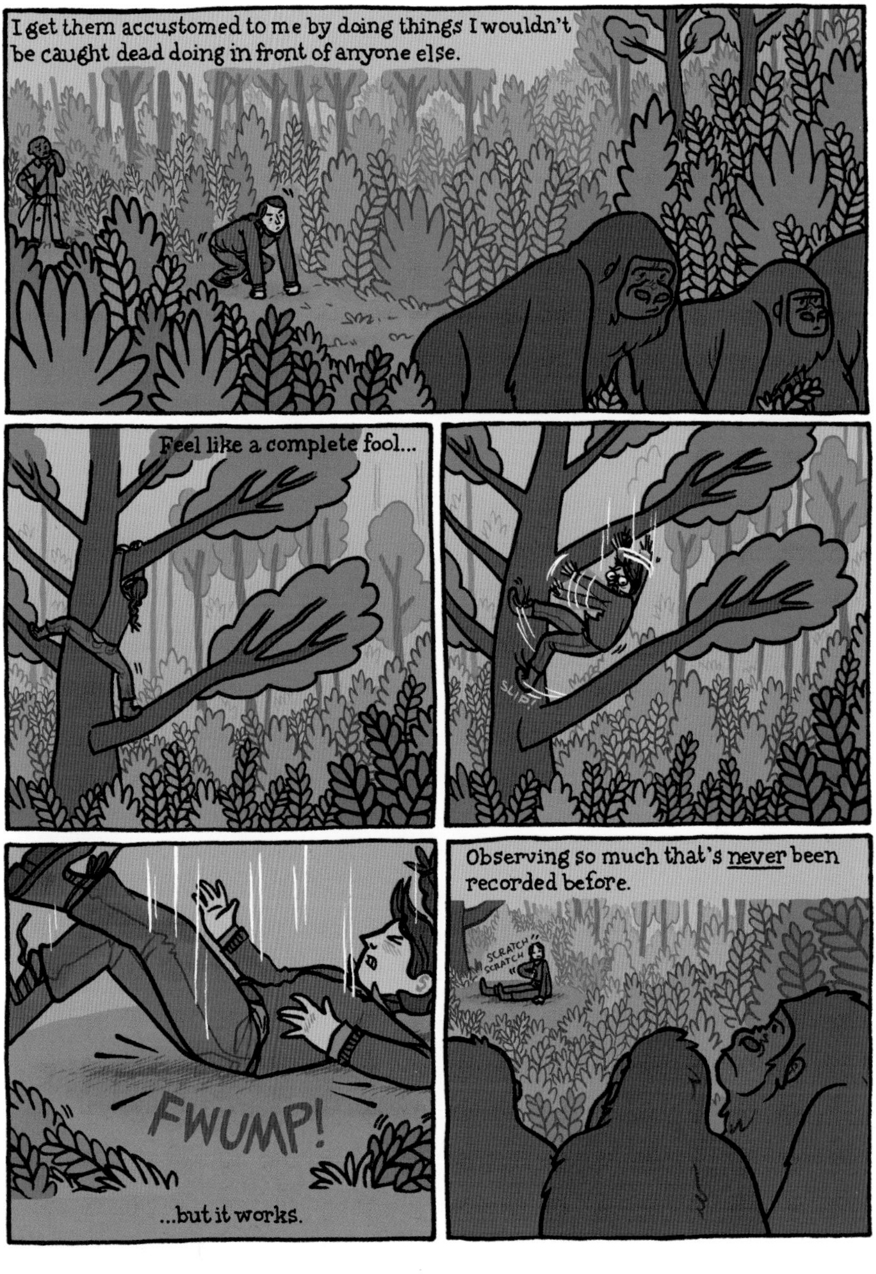
I get them accustomed to me by doing things I wouldn't be caught dead doing in front of anyone else.
Feel like a complete fool...
SLIP!
FWUMP!
...but it works.
Observing so much that's never been recorded before.
SCRATCH SCRATCH

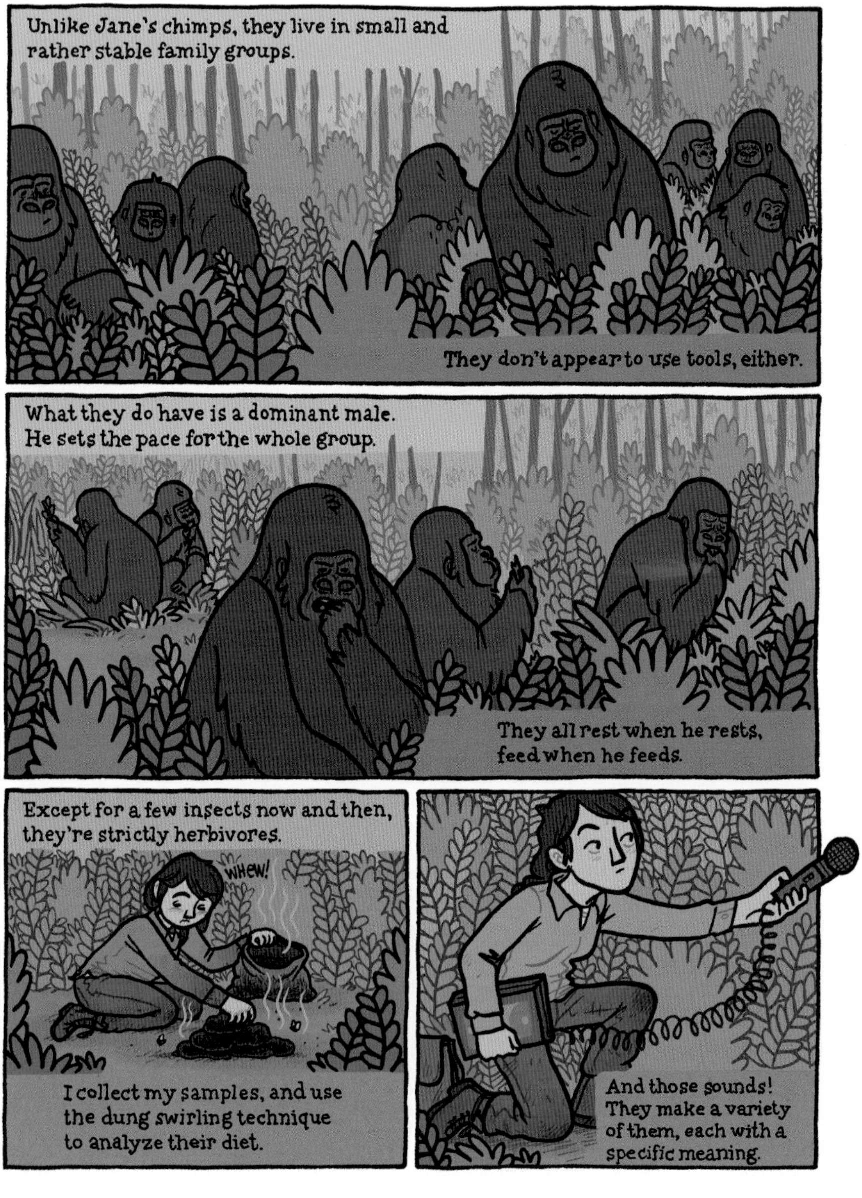
Unlike Jane's chimps, they live in small and rather stable family groups.
They don't appear to use tools, either.
What they do have is a dominant male. He sets the pace for the whole group.
They all rest when he rests, feed when he feeds.
Except for a few insects now and then, they're strictly herbivores.
WHEW!
I collect my samples, and use the dung swirling technique to analyze their diet.
And those sounds! They make a variety of them, each with a specific meaning.

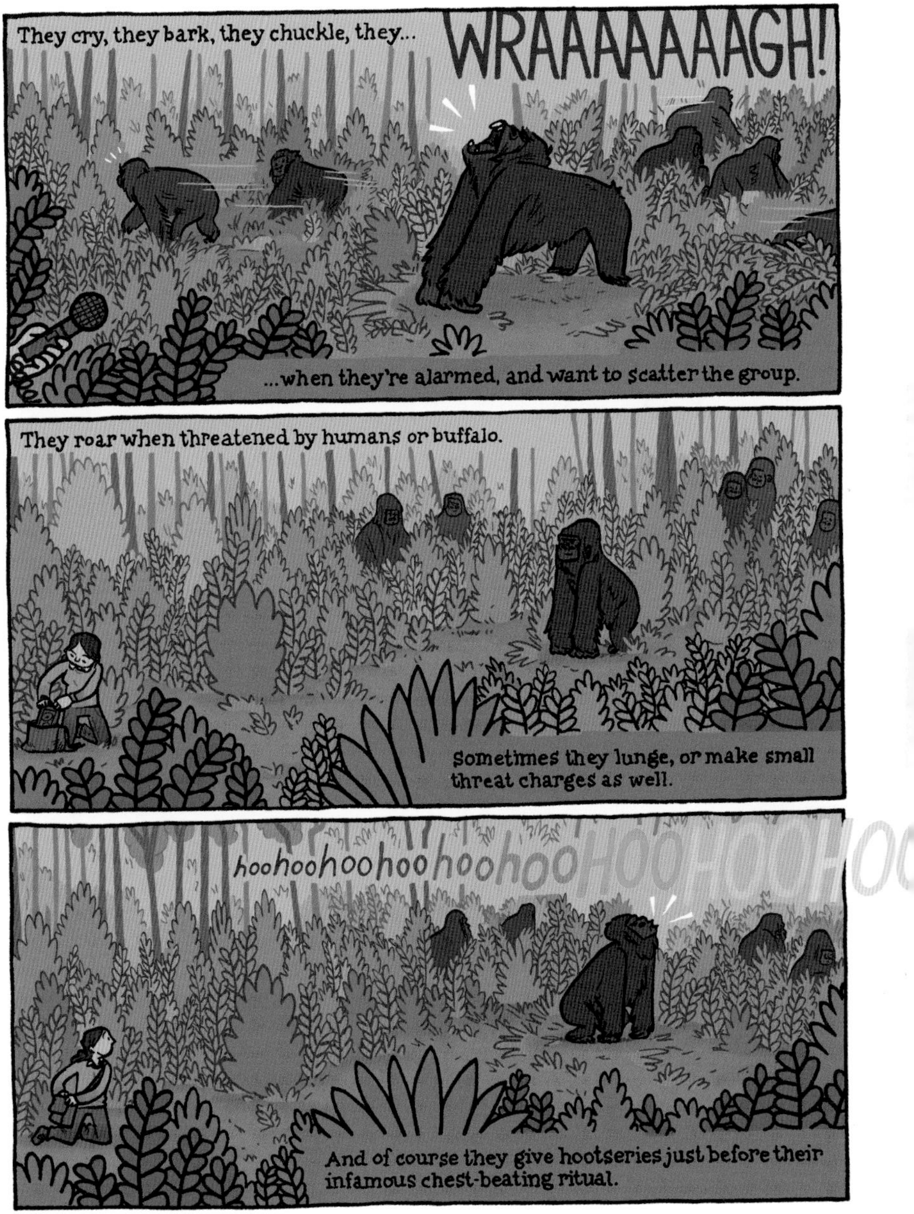
They cry, they bark, they chuckle, they...
WRAAAAAAAAGH!
...when they're alarmed, and want to scatter the group.
They roar when threatened by humans or buffalo.
Sometimes they lunge, or make small threat charges as well.
hoohoohoohoohoohooHOOHOOHOO
And of course they give hootseries just before their infamous chest-beating ritual.

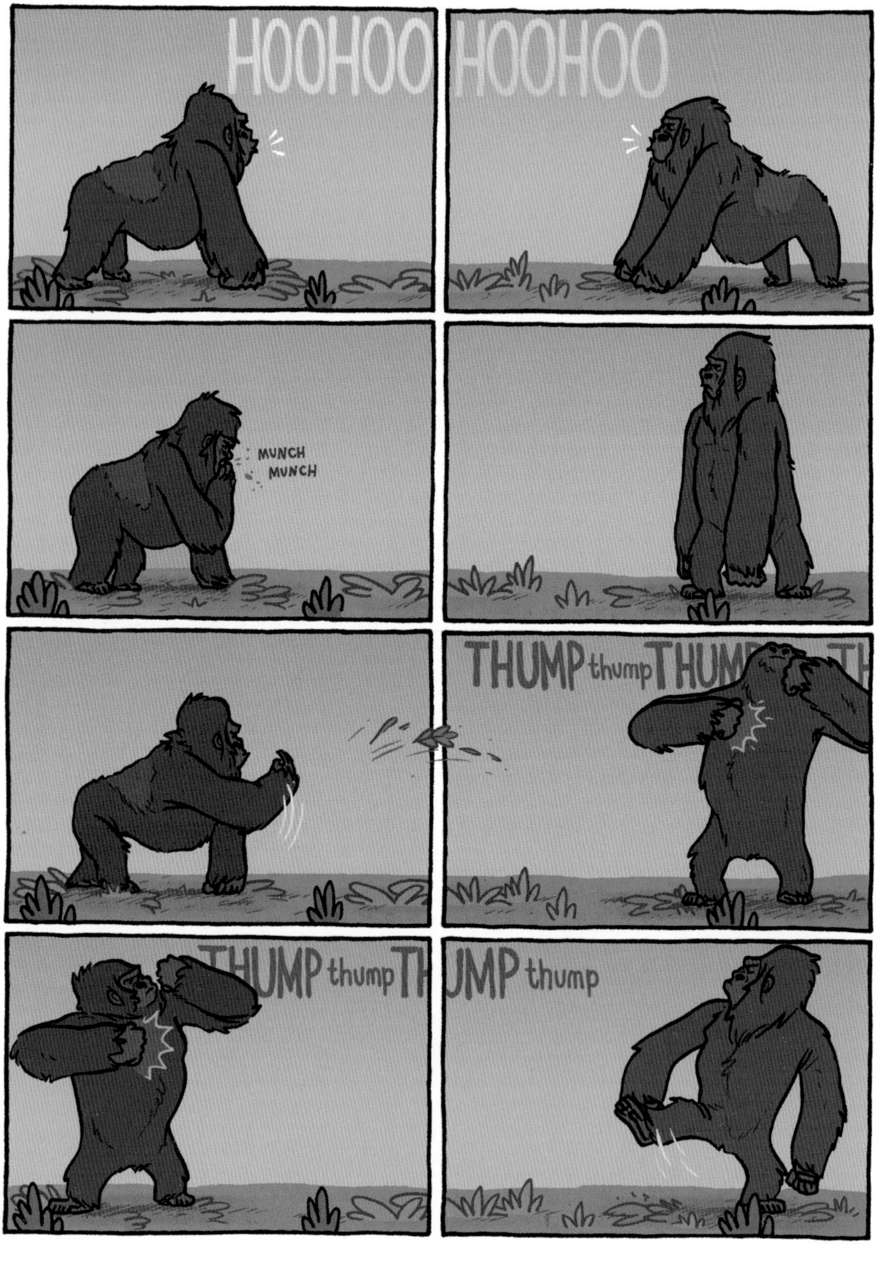
HOOHOO
HOOHOO
MUNCH
MUNCH
THUMP thump THUM
THUMP thump TH
UMP thump

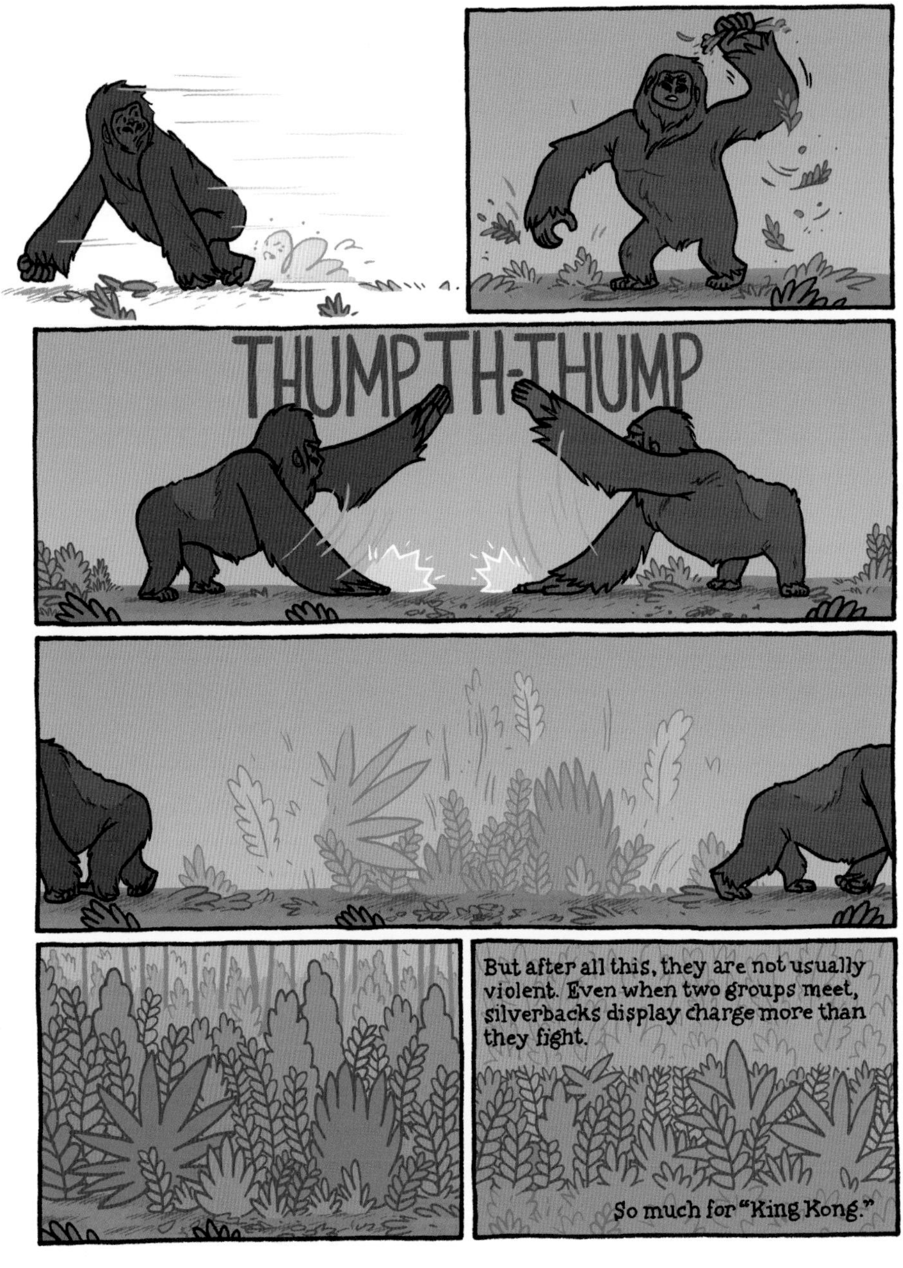
THUMP TH-THUMP
But after all this, they are not usually violent. Even when two groups meet, silverbacks display charge more than they fight.
So much for "King Kong."

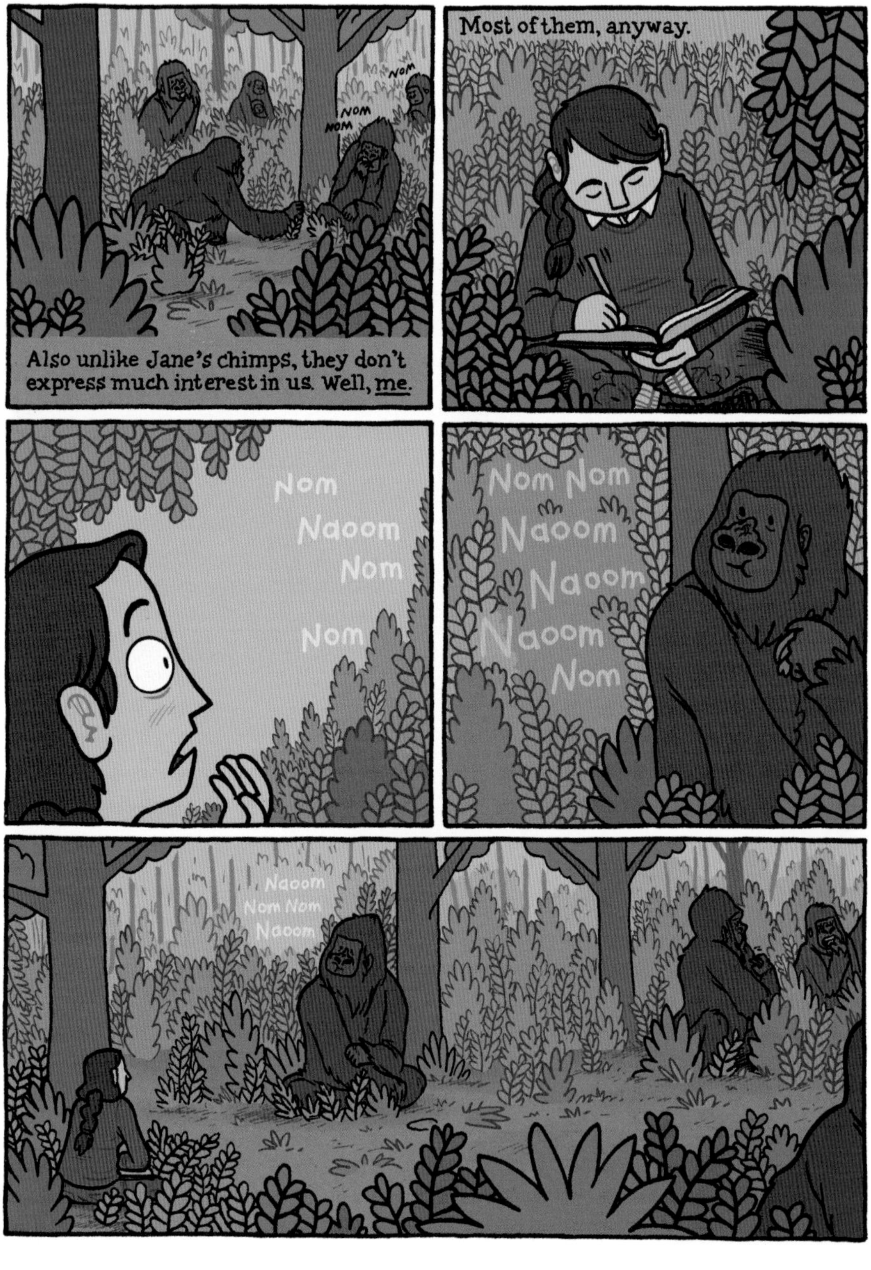
NOM
NOM NOM
Also unlike Jane's chimps, they don't express much interest in us. Well, me.
Most of them, anyway.
Nom
Naoom
Nom
Nom
Nom Nom
Naoom
Naoom
Naoom
Nom
Naoom
Nom Nom
Naoom

I named him Peanuts.

Nom
Naoom
Nom

He was my breakthrough.

TAKETA TAKETA tck tck tak
tck tck—ding! TAKETA tck tak
tak TAKETA tak   tak tck
—ding tak TAKETA   TAKETA
tck TAKETA tck   tck
          tak

"I'VE FINALLY
BEEN ACCEPTED
BY A GORILLA."

TOSS!

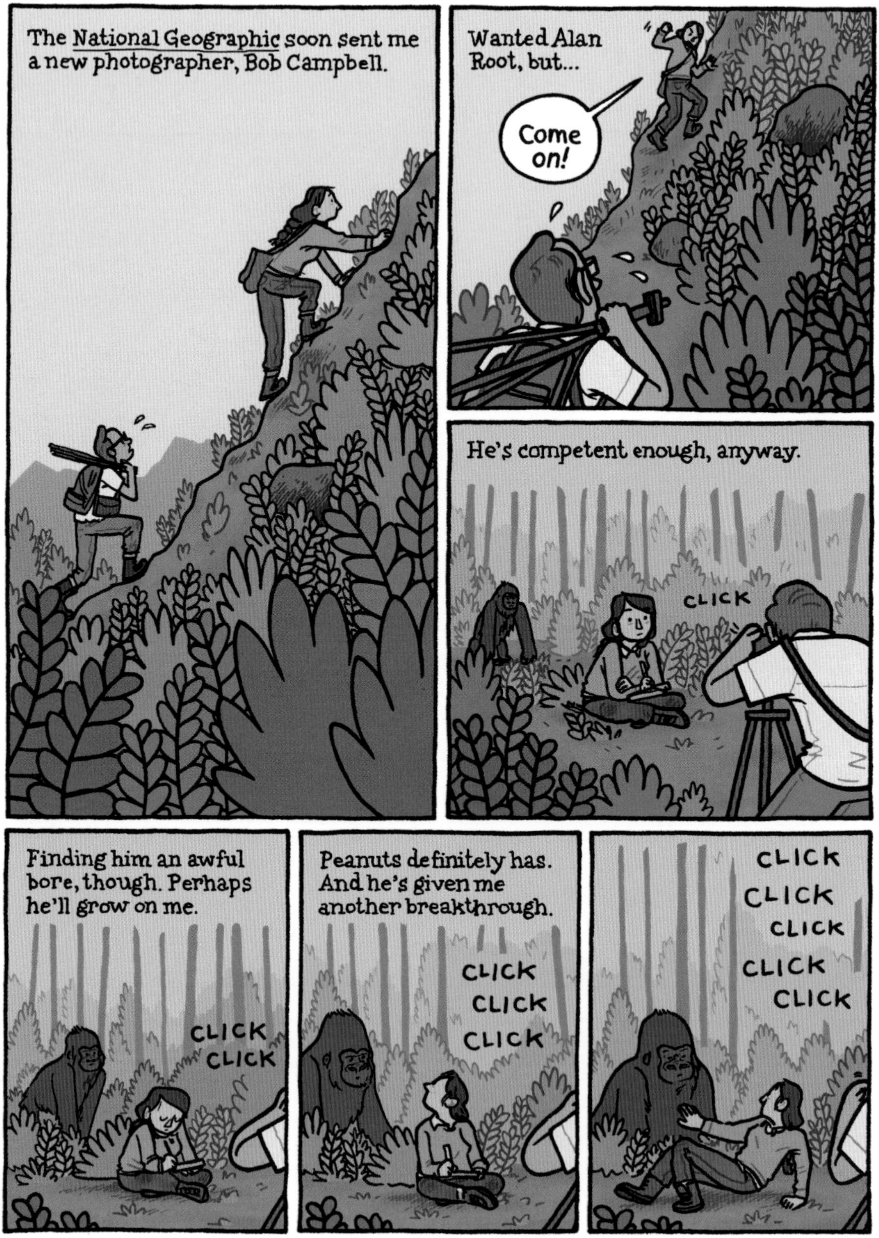
The National Geographic soon sent me a new photographer, Bob Campbell.
Wanted Alan Root, but...
Come on!
He's competent enough, anyway.
CLICK
Finding him an awful bore, though. Perhaps he'll grow on me.
CLICK
CLICK
Peanuts definitely has. And he's given me another breakthrough.
CLICK
CLICK
CLICK
CLICK
CLICK
CLICK
CLICK
CLICK

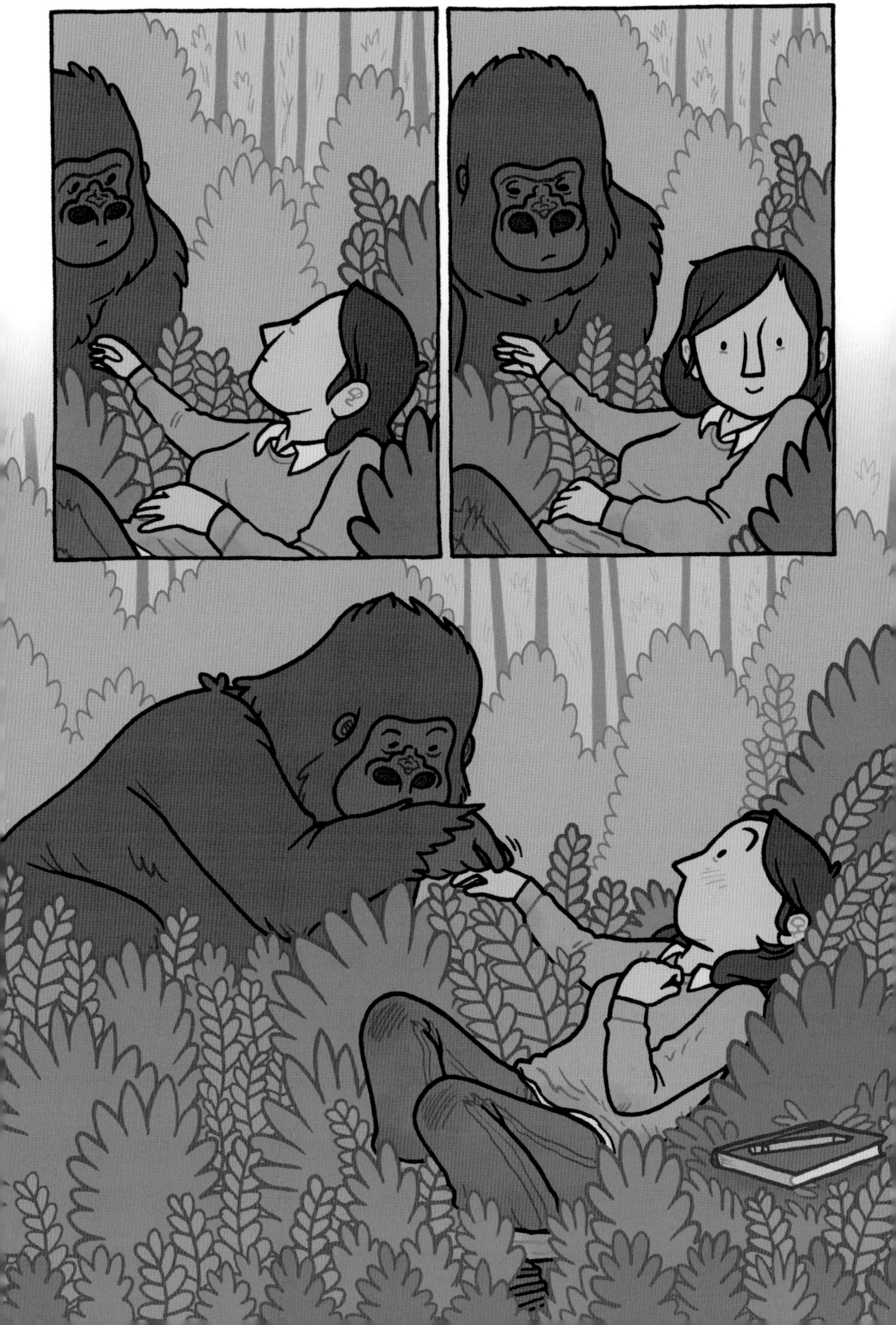

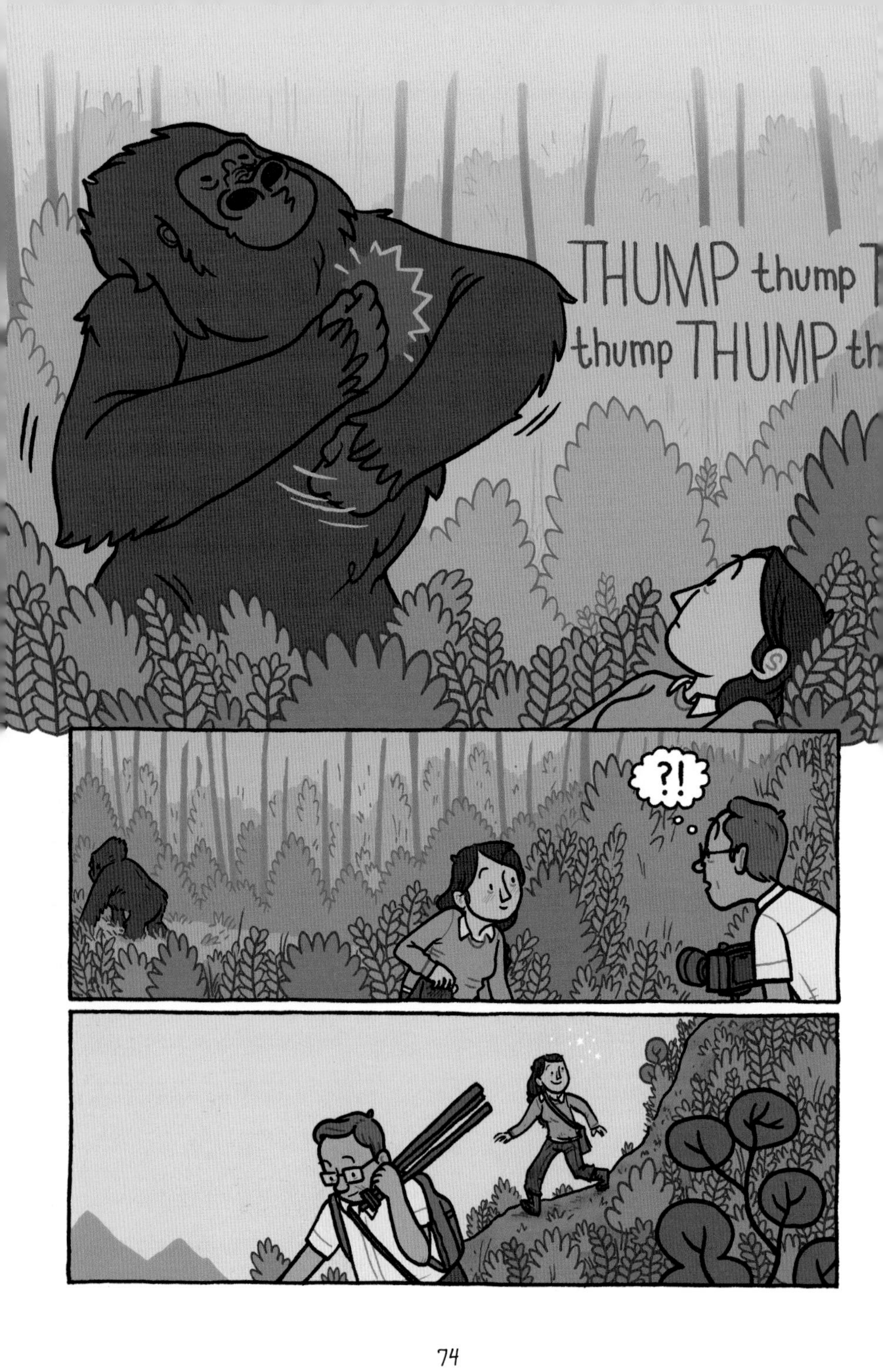
THUMP thump
thump THUMP
?!

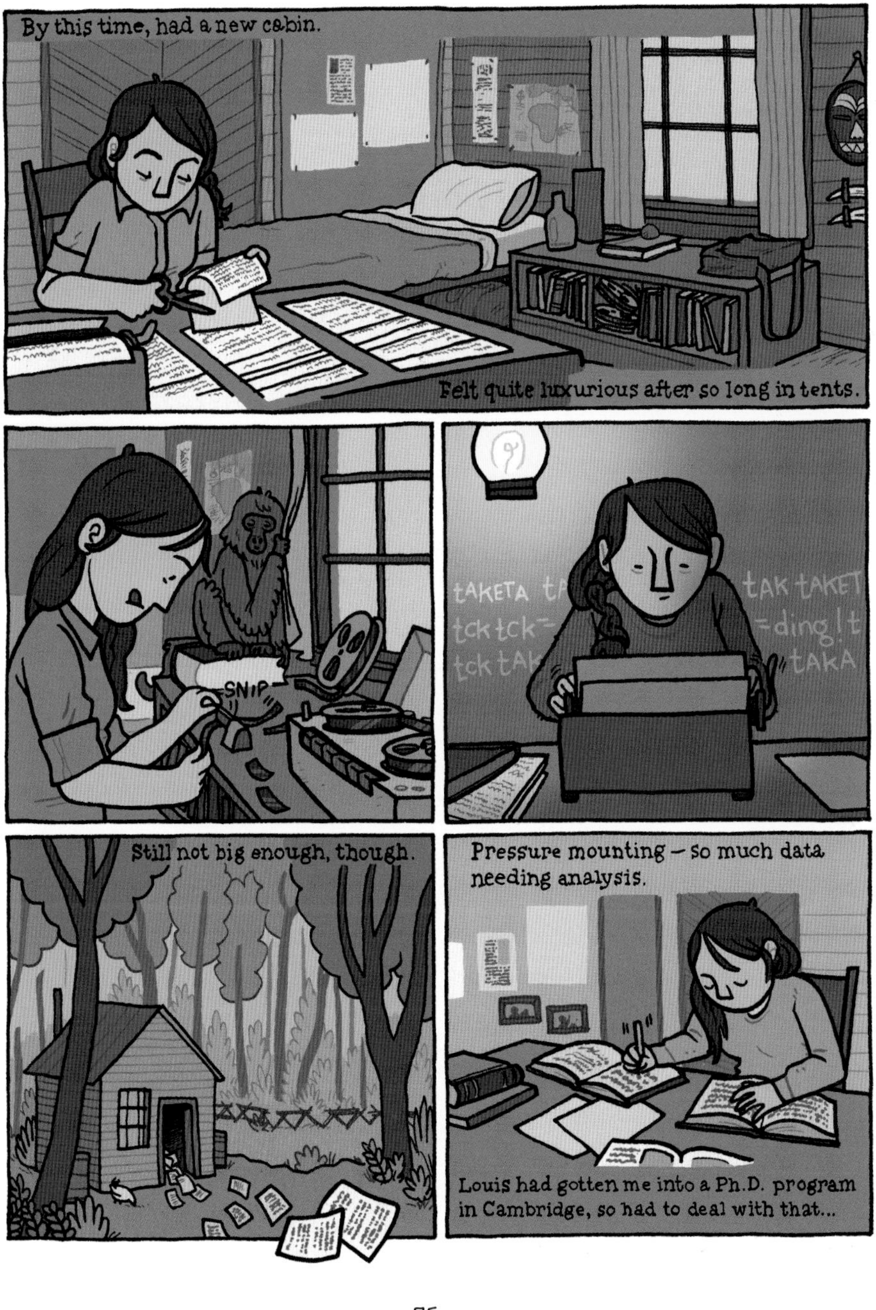
By this time, had a new cabin.
Felt quite luxurious after so long in tents.
SNIP
tAKETA
tck tck=
tck tAK
tAK tAKET
=ding! t
TAKA
Still not big enough, though.
Pressure mounting – so much data needing analysis.
Louis had gotten me into a Ph.D. program in Cambridge, so had to deal with that...

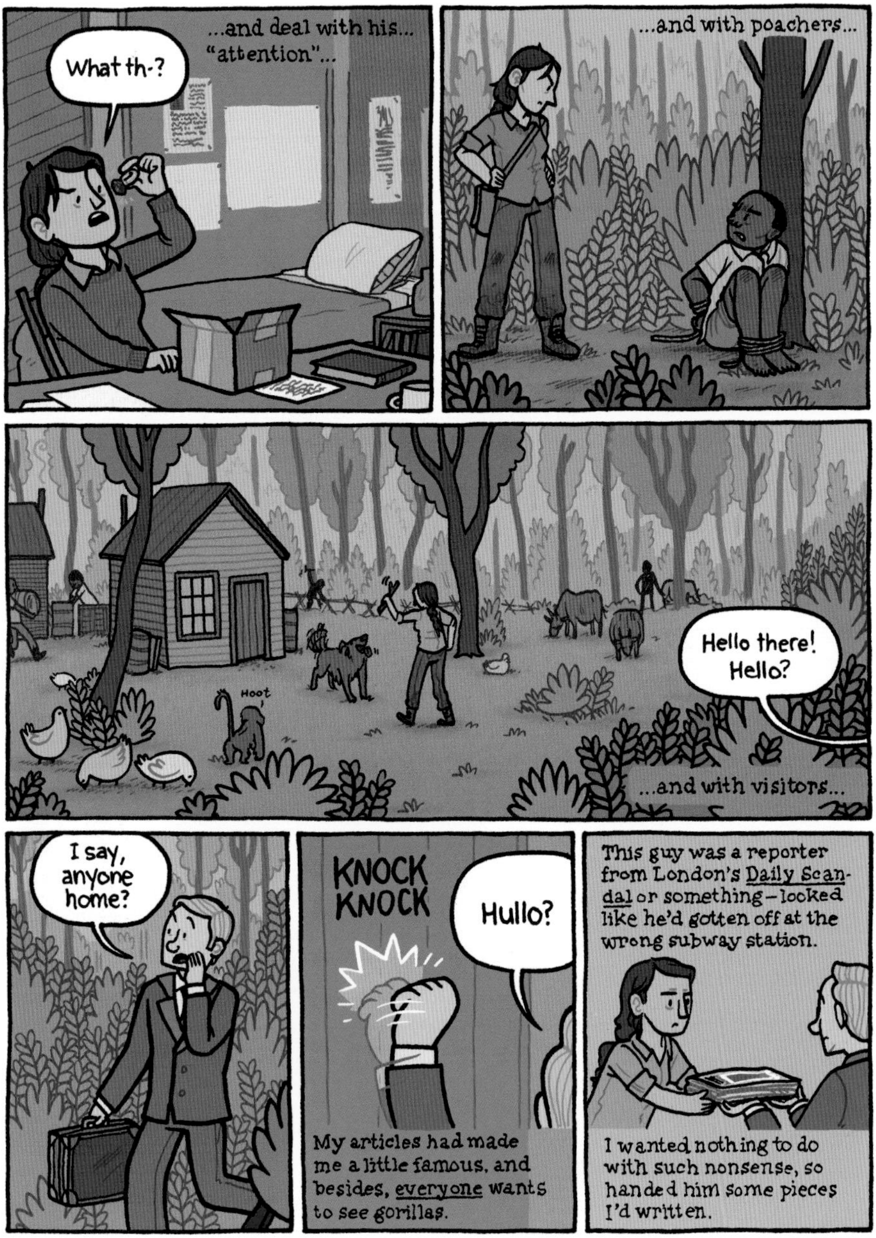
...and deal with his... "attention"...
What th-?
...and with poachers...
Hello there! Hello?
...and with visitors...
Hoot
I say, anyone home?
KNOCK KNOCK
Hullo?
My articles had made me a little famous, and besides, everyone wants to see gorillas.
This guy was a reporter from London's Daily Scandal or something—looked like he'd gotten off at the wrong subway station.
I wanted nothing to do with such nonsense, so handed him some pieces I'd written.

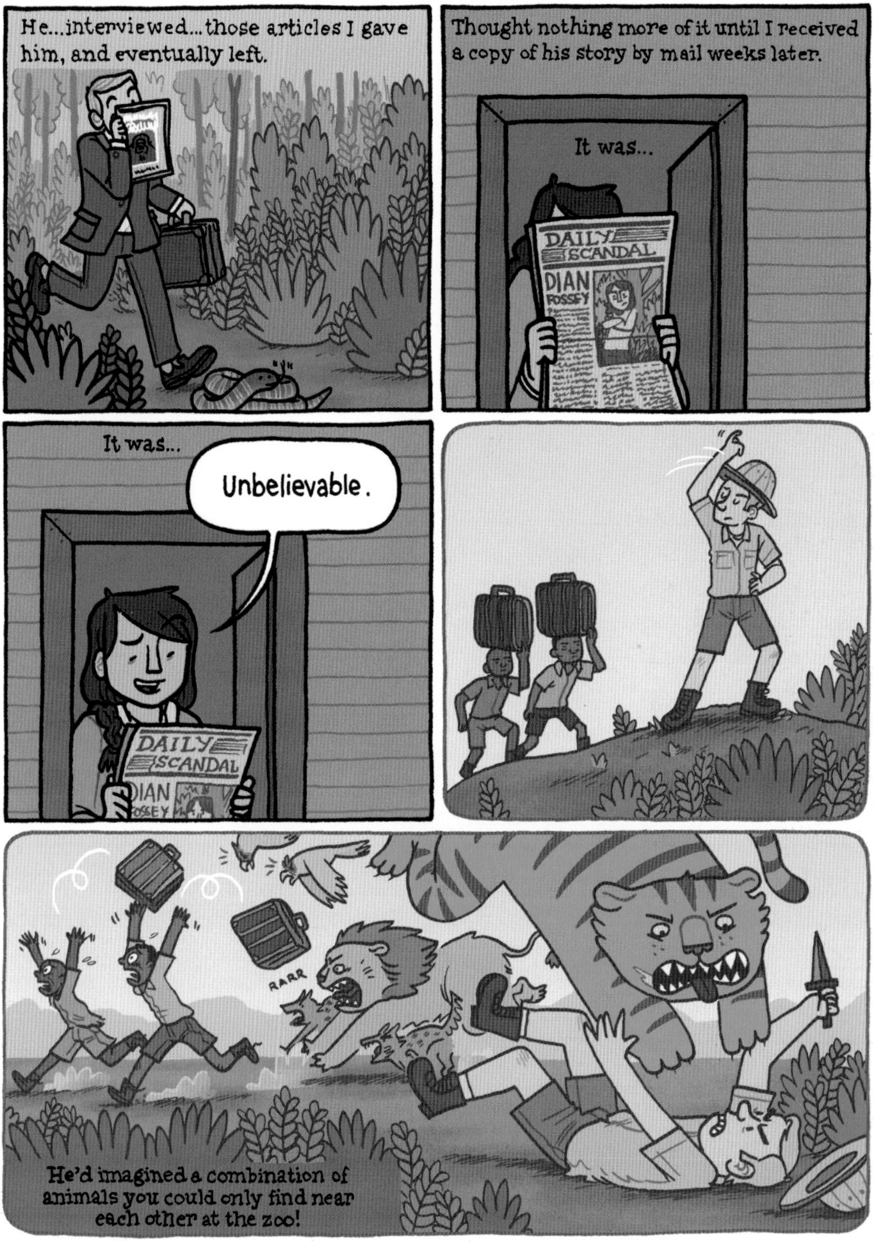
He...interviewed...those articles I gave him, and eventually left.
Thought nothing more of it until I received a copy of his story by mail weeks later.
It was...
DAILY SCANDAL
DIAN FOSSEY
It was...
Unbelievable.
DAILY SCANDAL
DIAN FOSSEY
RARR
He'd imagined a combination of animals you could only find near each other at the zoo!

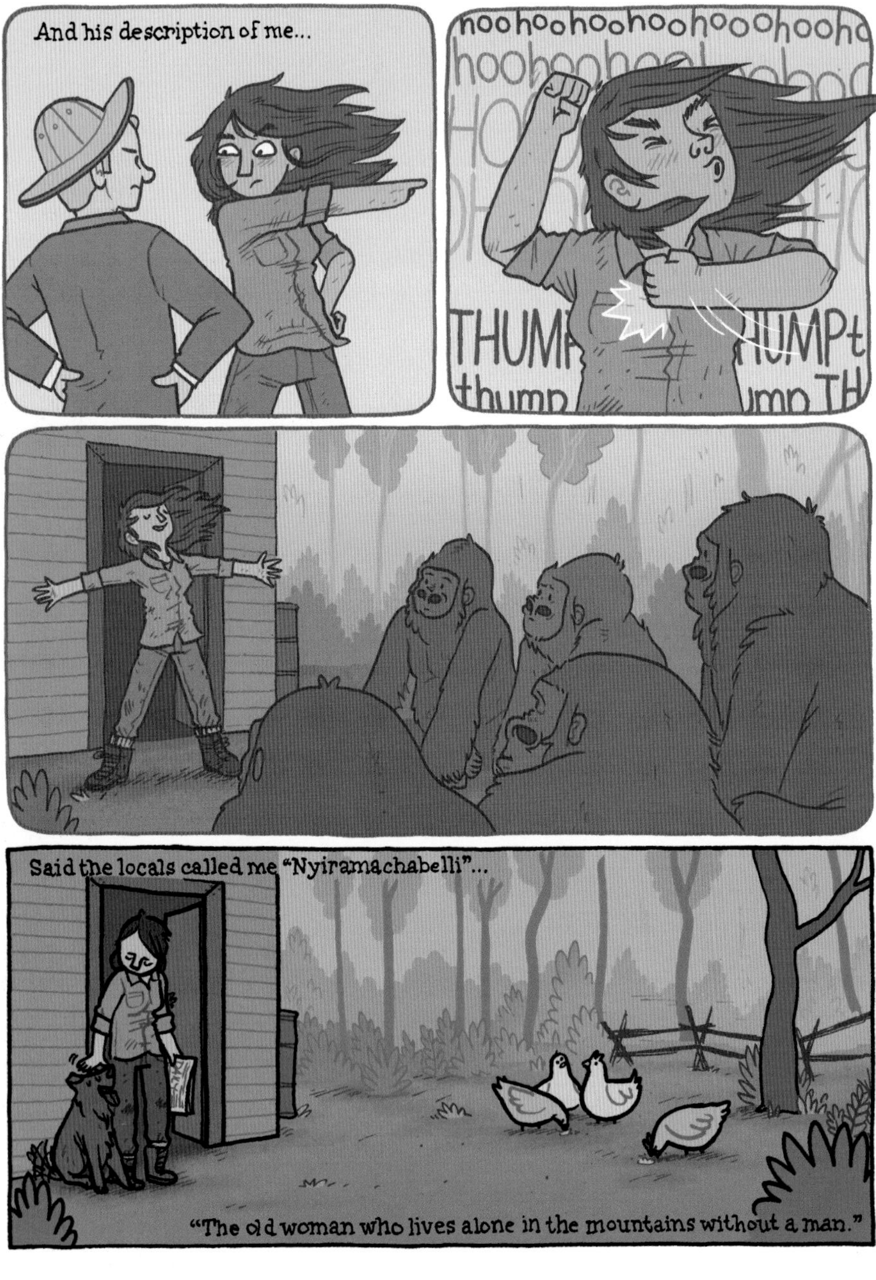
And his description of me...
hoohoohoohoohooohooho
THUMP
THUMPt
Said the locals called me "Nyiramachabelli"...
"The old woman who lives alone in the mountains without a man."

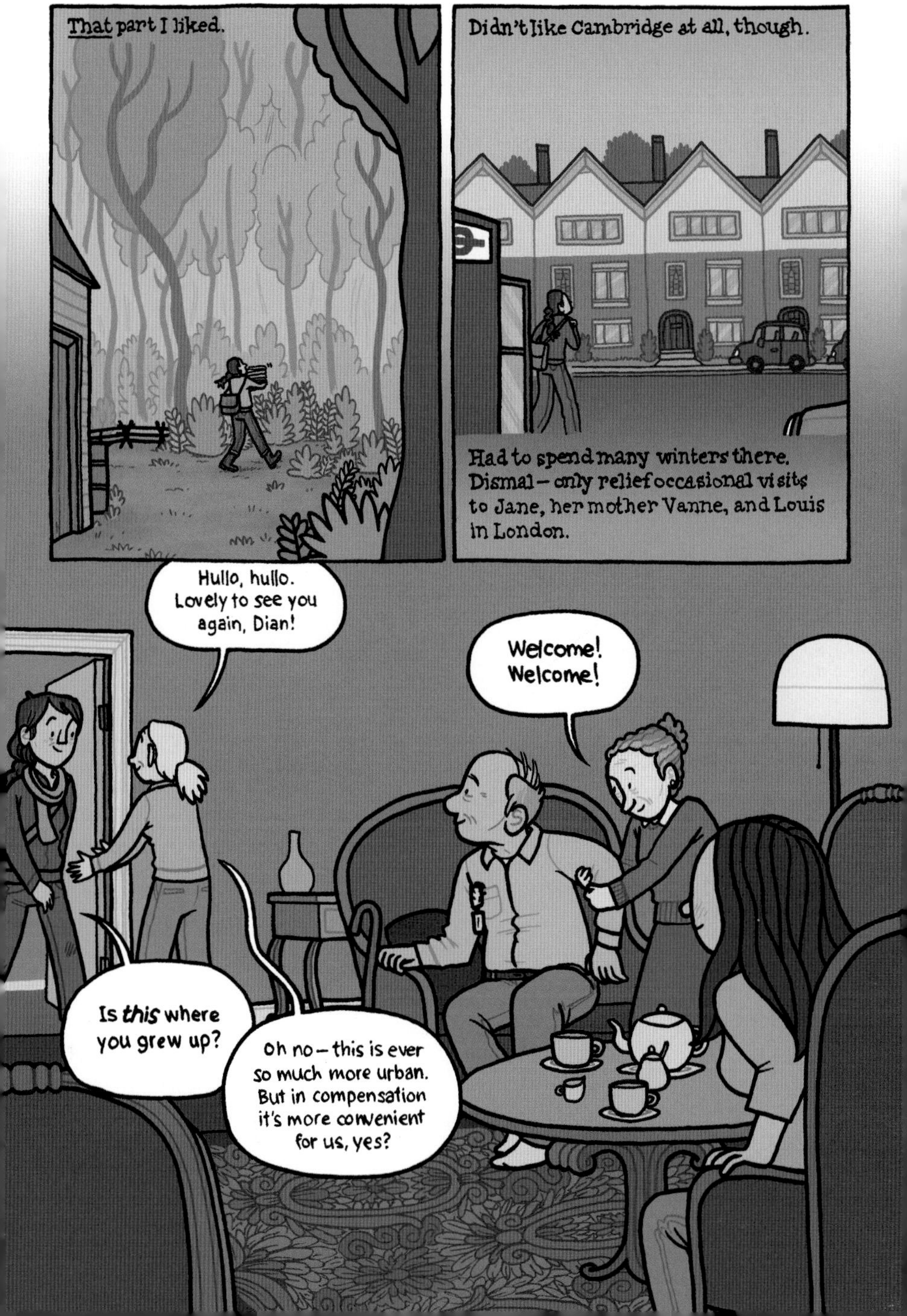
That part I liked.
Didn't like Cambridge at all, though.
Had to spend many winters there. Dismal—only relief occasional visits to Jane, her mother Vanne, and Louis in London.
Hullo, hullo. Lovely to see you again, Dian!
Welcome! Welcome!
Is *this* where you grew up?
Oh no—this is ever so much more urban. But in compensation it's more convenient for us, yes?

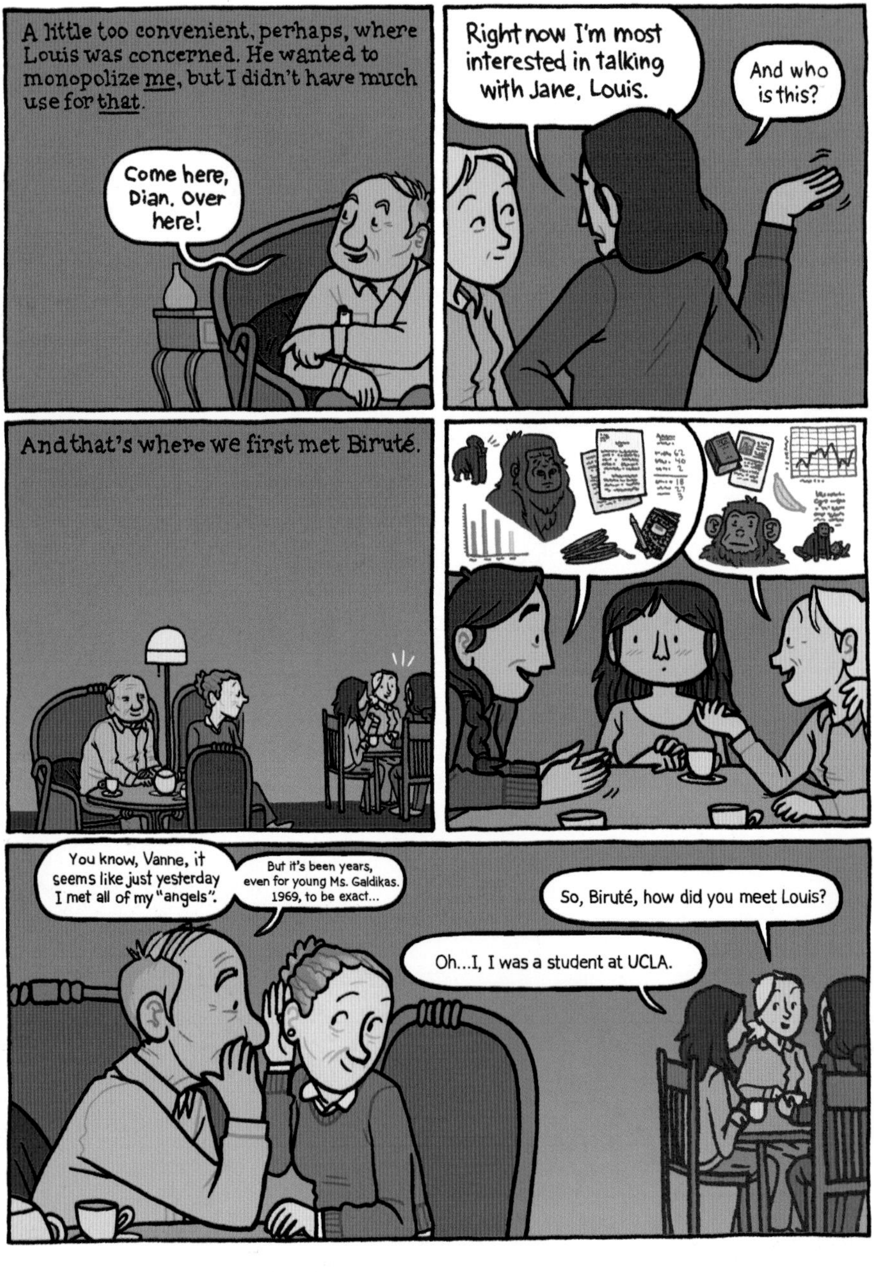
A little too convenient, perhaps, where Louis was concerned. He wanted to monopolize me, but I didn't have much use for that.
Come here, Dian. Over here!
Right now I'm most interested in talking with Jane, Louis.
And who is this?
And that's where we first met Biruté.
You know, Vanne, it seems like just yesterday I met all of my "angels".
But it's been years, even for young Ms. Galdikas. 1969, to be exact...
So, Biruté, how did you meet Louis?
Oh...I, I was a student at UCLA.

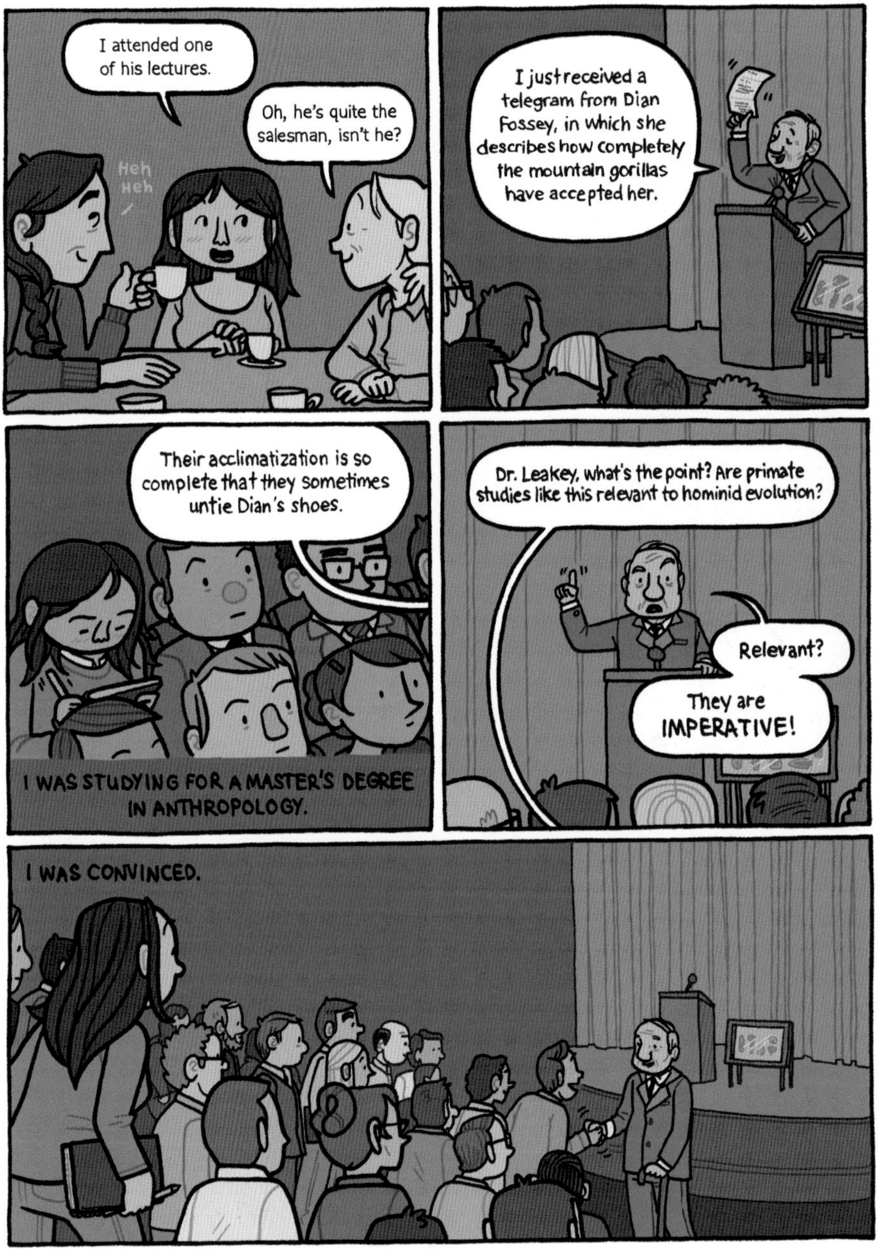
I attended one of his lectures.
Oh, he's quite the salesman, isn't he?
Heh Heh
I just received a telegram from Dian Fossey, in which she describes how completely the mountain gorillas have accepted her.
Their acclimatization is so complete that they sometimes untie Dian's shoes.
I WAS STUDYING FOR A MASTER'S DEGREE IN ANTHROPOLOGY.
Dr. Leakey, what's the point? Are primate studies like this relevant to hominid evolution?
Relevant?
They are IMPERATIVE!
I WAS CONVINCED.

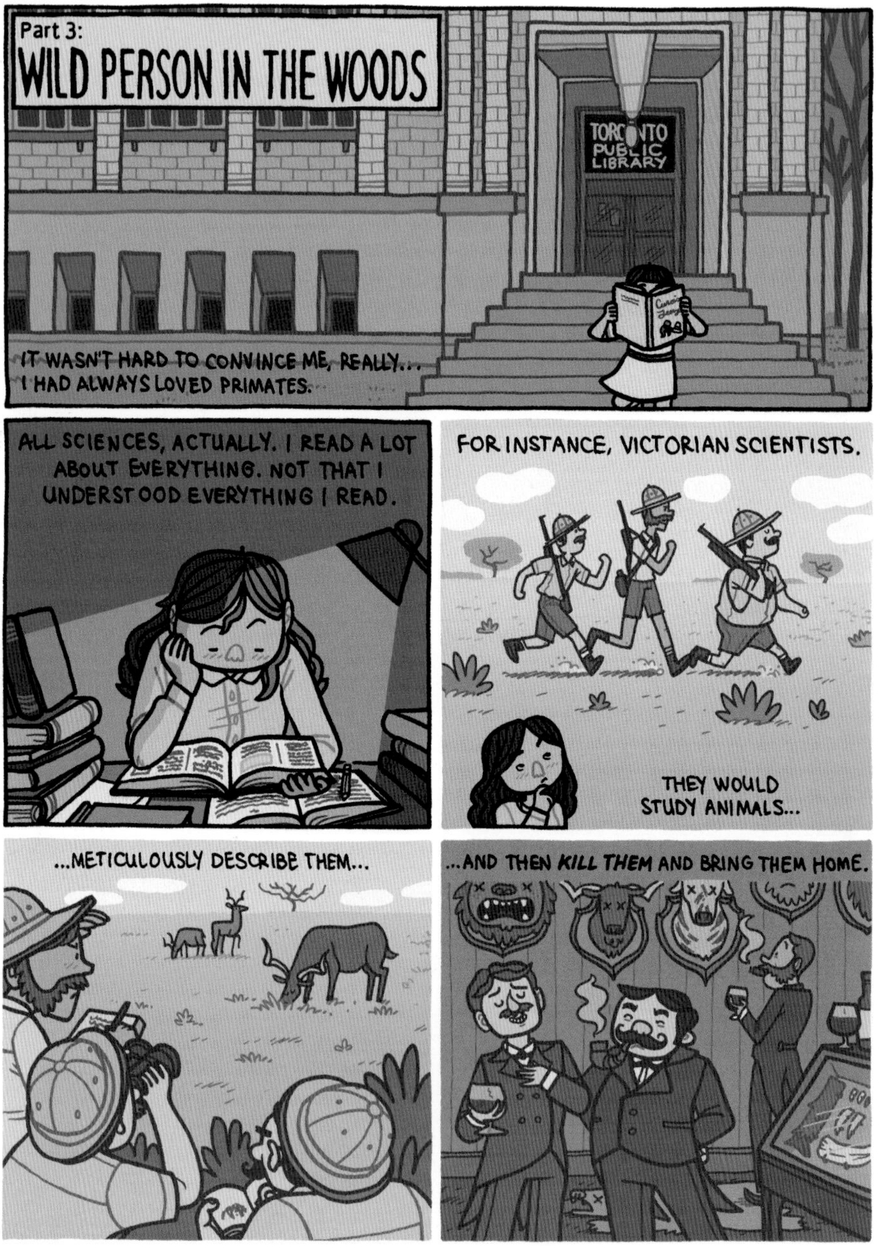
Part 3:
WILD PERSON IN THE WOODS
TORONTO PUBLIC LIBRARY
IT WASN'T HARD TO CONVINCE ME, REALLY...
I HAD ALWAYS LOVED PRIMATES.
ALL SCIENCES, ACTUALLY. I READ A LOT ABOUT EVERYTHING. NOT THAT I UNDERSTOOD EVERYTHING I READ.
FOR INSTANCE, VICTORIAN SCIENTISTS.
THEY WOULD STUDY ANIMALS...
...METICULOUSLY DESCRIBE THEM...
...AND THEN KILL THEM AND BRING THEM HOME.

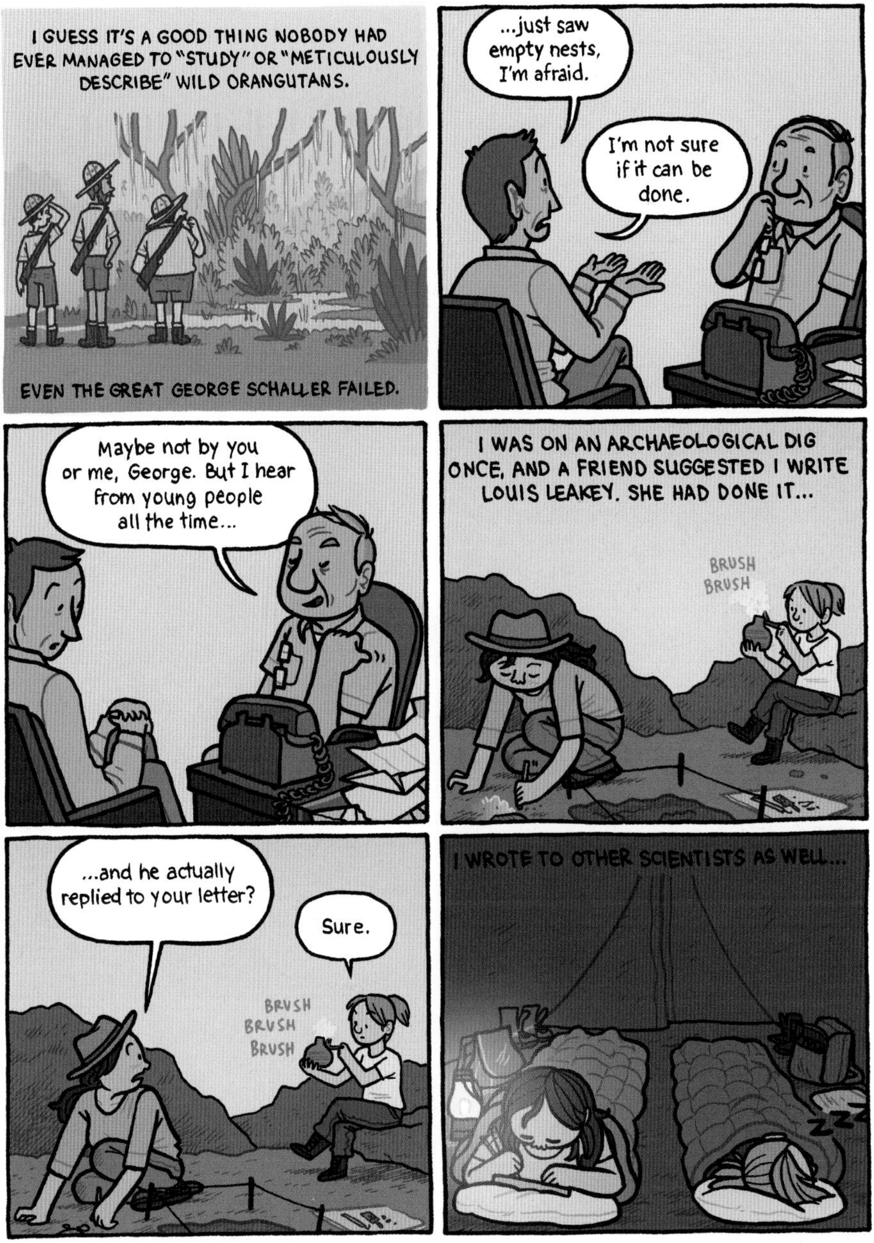
I GUESS IT'S A GOOD THING NOBODY HAD EVER MANAGED TO "STUDY" OR "METICULOUSLY DESCRIBE" WILD ORANGUTANS.
EVEN THE GREAT GEORGE SCHALLER FAILED.
...just saw empty nests, I'm afraid.
I'm not sure if it can be done.
Maybe not by you or me, George. But I hear from young people all the time...
I WAS ON AN ARCHAEOLOGICAL DIG ONCE, AND A FRIEND SUGGESTED I WRITE LOUIS LEAKEY. SHE HAD DONE IT...
BRUSH BRUSH
...and he actually replied to your letter?
Sure.
BRUSH BRUSH BRUSH
I WROTE TO OTHER SCIENTISTS AS WELL...
ZZZ

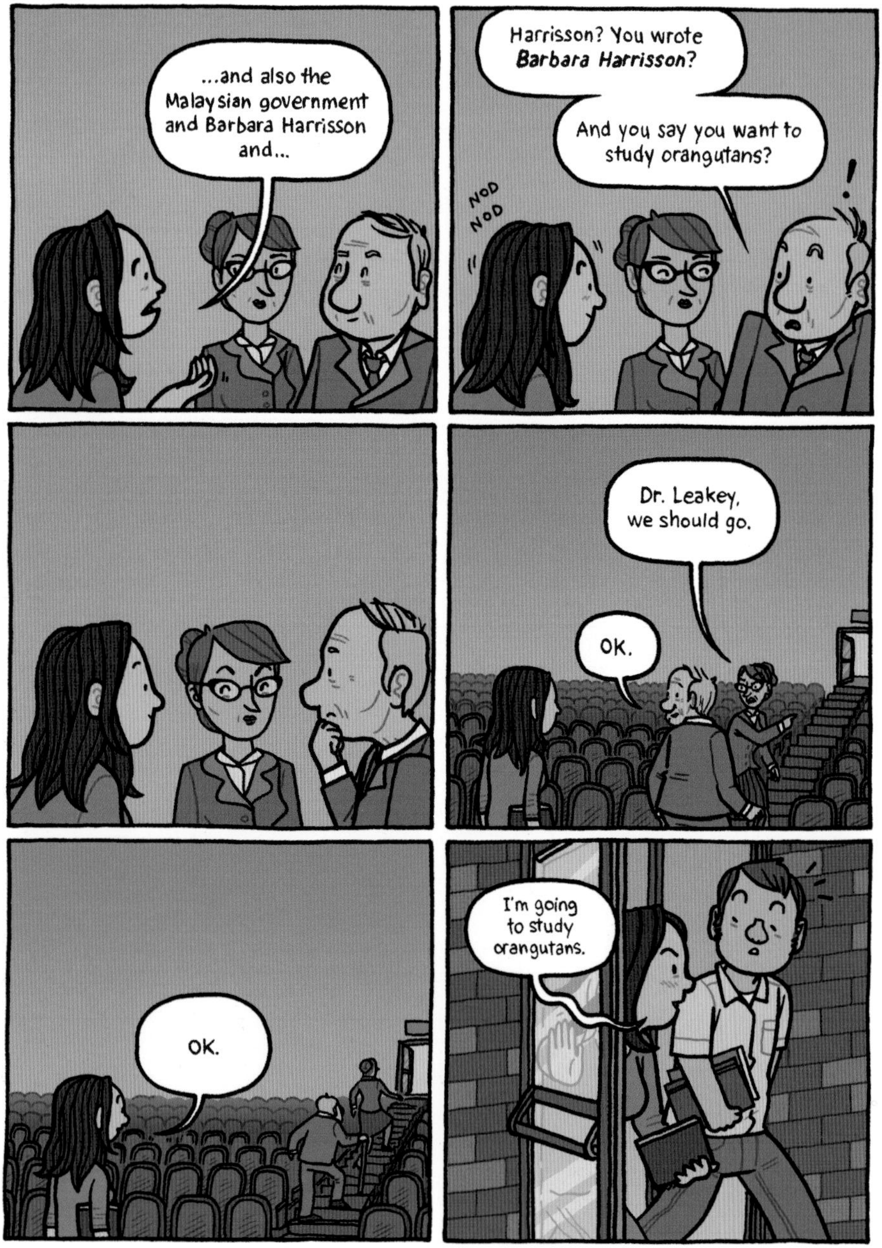
...and also the Malaysian government and Barbara Harrisson and...
Harrisson? You wrote **Barbara Harrisson**?
And you say you want to study orangutans?
NOD NOD
!
Dr. Leakey, we should go.
OK.
OK.
I'm going to study orangutans.

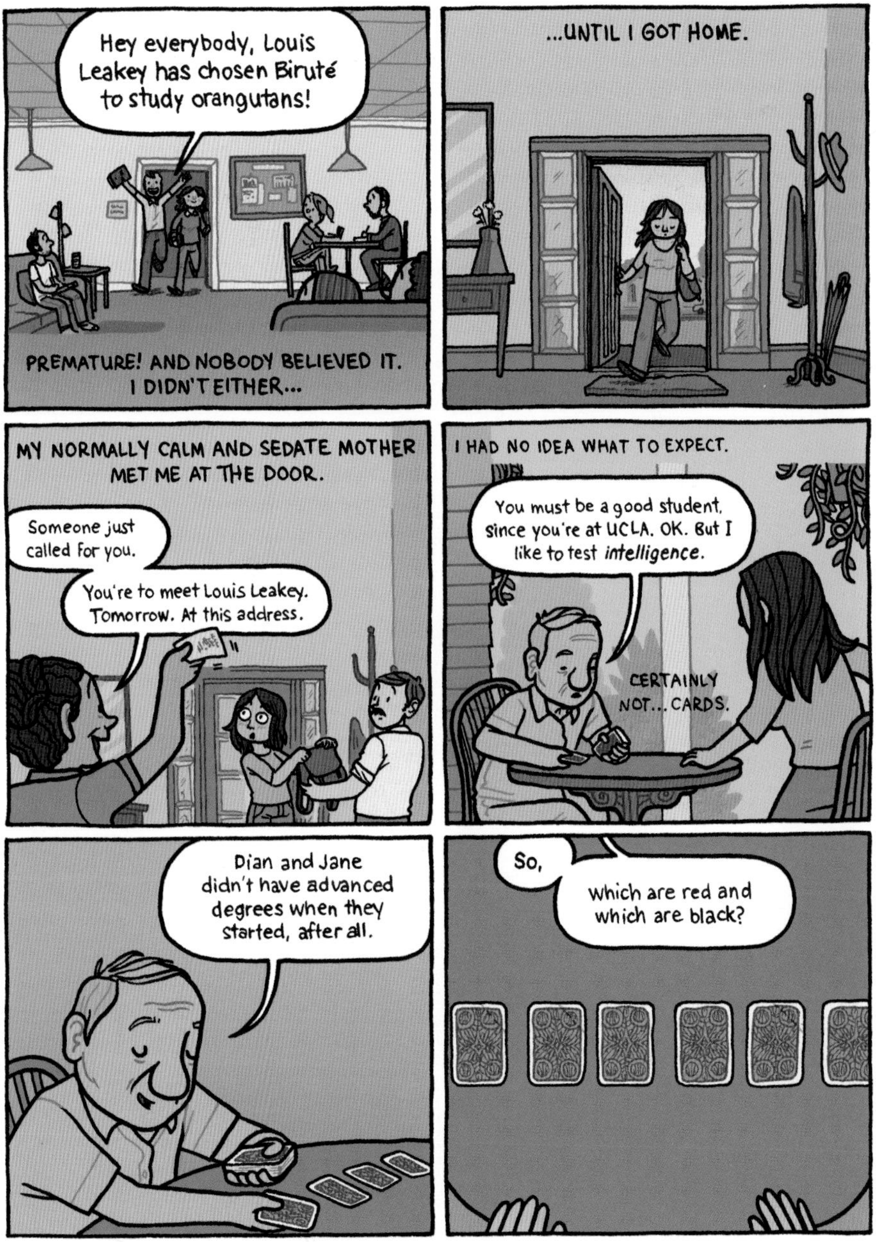
Hey everybody, Louis Leakey has chosen Biruté to study orangutans!
PREMATURE! AND NOBODY BELIEVED IT. I DIDN'T EITHER...
...UNTIL I GOT HOME.
MY NORMALLY CALM AND SEDATE MOTHER MET ME AT THE DOOR.
Someone just called for you.
You're to meet Louis Leakey. Tomorrow. At this address.
I HAD NO IDEA WHAT TO EXPECT.
You must be a good student, since you're at UCLA. OK. But I like to test *intelligence*.
CERTAINLY NOT... CARDS.
Dian and Jane didn't have advanced degrees when they started, after all.
So,
Which are red and which are black?

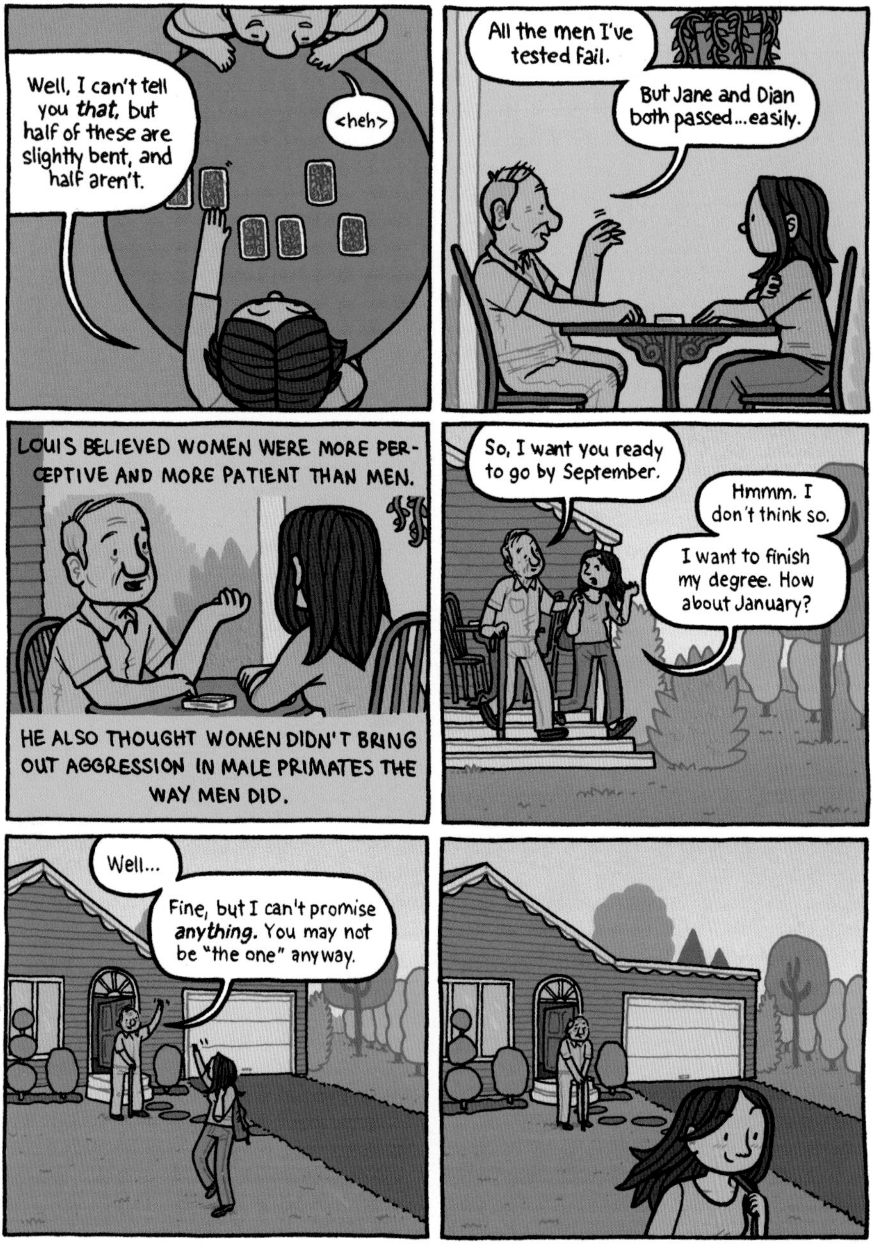
Well, I can't tell you *that,* but half of these are slightly bent, and half aren't.
<heh>
All the men I've tested fail.
But Jane and Dian both passed...easily.
LOUIS BELIEVED WOMEN WERE MORE PERCEPTIVE AND MORE PATIENT THAN MEN.
HE ALSO THOUGHT WOMEN DIDN'T BRING OUT AGGRESSION IN MALE PRIMATES THE WAY MEN DID.
So, I want you ready to go by September.
Hmmm. I don't think so.
I want to finish my degree. How about January?
Well...
Fine, but I can't promise *anything.* You may not be "the one" anyway.

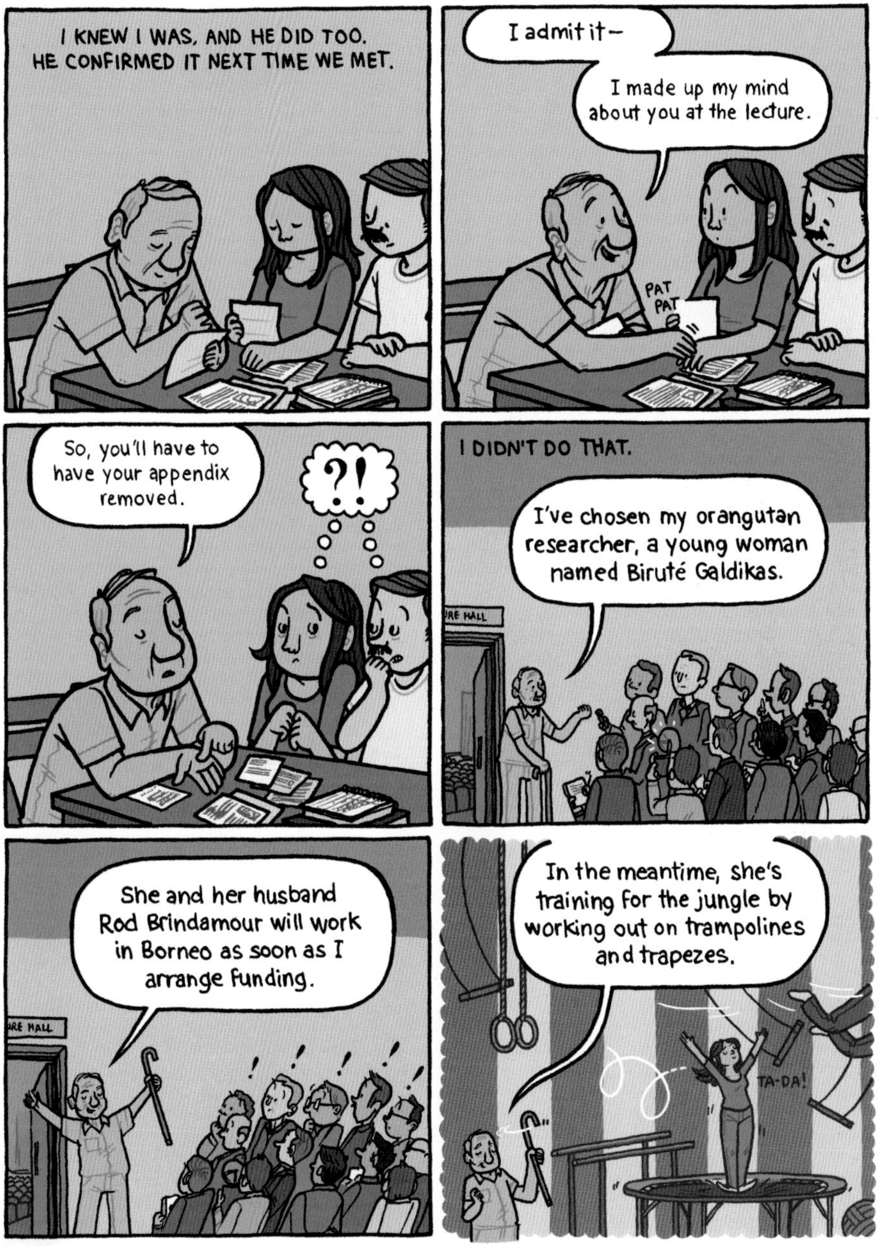
I KNEW I WAS, AND HE DID TOO.
HE CONFIRMED IT NEXT TIME WE MET.
I admit it—
I made up my mind about you at the lecture.
PAT PAT
So, you'll have to have your appendix removed.
?!
I DIDN'T DO THAT.
I've chosen my orangutan researcher, a young woman named Biruté Galdikas.
She and her husband Rod Brindamour will work in Borneo as soon as I arrange funding.
In the meantime, she's training for the jungle by working out on trampolines and trapezes.
TA-DA!

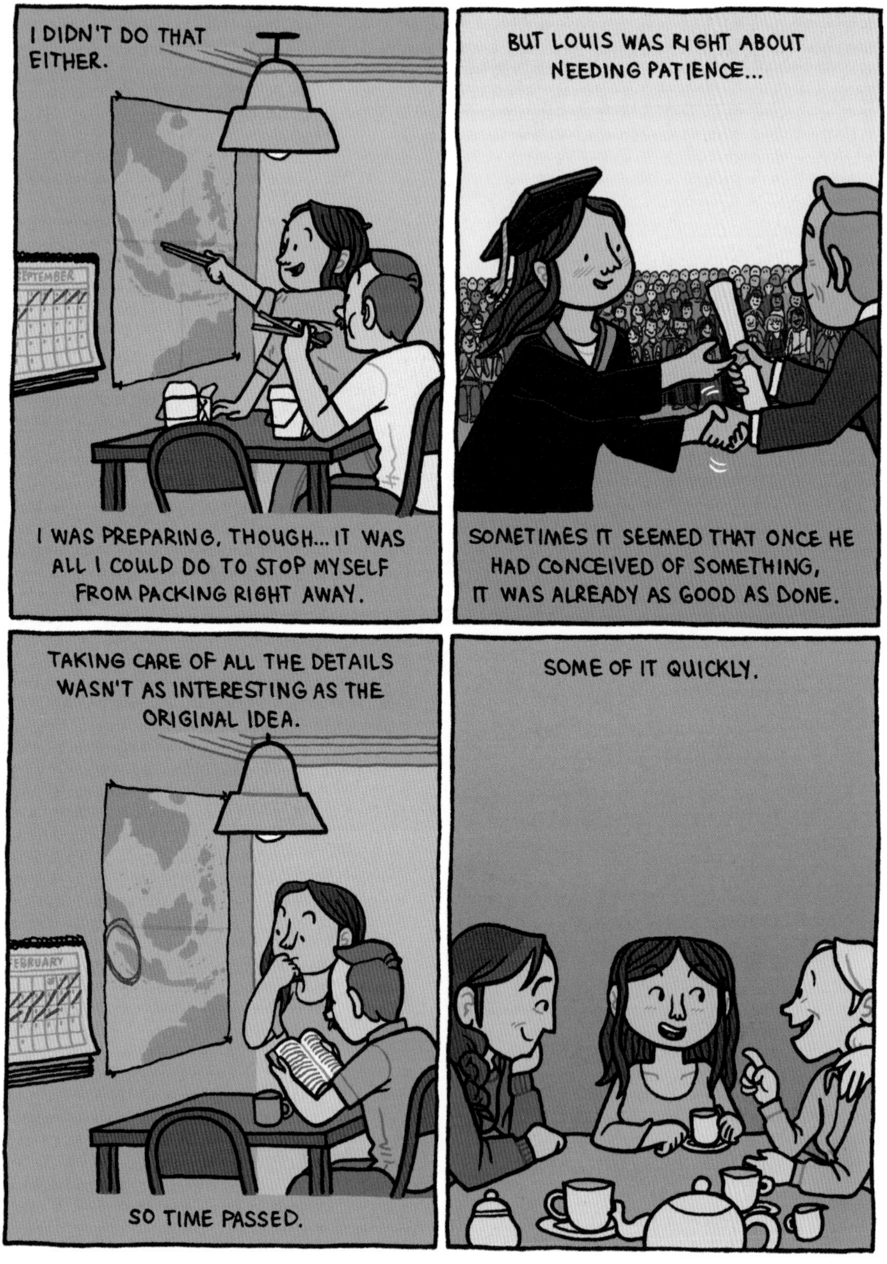
I DIDN'T DO THAT EITHER.
SEPTEMBER
I WAS PREPARING, THOUGH... IT WAS ALL I COULD DO TO STOP MYSELF FROM PACKING RIGHT AWAY.
BUT LOUIS WAS RIGHT ABOUT NEEDING PATIENCE...
SOMETIMES IT SEEMED THAT ONCE HE HAD CONCEIVED OF SOMETHING, IT WAS ALREADY AS GOOD AS DONE.
TAKING CARE OF ALL THE DETAILS WASN'T AS INTERESTING AS THE ORIGINAL IDEA.
FEBRUARY
SO TIME PASSED.
SOME OF IT QUICKLY.

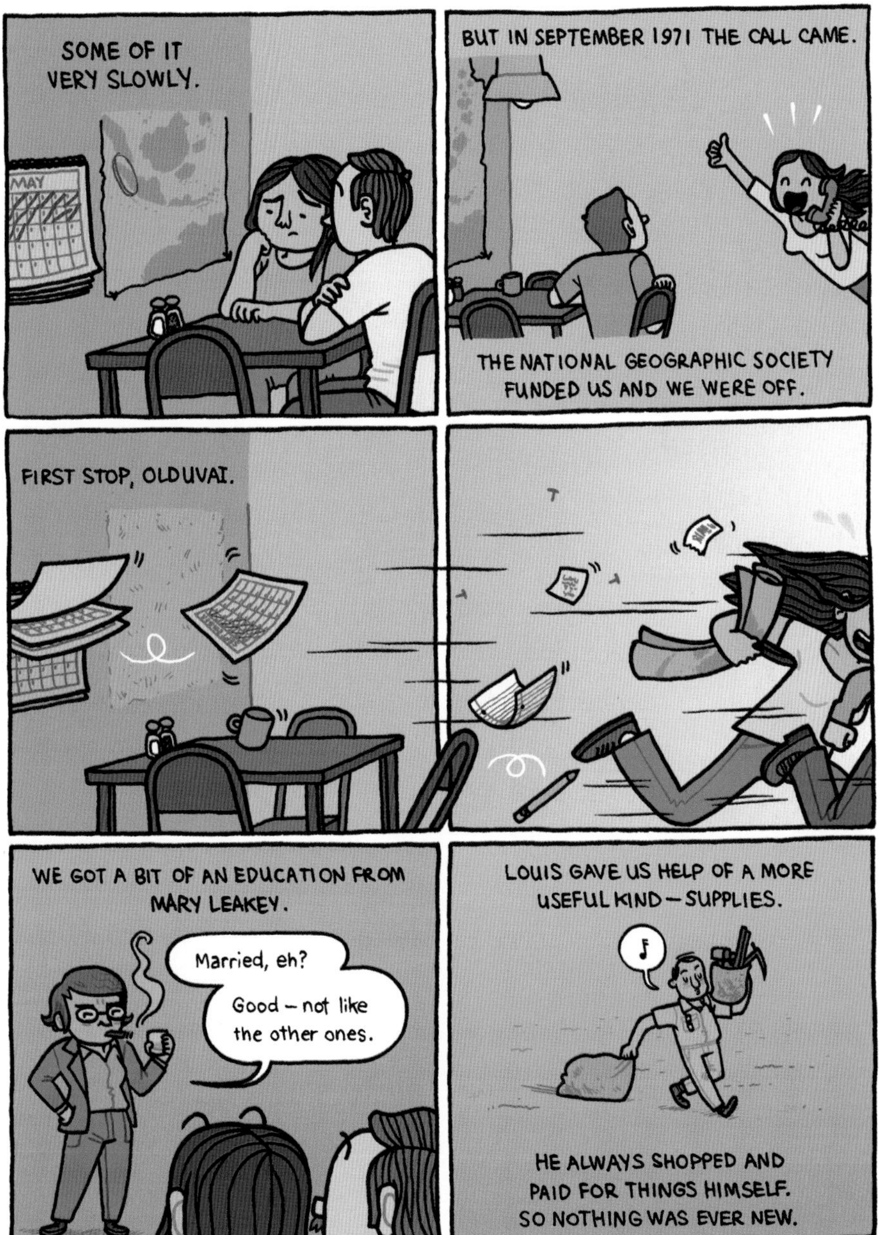
SOME OF IT VERY SLOWLY.
MAY
BUT IN SEPTEMBER 1971 THE CALL CAME.
THE NATIONAL GEOGRAPHIC SOCIETY FUNDED US AND WE WERE OFF.
FIRST STOP, OLDUVAI.
WE GOT A BIT OF AN EDUCATION FROM MARY LEAKEY.
Married, eh?
Good – not like the other ones.
LOUIS GAVE US HELP OF A MORE USEFUL KIND – SUPPLIES.
HE ALWAYS SHOPPED AND PAID FOR THINGS HIMSELF. SO NOTHING WAS EVER NEW.

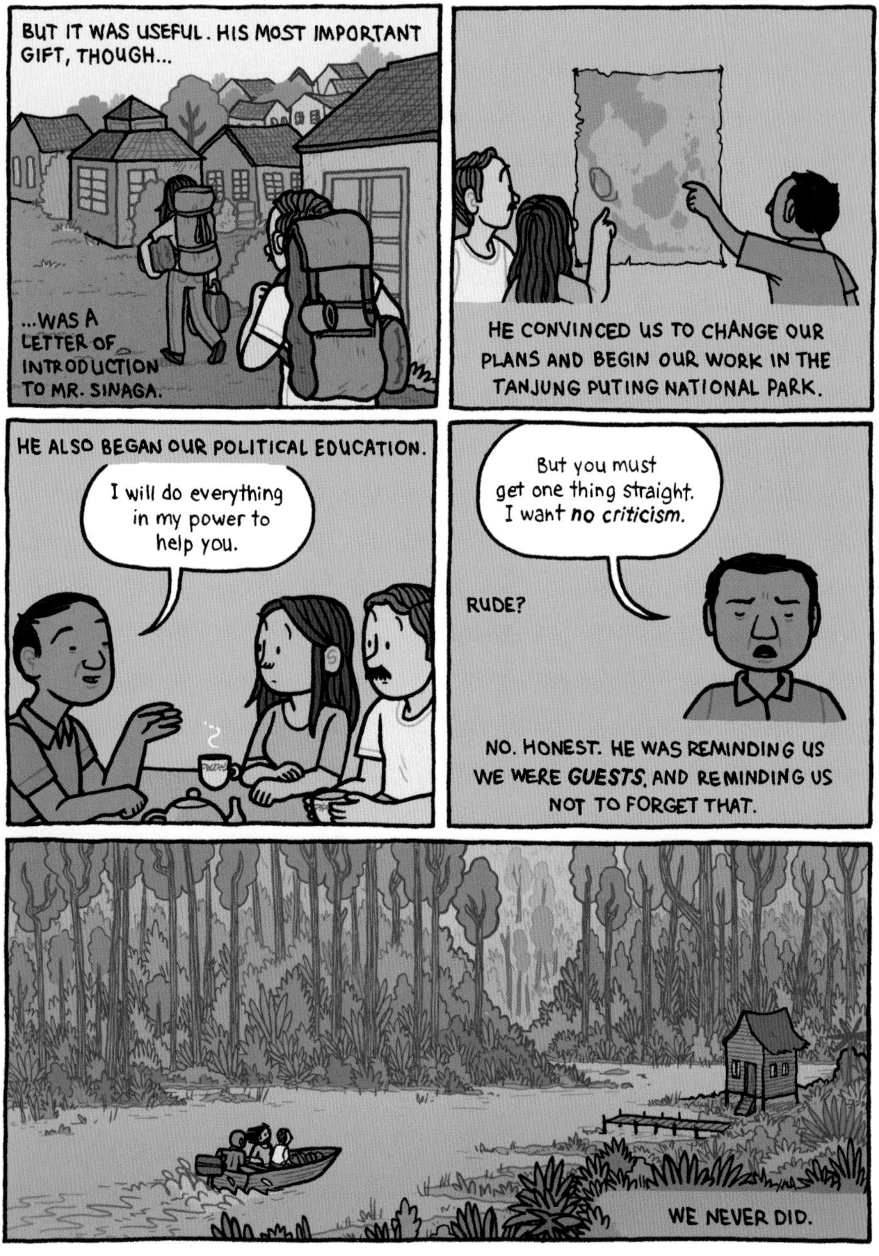
BUT IT WAS USEFUL. HIS MOST IMPORTANT GIFT, THOUGH...
...WAS A LETTER OF INTRODUCTION TO MR. SINAGA.
HE CONVINCED US TO CHANGE OUR PLANS AND BEGIN OUR WORK IN THE TANJUNG PUTING NATIONAL PARK.
HE ALSO BEGAN OUR POLITICAL EDUCATION.
I will do everything in my power to help you.
But you must get one thing straight. I want *no criticism.*
RUDE?
NO. HONEST. HE WAS REMINDING US WE WERE *GUESTS*, AND REMINDING US NOT TO FORGET THAT.
WE NEVER DID.

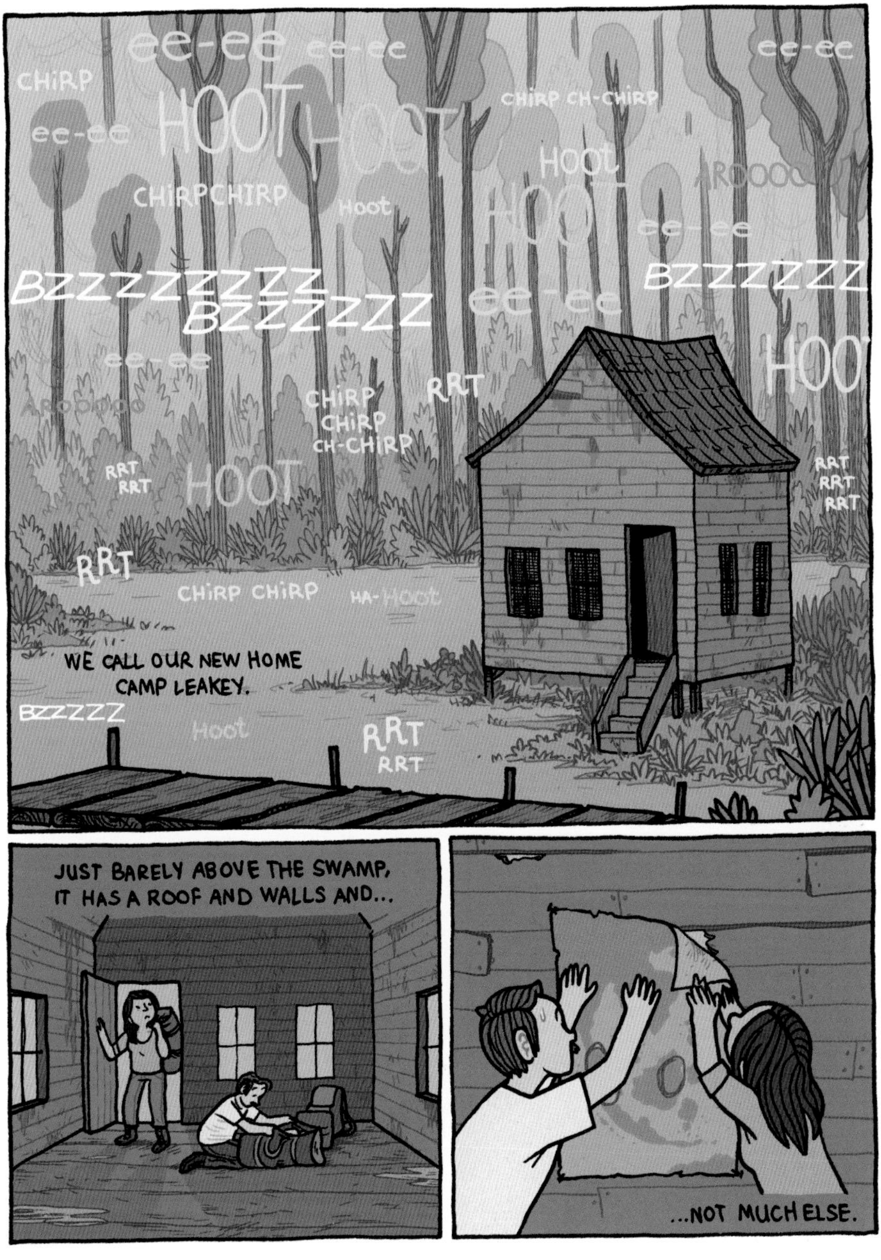
ee-ee ee-ee
ee-ee
CHIRP
HOOT HOOT
CHIRP CH-CHIRP
ee-ee
HOOT
CHIRPCHIRP
Hoot
HOOT
ee-ee
BZZZZZZZZ
BZZZZZZZ
BZZZZZZZ
ee-ee
HOOT
ee-ee
CHIRP
CHIRP
CH-CHIRP
RRT
RRT
RRT
HOOT
RRT
RRT
RRT
RRT
CHIRP CHIRP
HA-HOOT
WE CALL OUR NEW HOME CAMP LEAKEY.
BZZZZZ
Hoot
RRT
RRT
JUST BARELY ABOVE THE SWAMP, IT HAS A ROOF AND WALLS AND...
...NOT MUCH ELSE.

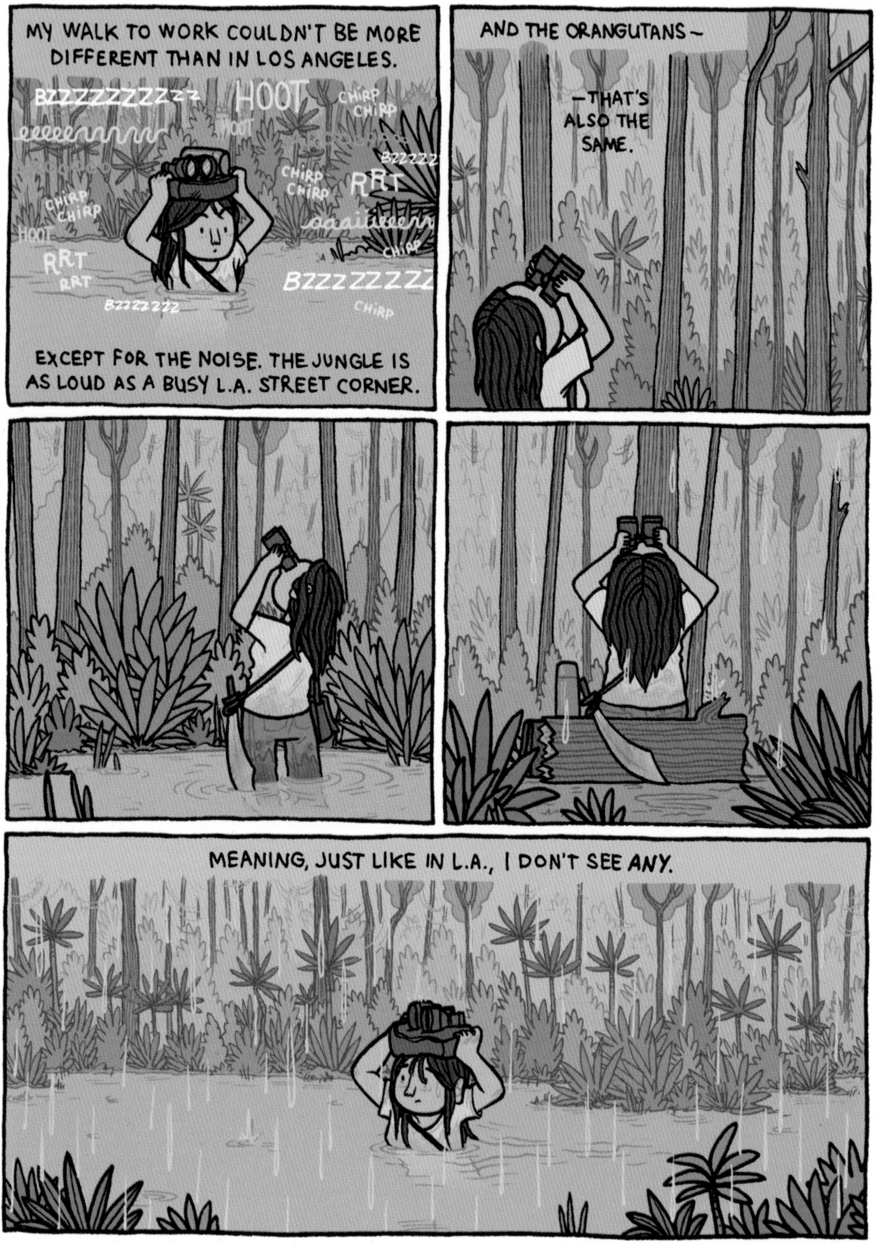
MY WALK TO WORK COULDN'T BE MORE DIFFERENT THAN IN LOS ANGELES.
BZZZZZZZZzz
HOOT
CHIRP CHIRP
HOOT
CHIRP CHIRP
RRT
CHIRP CHIRP
HOOT
RRT
RRT
CHIRP
BZZZZZZZZ
BZZZZZZ
CHIRP
EXCEPT FOR THE NOISE. THE JUNGLE IS AS LOUD AS A BUSY L.A. STREET CORNER.
AND THE ORANGUTANS—
—THAT'S ALSO THE SAME.
MEANING, JUST LIKE IN L.A., I DON'T SEE ANY.

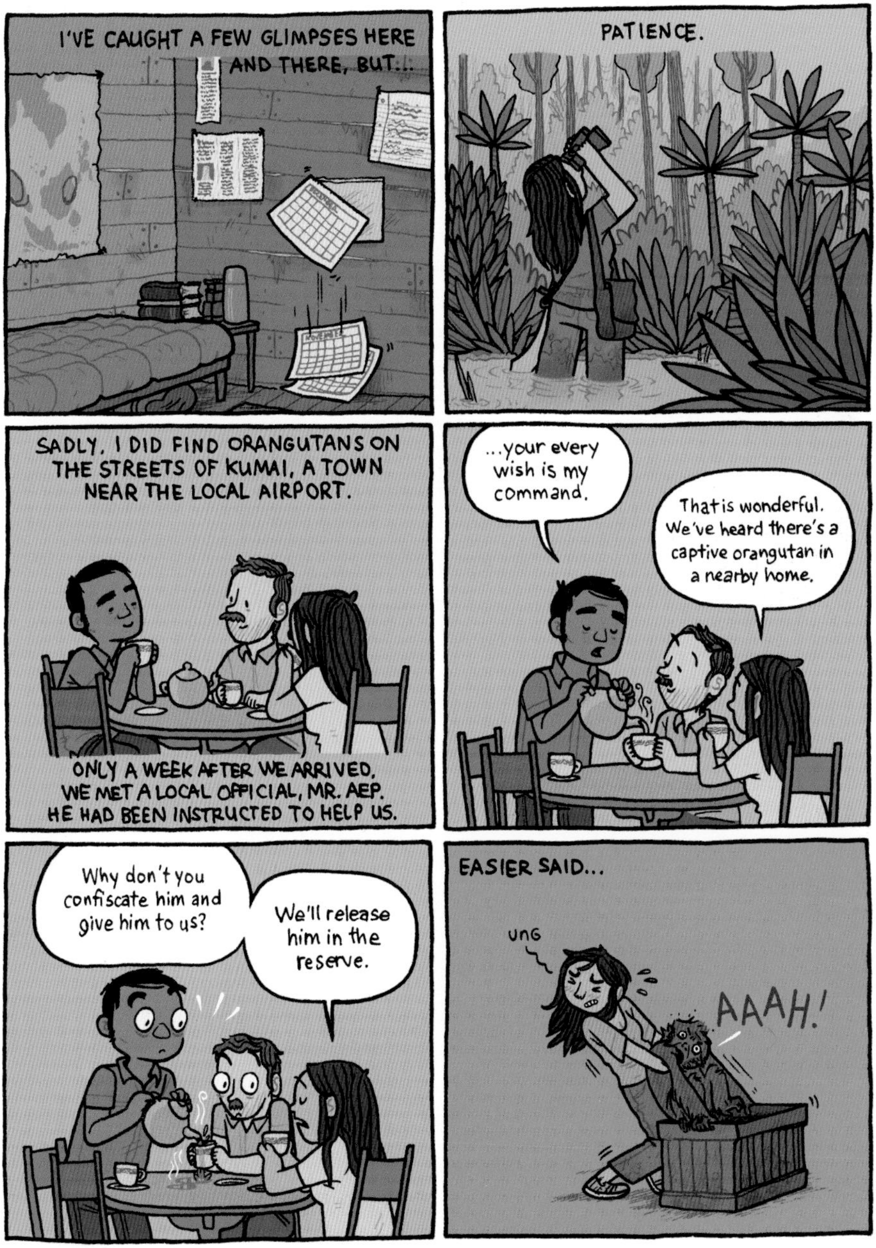
I'VE CAUGHT A FEW GLIMPSES HERE AND THERE, BUT...
PATIENCE.
SADLY, I DID FIND ORANGUTANS ON THE STREETS OF KUMAI, A TOWN NEAR THE LOCAL AIRPORT.
ONLY A WEEK AFTER WE ARRIVED, WE MET A LOCAL OFFICIAL, MR. AEP. HE HAD BEEN INSTRUCTED TO HELP US.
...your every wish is my command.
That is wonderful. We've heard there's a captive orangutan in a nearby home.
Why don't you confiscate him and give him to us?
We'll release him in the reserve.
EASIER SAID...
UNG
AAAH!

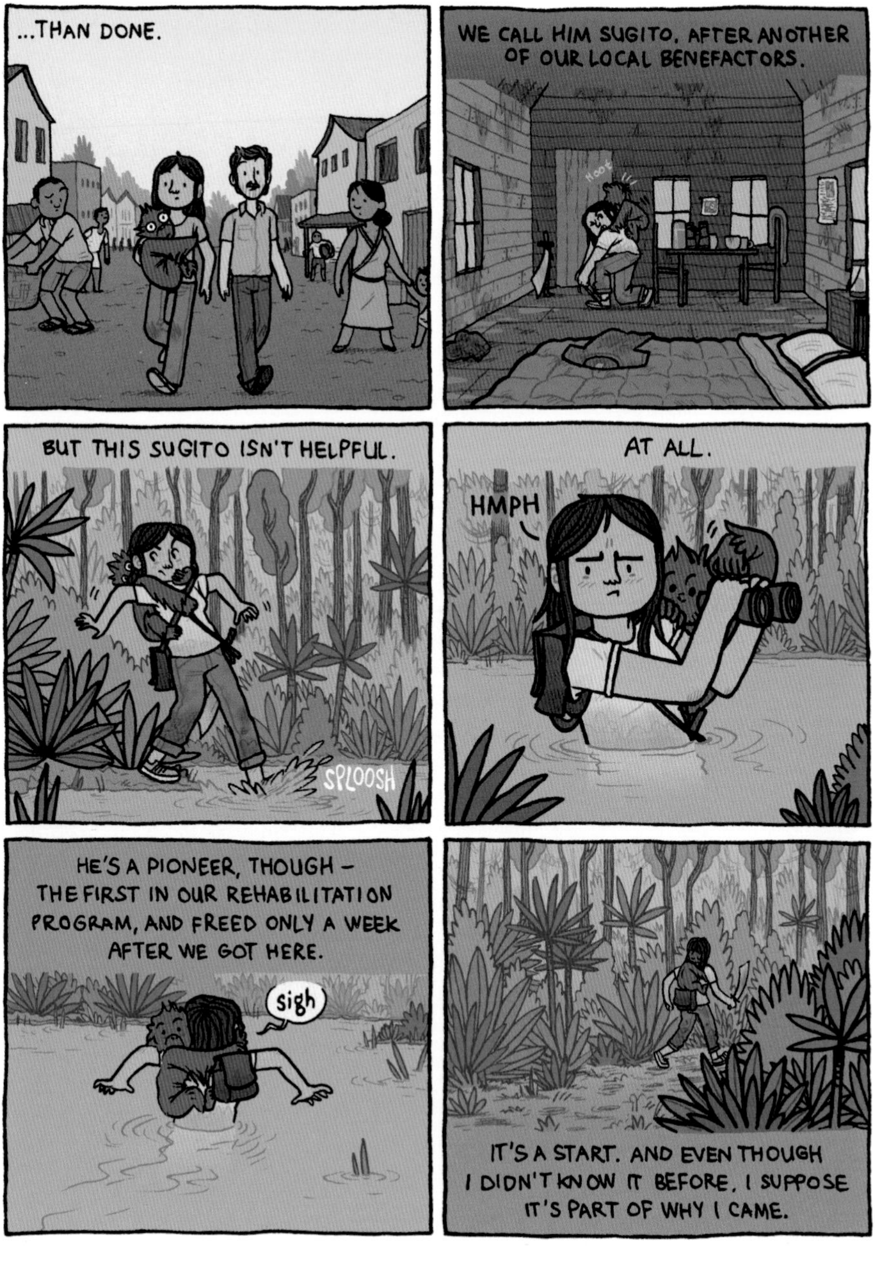
...THAN DONE.
WE CALL HIM SUGITO, AFTER ANOTHER OF OUR LOCAL BENEFACTORS.
HOOT
BUT THIS SUGITO ISN'T HELPFUL.
SPLOOSH
AT ALL.
HMPH
HE'S A PIONEER, THOUGH – THE FIRST IN OUR REHABILITATION PROGRAM, AND FREED ONLY A WEEK AFTER WE GOT HERE.
sigh
IT'S A START. AND EVEN THOUGH I DIDN'T KNOW IT BEFORE, I SUPPOSE IT'S PART OF WHY I CAME.

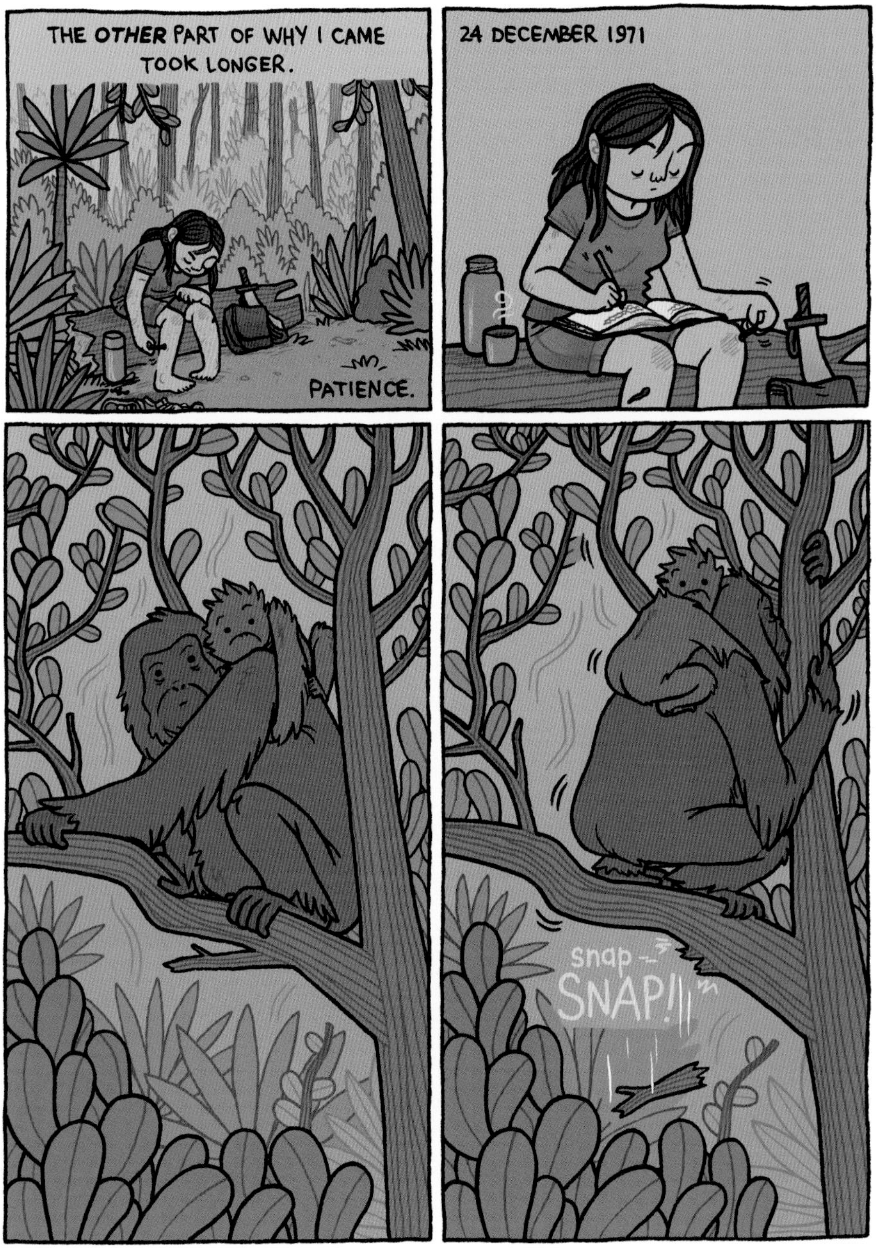
THE OTHER PART OF WHY I CAME TOOK LONGER.
PATIENCE.
24 DECEMBER 1971
snap
SNAP!

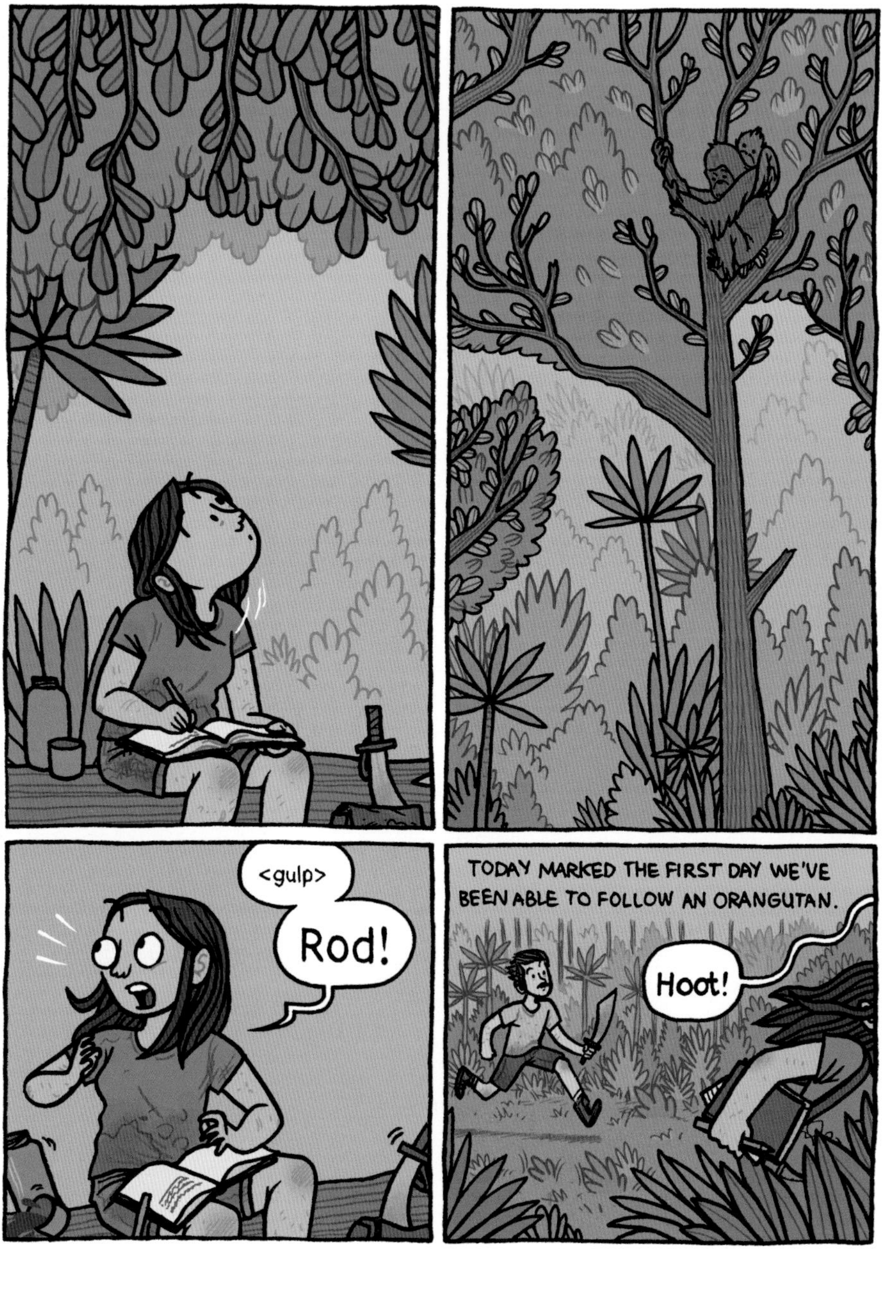
<gulp>
Rod!
TODAY MARKED THE FIRST DAY WE'VE BEEN ABLE TO FOLLOW AN ORANGUTAN.
Hoot!

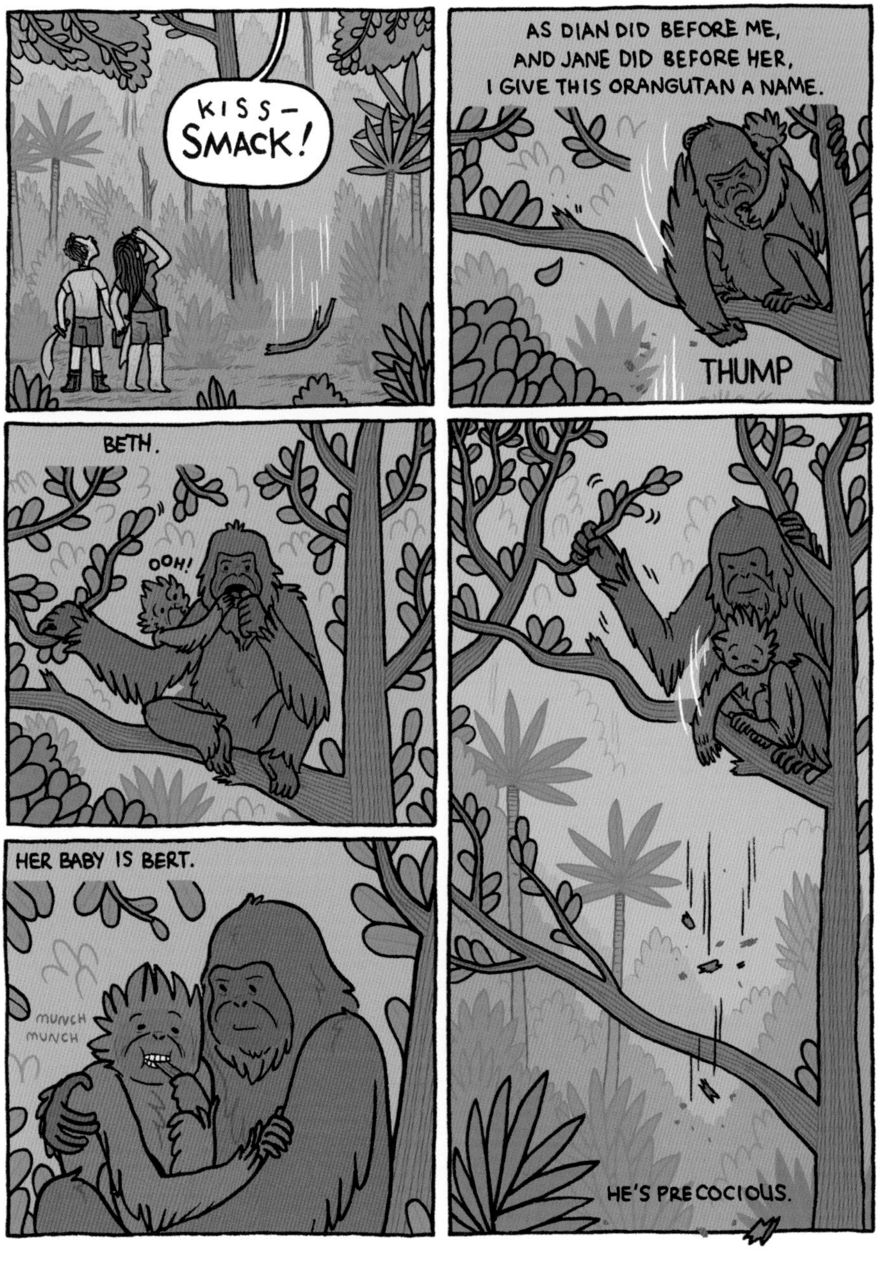
KISS–
SMACK!
AS DIAN DID BEFORE ME,
AND JANE DID BEFORE HER,
I GIVE THIS ORANGUTAN A NAME.
THUMP
BETH.
OOH!
HER BABY IS BERT.
MUNCH
MUNCH
HE'S PRECOCIOUS.

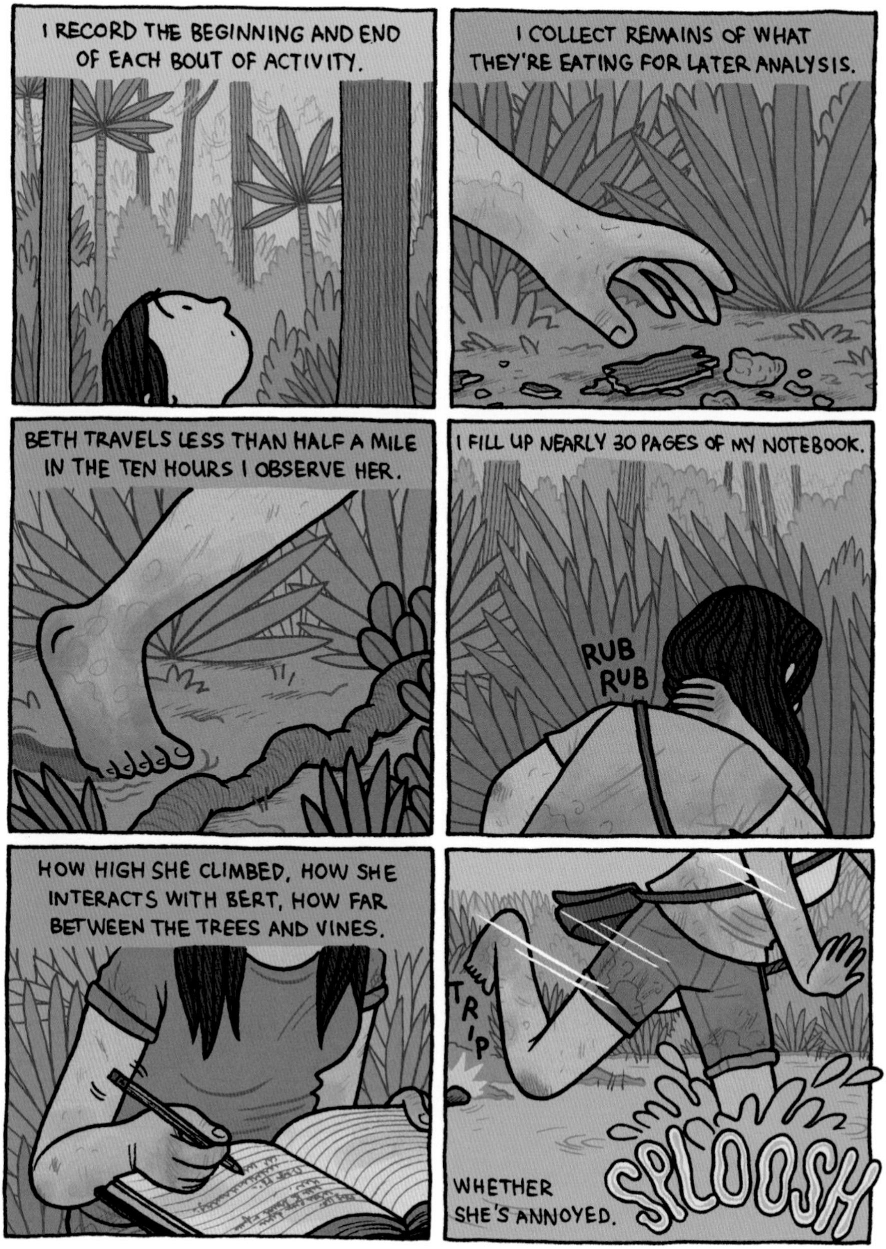
I RECORD THE BEGINNING AND END OF EACH BOUT OF ACTIVITY.
I COLLECT REMAINS OF WHAT THEY'RE EATING FOR LATER ANALYSIS.
BETH TRAVELS LESS THAN HALF A MILE IN THE TEN HOURS I OBSERVE HER.
I FILL UP NEARLY 30 PAGES OF MY NOTEBOOK.
RUB RUB
HOW HIGH SHE CLIMBED, HOW SHE INTERACTS WITH BERT, HOW FAR BETWEEN THE TREES AND VINES.
TRIP
WHETHER SHE'S ANNOYED.
SPLOOSH

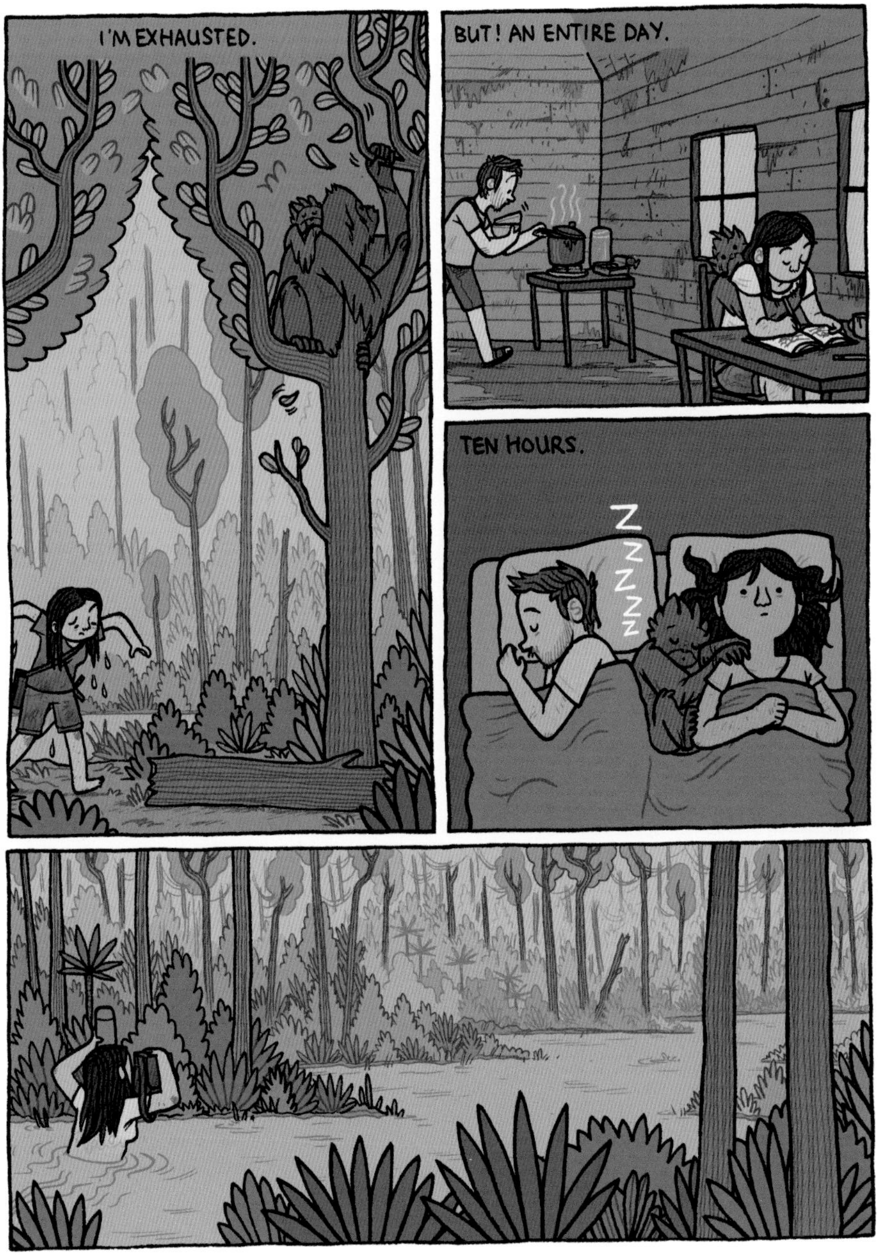
I'M EXHAUSTED.
BUT! AN ENTIRE DAY.
TEN HOURS.
ZZZZZ

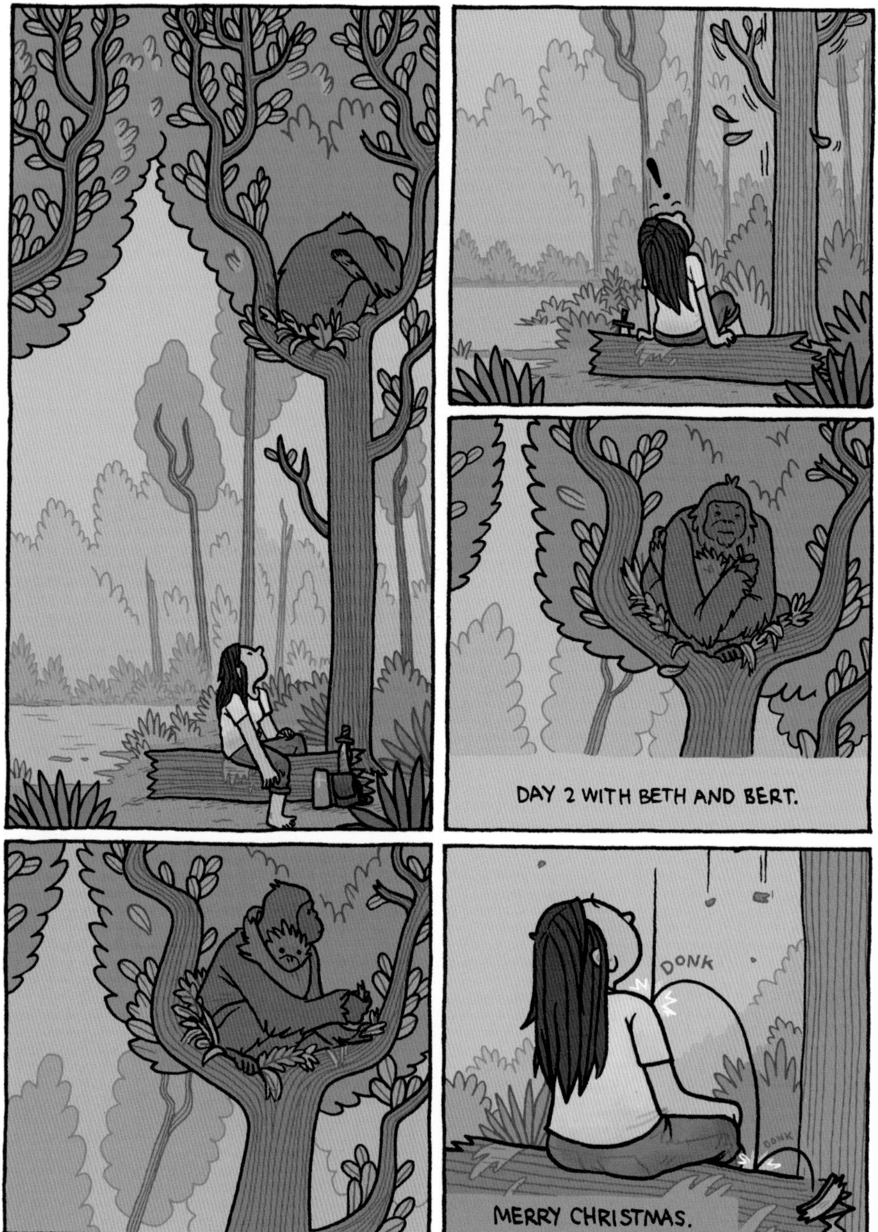
!
DAY 2 WITH BETH AND BERT.
DONK
DONK
MERRY CHRISTMAS.

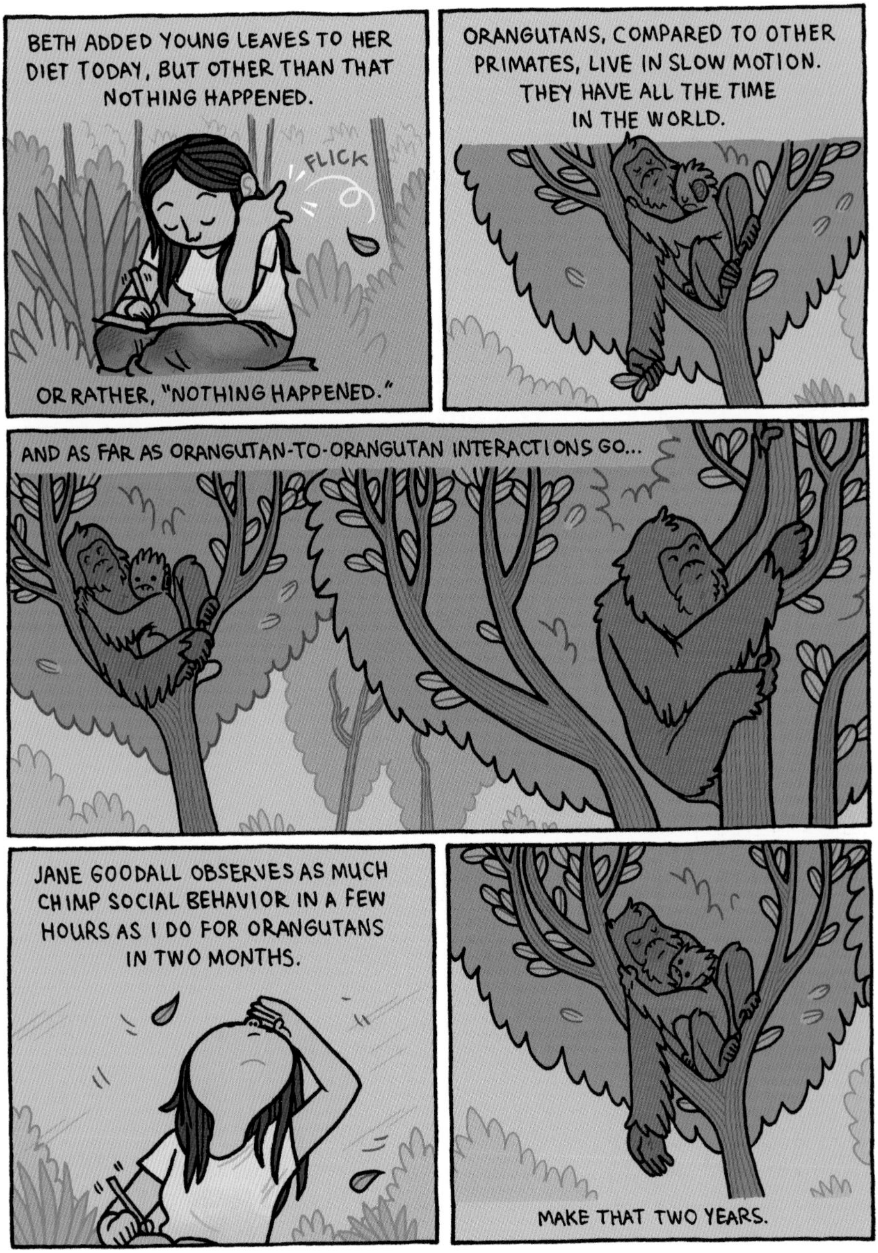
BETH ADDED YOUNG LEAVES TO HER DIET TODAY, BUT OTHER THAN THAT NOTHING HAPPENED.
FLICK
OR RATHER, "NOTHING HAPPENED."
ORANGUTANS, COMPARED TO OTHER PRIMATES, LIVE IN SLOW MOTION. THEY HAVE ALL THE TIME IN THE WORLD.
AND AS FAR AS ORANGUTAN-TO-ORANGUTAN INTERACTIONS GO...
JANE GOODALL OBSERVES AS MUCH CHIMP SOCIAL BEHAVIOR IN A FEW HOURS AS I DO FOR ORANGUTANS IN TWO MONTHS.
MAKE THAT TWO YEARS.

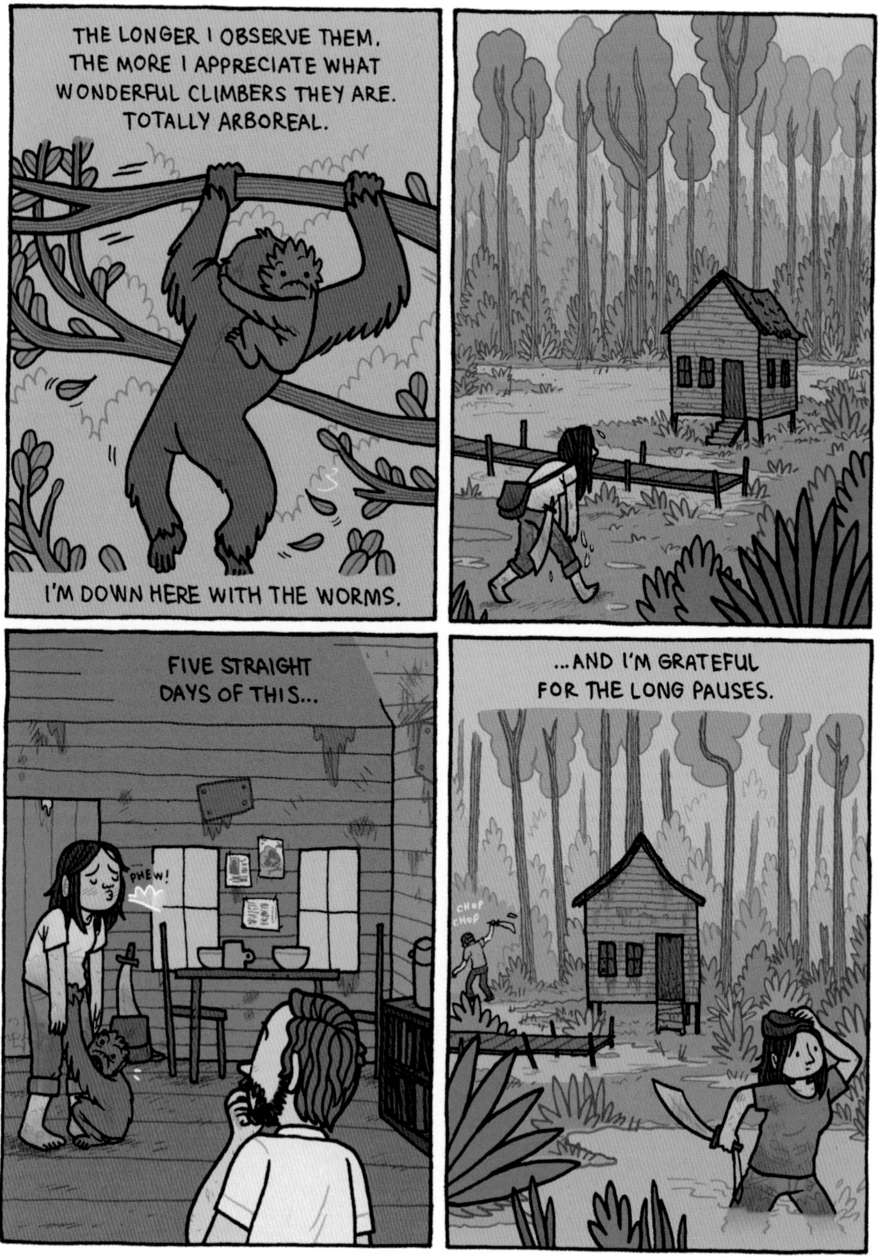
THE LONGER I OBSERVE THEM, THE MORE I APPRECIATE WHAT WONDERFUL CLIMBERS THEY ARE. TOTALLY ARBOREAL.
I'M DOWN HERE WITH THE WORMS.
FIVE STRAIGHT DAYS OF THIS...
PHEW!
...AND I'M GRATEFUL FOR THE LONG PAUSES.
CHOP CHOP

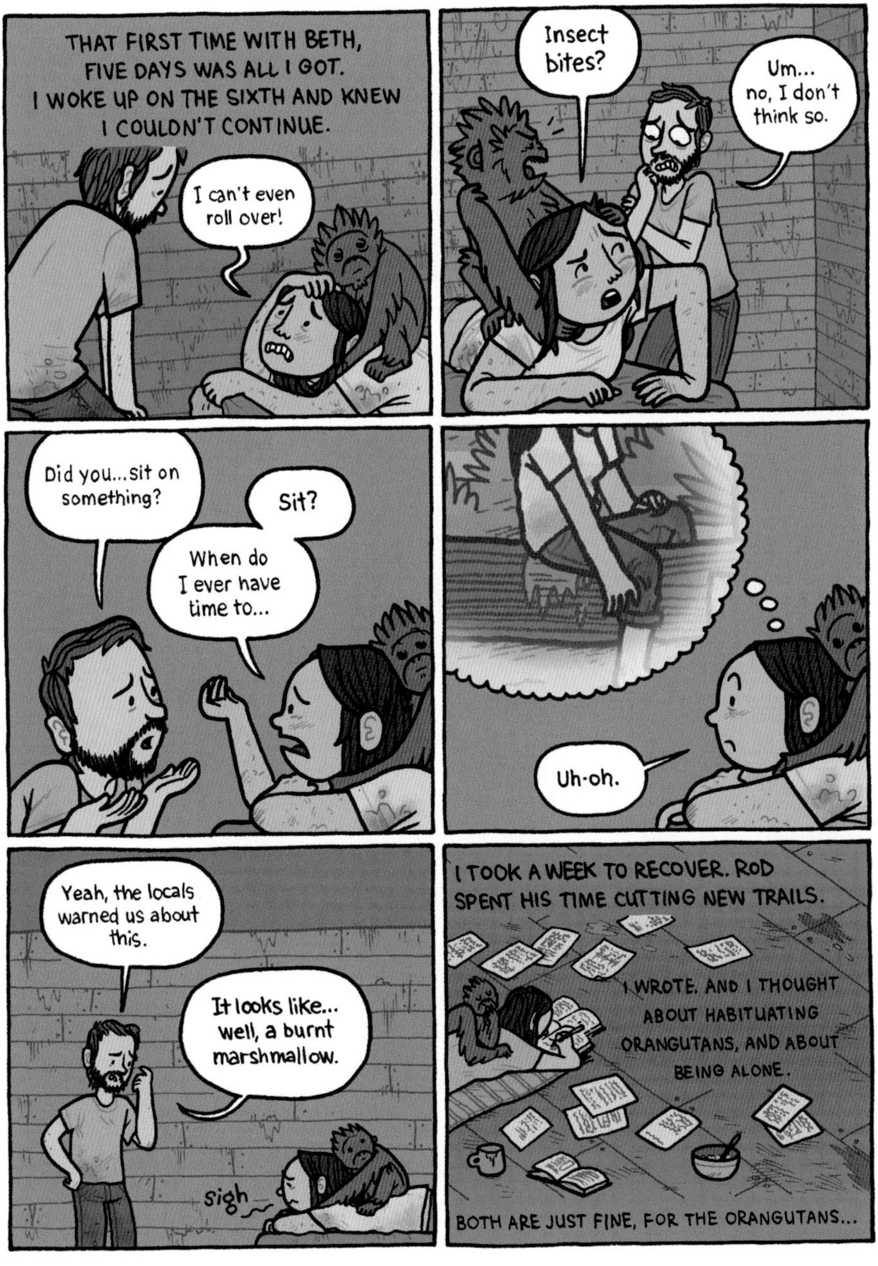
THAT FIRST TIME WITH BETH, FIVE DAYS WAS ALL I GOT. I WOKE UP ON THE SIXTH AND KNEW I COULDN'T CONTINUE.
I can't even roll over!
Insect bites?
Um... no, I don't think so.
Did you...sit on something?
Sit?
When do I ever have time to...
Uh-oh.
Yeah, the locals warned us about this.
It looks like... well, a burnt marshmallow.
sigh
I TOOK A WEEK TO RECOVER. ROD SPENT HIS TIME CUTTING NEW TRAILS.
I WROTE. AND I THOUGHT ABOUT HABITUATING ORANGUTANS, AND ABOUT BEING ALONE.
BOTH ARE JUST FINE, FOR THE ORANGUTANS...

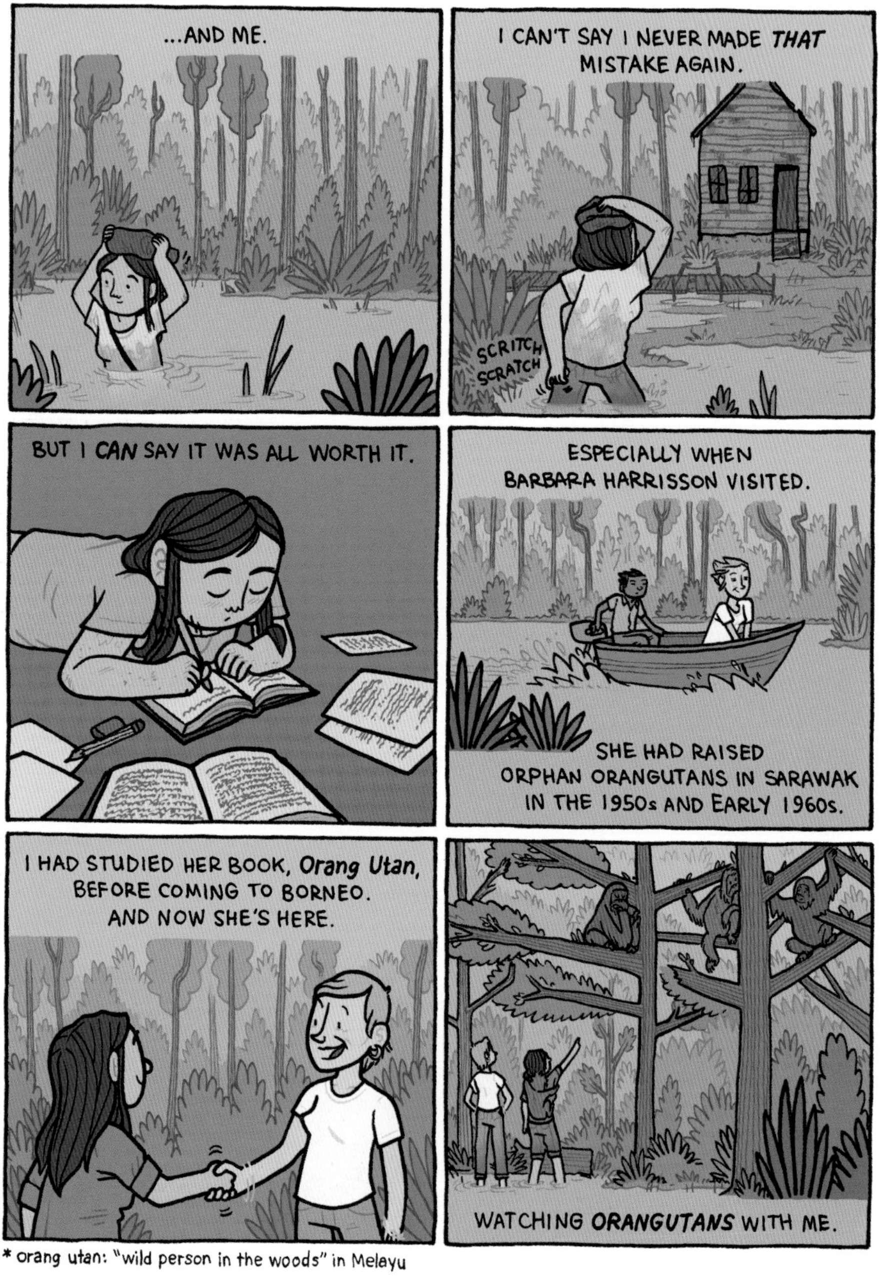
...AND ME.
I CAN'T SAY I NEVER MADE *THAT* MISTAKE AGAIN.
SCRITCH SCRATCH
BUT I *CAN* SAY IT WAS ALL WORTH IT.
ESPECIALLY WHEN BARBARA HARRISSON VISITED.
SHE HAD RAISED ORPHAN ORANGUTANS IN SARAWAK IN THE 1950s AND EARLY 1960s.
I HAD STUDIED HER BOOK, *Orang Utan*, BEFORE COMING TO BORNEO. AND NOW SHE'S HERE.
WATCHING ***ORANGUTANS*** WITH ME.

* orang utan: "wild person in the woods" in Melayu

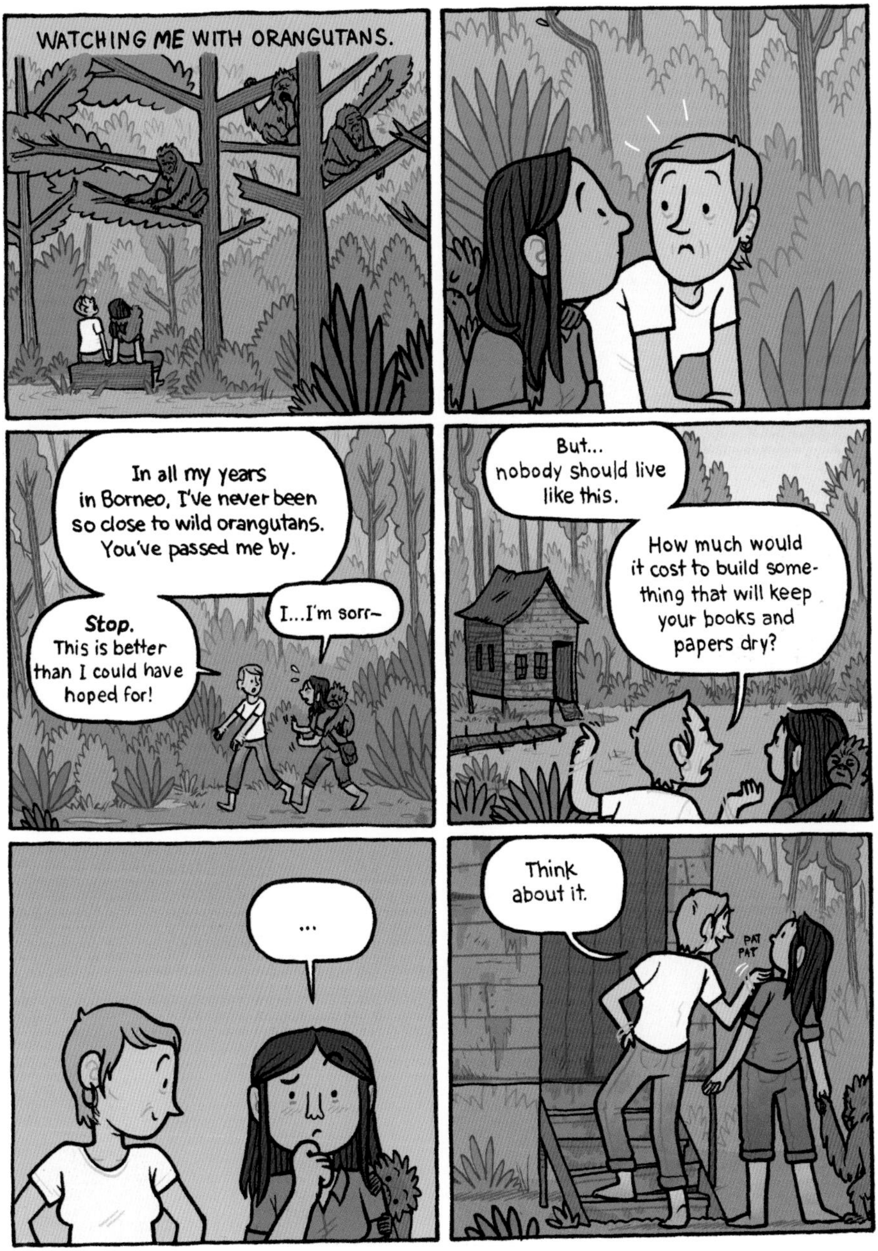
WATCHING ME WITH ORANGUTANS.
In all my years in Borneo, I've never been so close to wild orangutans. You've passed me by.
I...I'm sorr–
Stop. This is better than I could have hoped for!
But... nobody should live like this.
How much would it cost to build something that will keep your books and papers dry?
...
Think about it.
PAT PAT

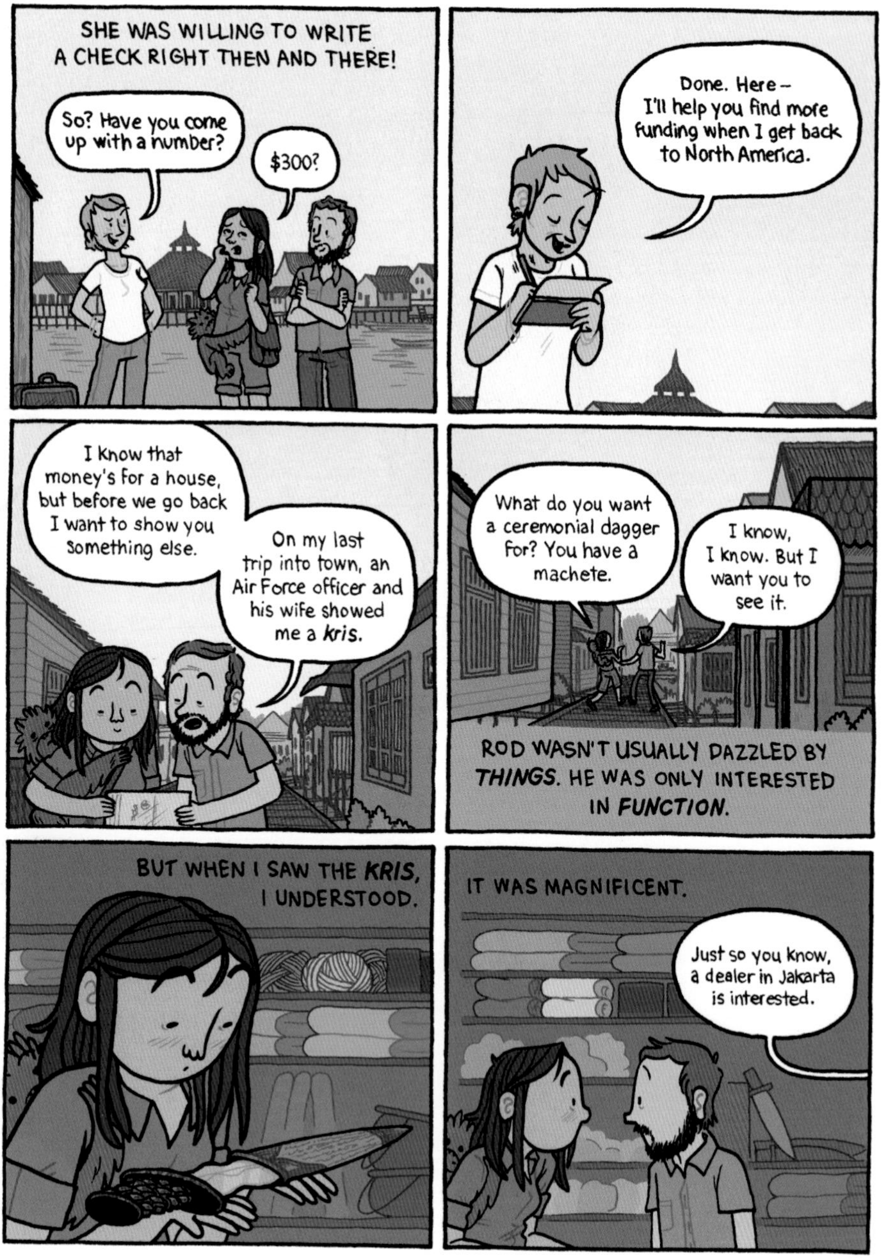
SHE WAS WILLING TO WRITE A CHECK RIGHT THEN AND THERE!
So? Have you come up with a number?
$300?
Done. Here– I'll help you find more funding when I get back to North America.
I know that money's for a house, but before we go back I want to show you something else.
On my last trip into town, an Air Force officer and his wife showed me a *kris*.
What do you want a ceremonial dagger for? You have a machete.
I know, I know. But I want you to see it.
ROD WASN'T USUALLY DAZZLED BY *THINGS*. HE WAS ONLY INTERESTED IN *FUNCTION*.
BUT WHEN I SAW THE *KRIS*, I UNDERSTOOD.
IT WAS MAGNIFICENT.
Just so you know, a dealer in Jakarta is interested.

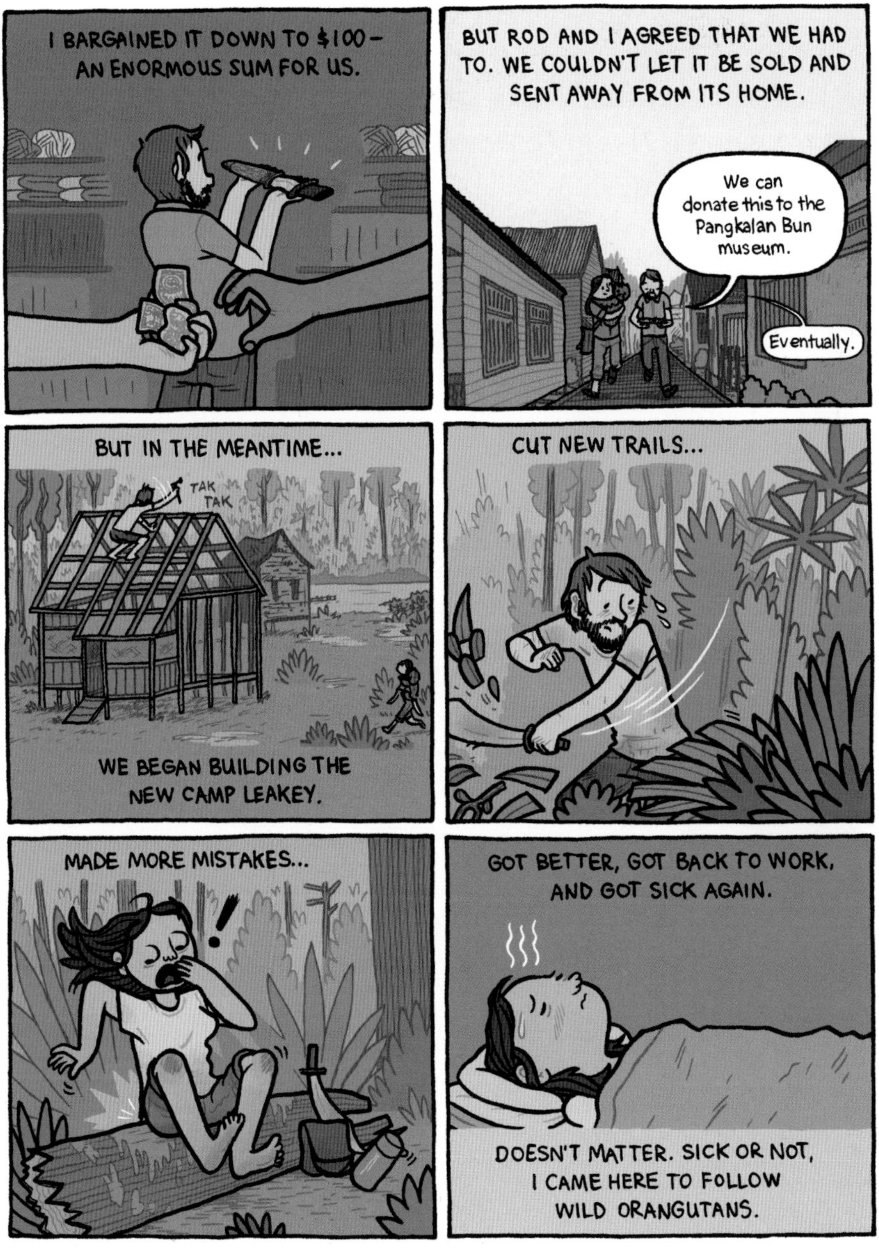
I BARGAINED IT DOWN TO $100 – AN ENORMOUS SUM FOR US.
BUT ROD AND I AGREED THAT WE HAD TO. WE COULDN'T LET IT BE SOLD AND SENT AWAY FROM ITS HOME.
We can donate this to the Pangkalan Bun museum.
Eventually.
BUT IN THE MEANTIME...
TAK TAK
WE BEGAN BUILDING THE NEW CAMP LEAKEY.
CUT NEW TRAILS...
MADE MORE MISTAKES...
!
GOT BETTER, GOT BACK TO WORK, AND GOT SICK AGAIN.
DOESN'T MATTER. SICK OR NOT, I CAME HERE TO FOLLOW WILD ORANGUTANS.

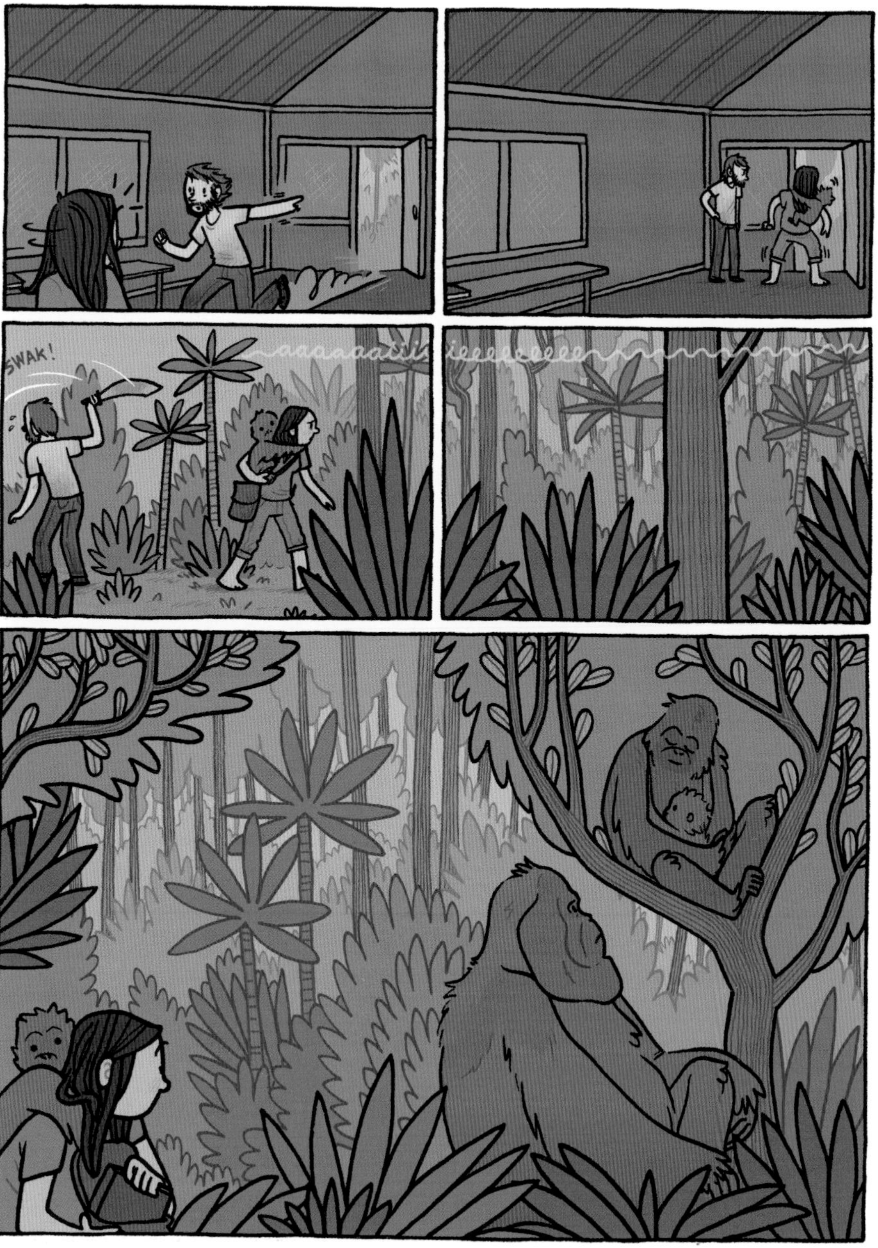
SWAK!
aaaaaaaiiii
ieeeeeeeee

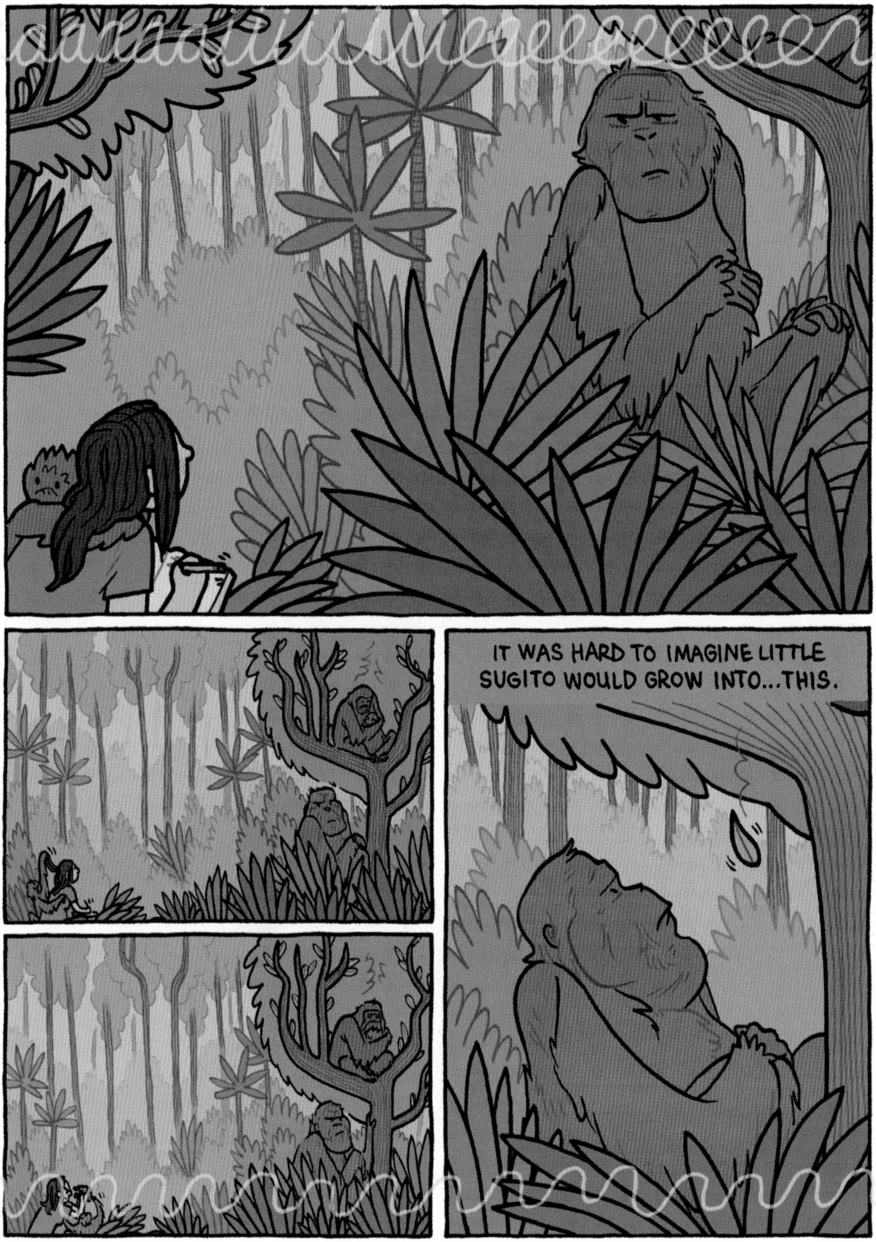
IT WAS HARD TO IMAGINE LITTLE SUGITO WOULD GROW INTO...THIS.

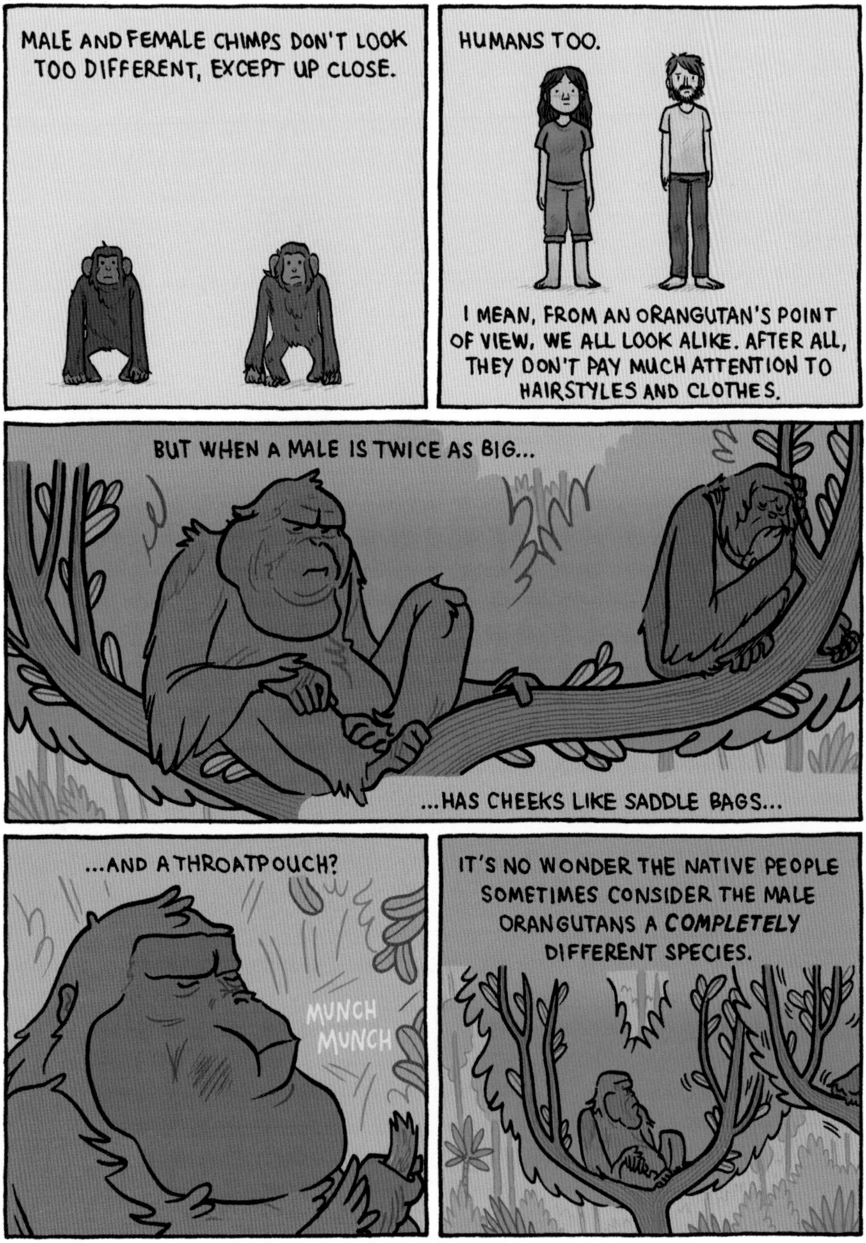
MALE AND FEMALE CHIMPS DON'T LOOK TOO DIFFERENT, EXCEPT UP CLOSE.
HUMANS TOO.
I MEAN, FROM AN ORANGUTAN'S POINT OF VIEW, WE ALL LOOK ALIKE. AFTER ALL, THEY DON'T PAY MUCH ATTENTION TO HAIRSTYLES AND CLOTHES.
BUT WHEN A MALE IS TWICE AS BIG...
...HAS CHEEKS LIKE SADDLE BAGS...
...AND A THROAT POUCH?
MUNCH MUNCH
IT'S NO WONDER THE NATIVE PEOPLE SOMETIMES CONSIDER THE MALE ORANGUTANS A COMPLETELY DIFFERENT SPECIES.

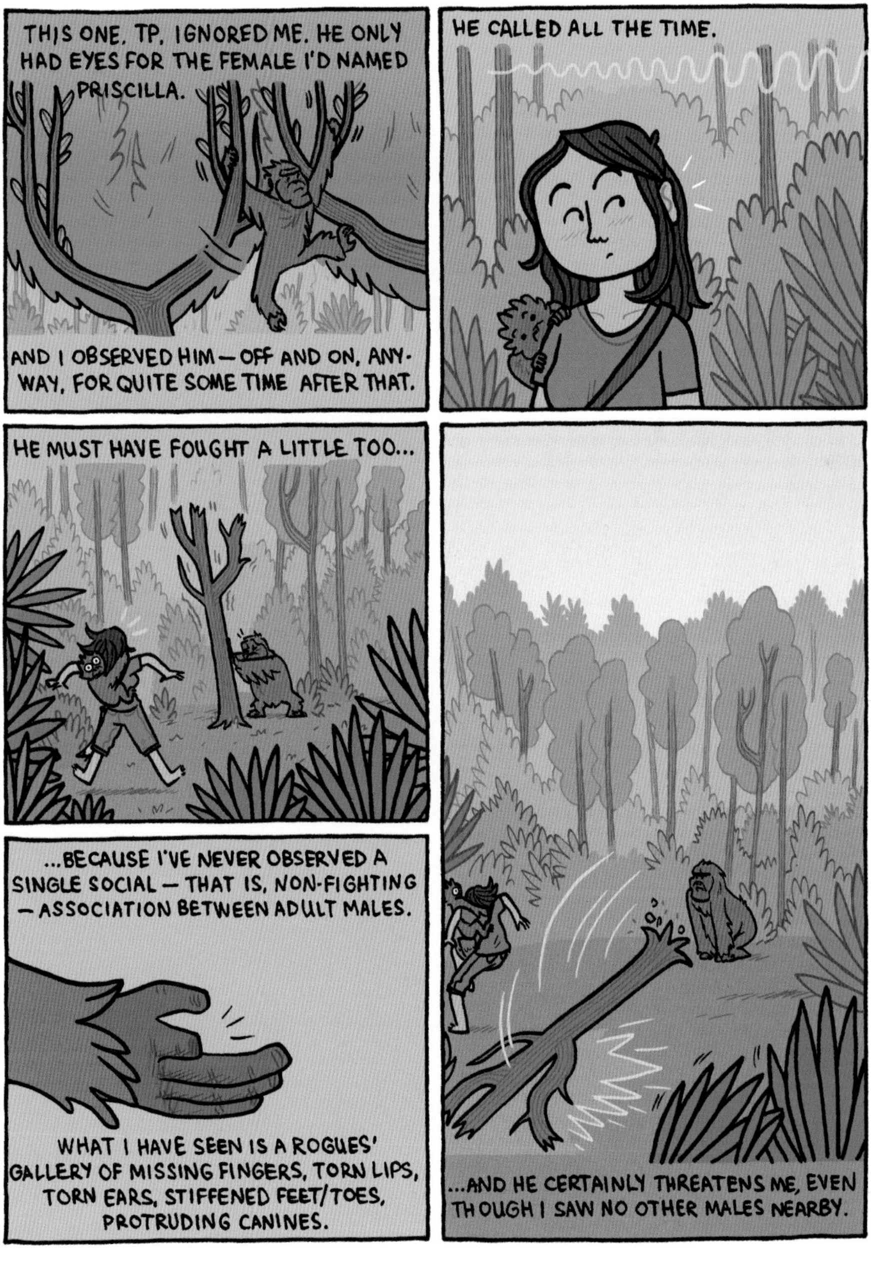

THIS ONE, TP, IGNORED ME. HE ONLY HAD EYES FOR THE FEMALE I'D NAMED PRISCILLA.
AND I OBSERVED HIM—OFF AND ON, ANYWAY, FOR QUITE SOME TIME AFTER THAT.
HE CALLED ALL THE TIME.
HE MUST HAVE FOUGHT A LITTLE TOO...
...BECAUSE I'VE NEVER OBSERVED A SINGLE SOCIAL—THAT IS, NON-FIGHTING—ASSOCIATION BETWEEN ADULT MALES.
WHAT I HAVE SEEN IS A ROGUES' GALLERY OF MISSING FINGERS, TORN LIPS, TORN EARS, STIFFENED FEET/TOES, PROTRUDING CANINES.
...AND HE CERTAINLY THREATENS ME, EVEN THOUGH I SAW NO OTHER MALES NEARBY.

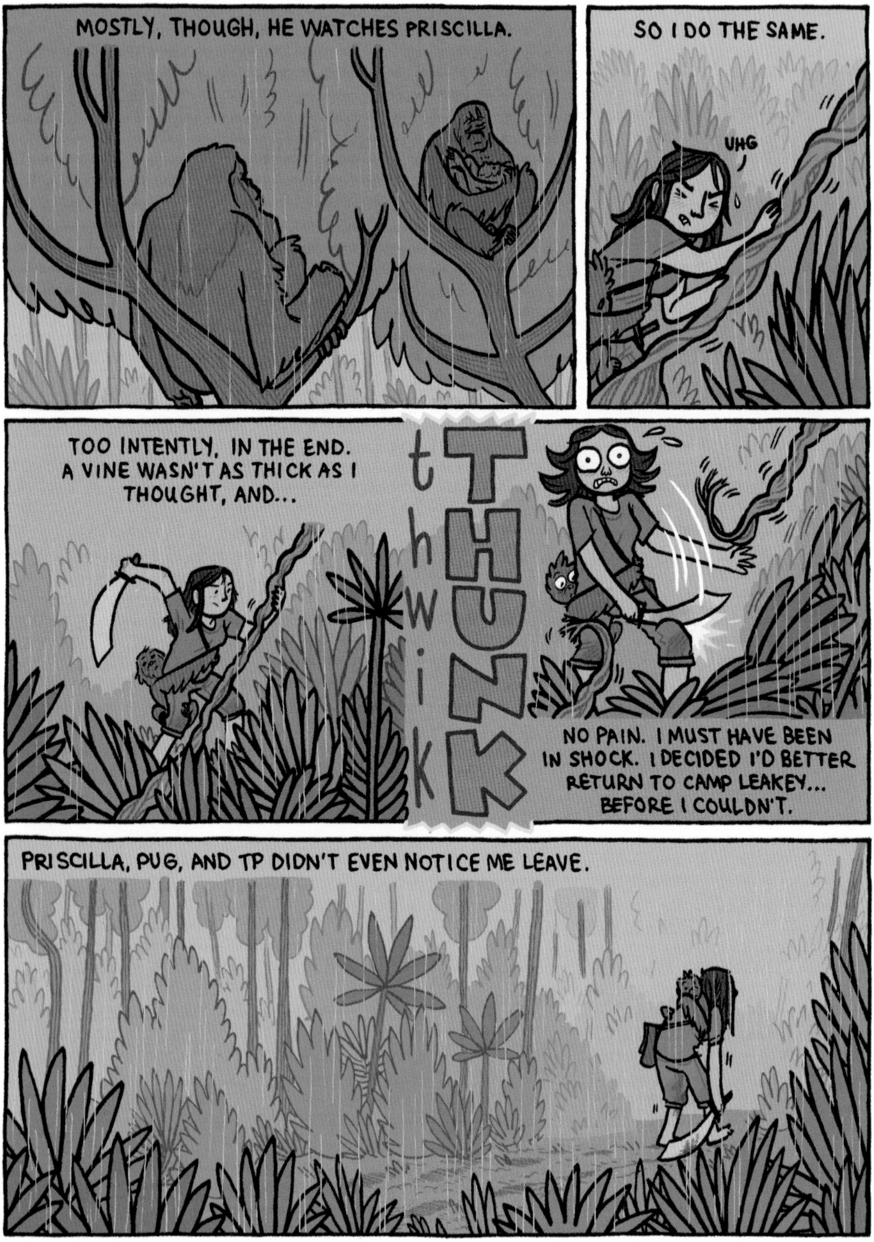
MOSTLY, THOUGH, HE WATCHES PRISCILLA.
SO I DO THE SAME.
UHG
TOO INTENTLY, IN THE END. A VINE WASN'T AS THICK AS I THOUGHT, AND...
thwik
THUNK
NO PAIN. I MUST HAVE BEEN IN SHOCK. I DECIDED I'D BETTER RETURN TO CAMP LEAKEY... BEFORE I COULDN'T.
PRISCILLA, PUG, AND TP DIDN'T EVEN NOTICE ME LEAVE.

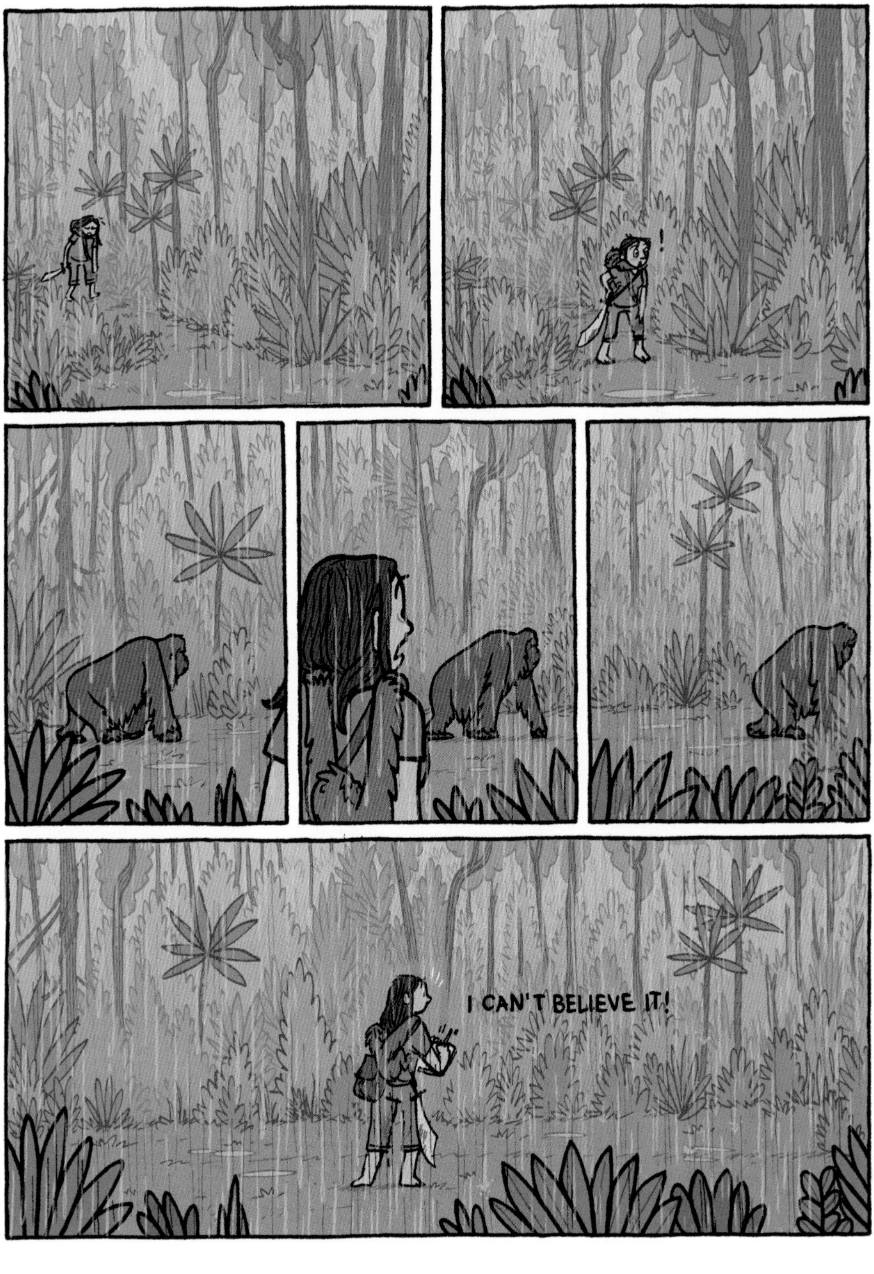
!
I CAN'T BELIEVE IT!

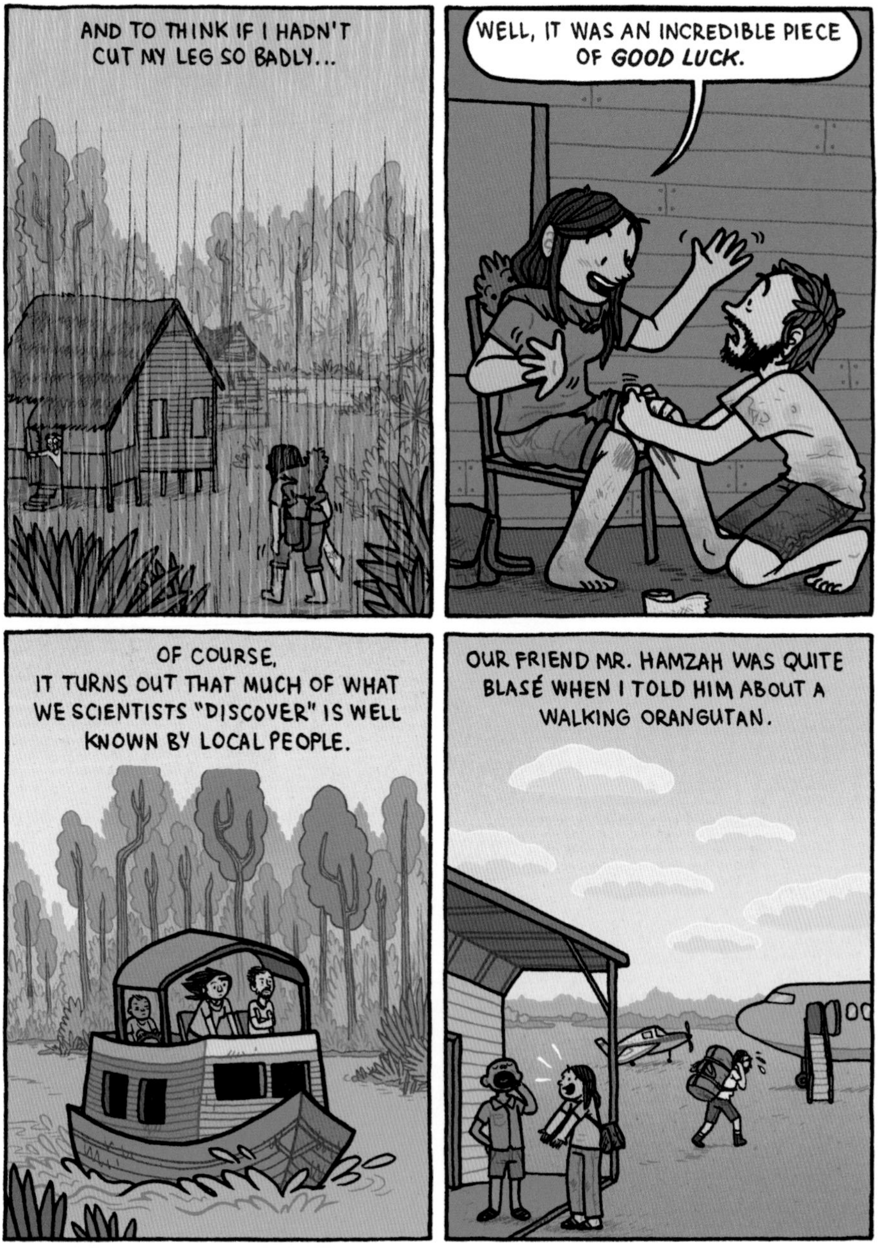
AND TO THINK IF I HADN'T CUT MY LEG SO BADLY...
WELL, IT WAS AN INCREDIBLE PIECE OF GOOD LUCK.
OF COURSE, IT TURNS OUT THAT MUCH OF WHAT WE SCIENTISTS "DISCOVER" IS WELL KNOWN BY LOCAL PEOPLE.
OUR FRIEND MR. HAMZAH WAS QUITE BLASÉ WHEN I TOLD HIM ABOUT A WALKING ORANGUTAN.

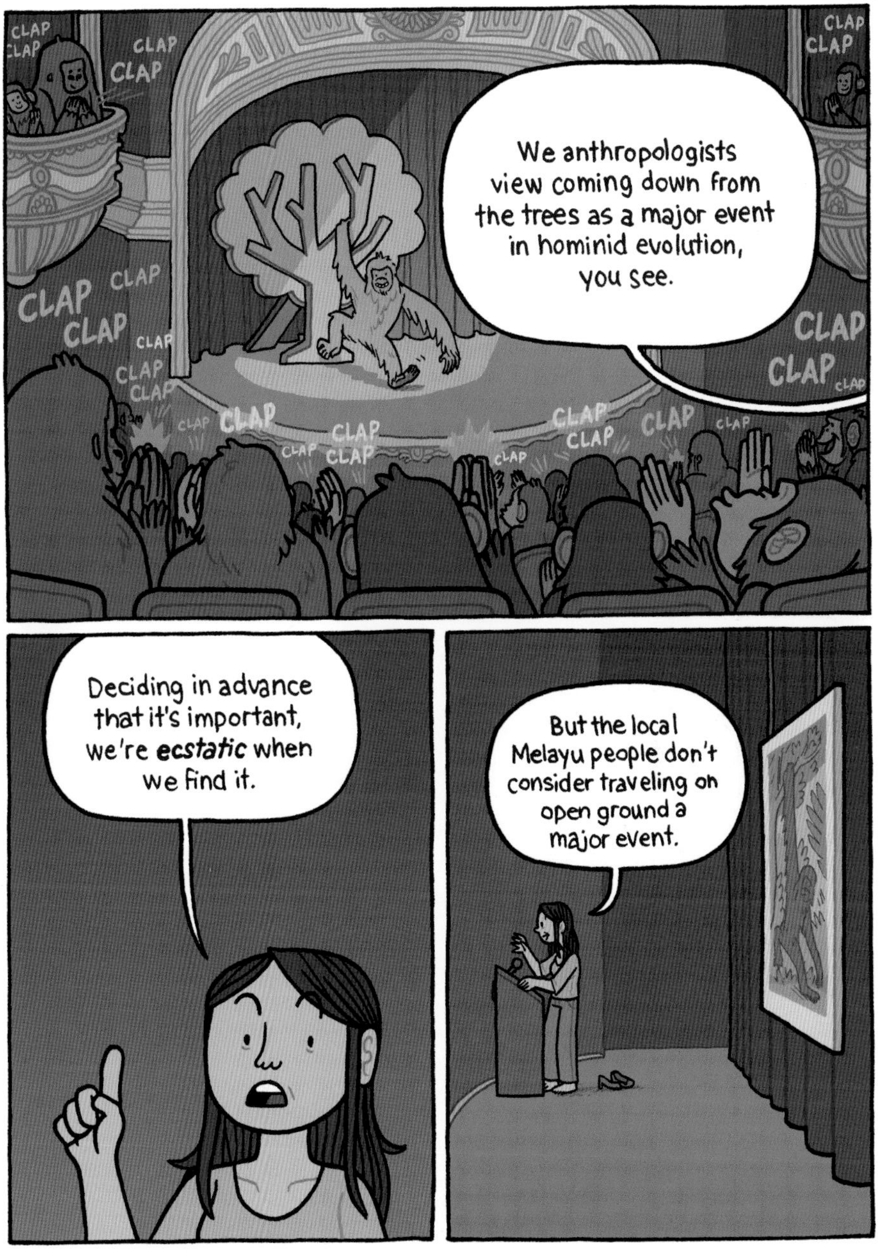
CLAP CLAP
CLAP CLAP
We anthropologists view coming down from the trees as a major event in hominid evolution, you see.
CLAP CLAP
CLAP CLAP
CLAP CLAP
CLAP CLAP
Deciding in advance that it's important, we're *ecstatic* when we find it.
But the local Melayu people don't consider traveling on open ground a major event.

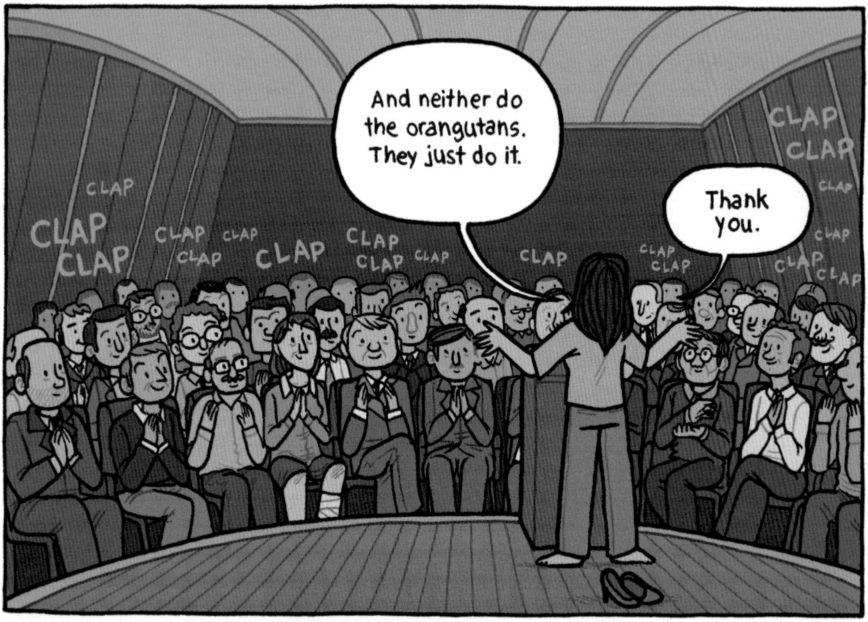
CLAP
CLAP
CLAP
CLAP
CLAP
CLAP
CLAP
CLAP
CLAP
CLAP
CLAP
CLAP
And neither do the orangutans. They just do it.
Thank you.

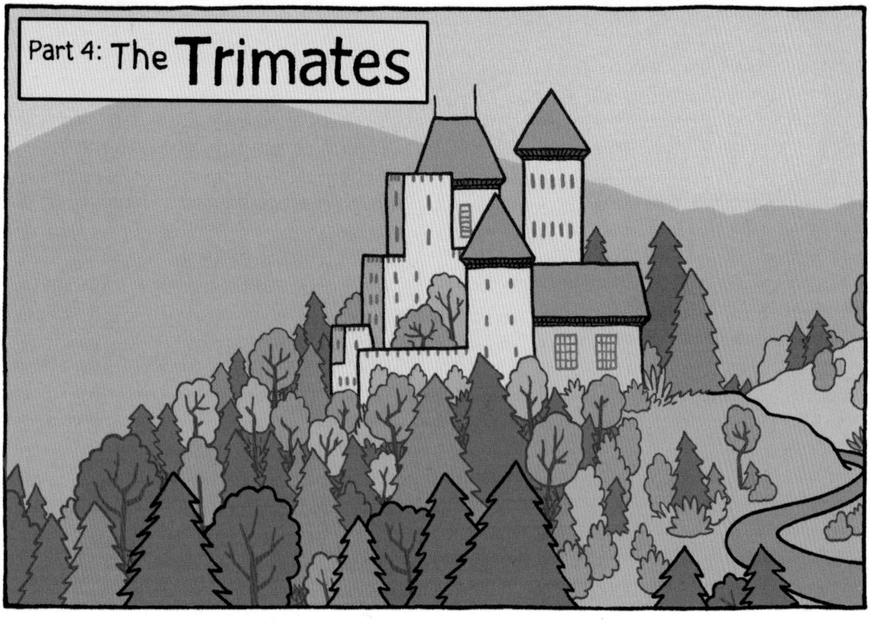
Part 4: The Trimates

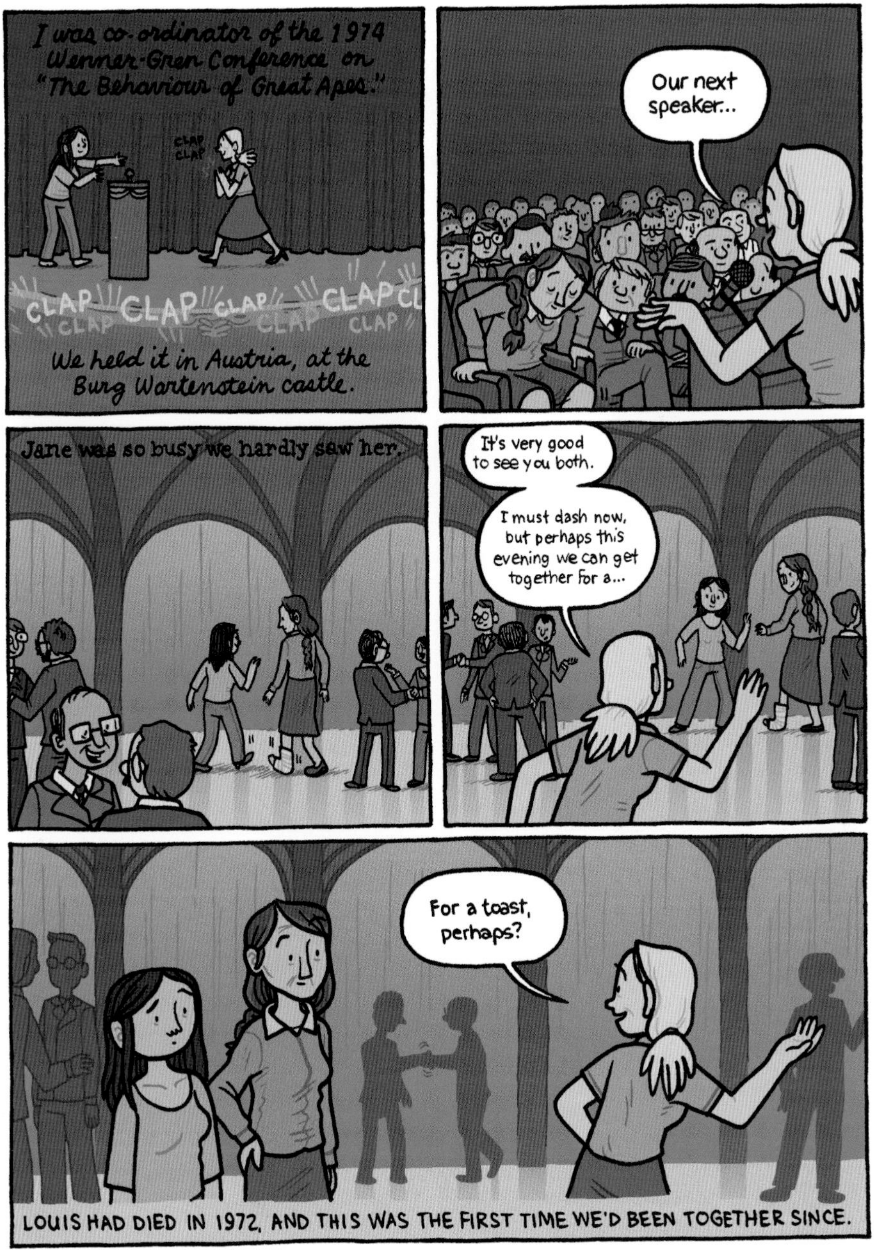

I was co-ordinator of the 1974 Wenner-Gren Conference on "The Behaviour of Great Apes."
CLAP CLAP
CLAP CLAP CLAP CLAP CLAP CL
CLAP CLAP CLAP
We held it in Austria, at the Burg Wartenstein castle.
Our next speaker...
Jane was so busy we hardly saw her.
It's very good to see you both.
I must dash now, but perhaps this evening we can get together for a...
For a toast, perhaps?
LOUIS HAD DIED IN 1972, AND THIS WAS THE FIRST TIME WE'D BEEN TOGETHER SINCE.

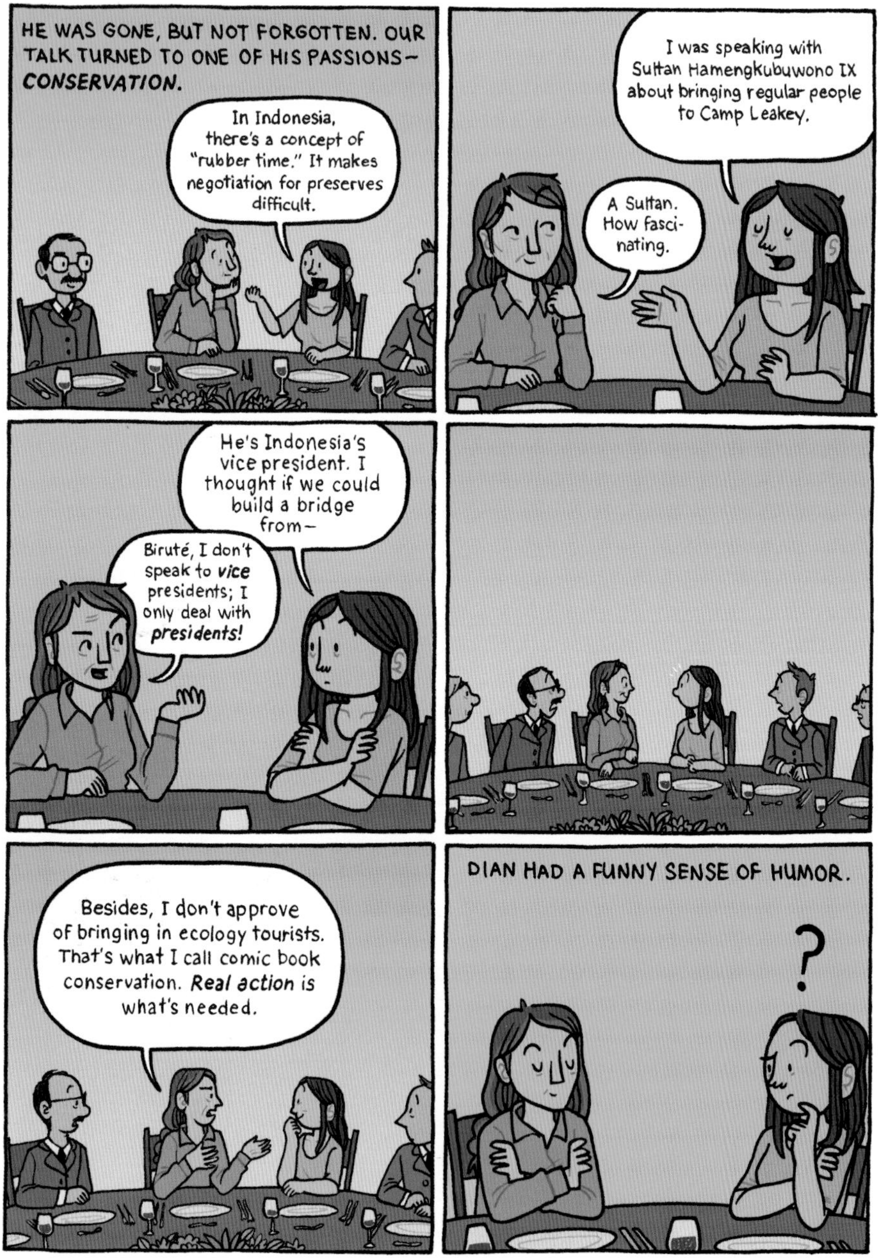

HE WAS GONE, BUT NOT FORGOTTEN. OUR TALK TURNED TO ONE OF HIS PASSIONS—*CONSERVATION*.
In Indonesia, there's a concept of "rubber time." It makes negotiation for preserves difficult.
I was speaking with Sultan Hamengkubuwono IX about bringing regular people to Camp Leakey.
A Sultan. How fascinating.
He's Indonesia's vice president. I thought if we could build a bridge from—
Biruté, I don't speak to *vice* presidents; I only deal with *presidents!*
Besides, I don't approve of bringing in ecology tourists. That's what I call comic book conservation. *Real action* is what's needed.
DIAN HAD A FUNNY SENSE OF HUMOR.
?

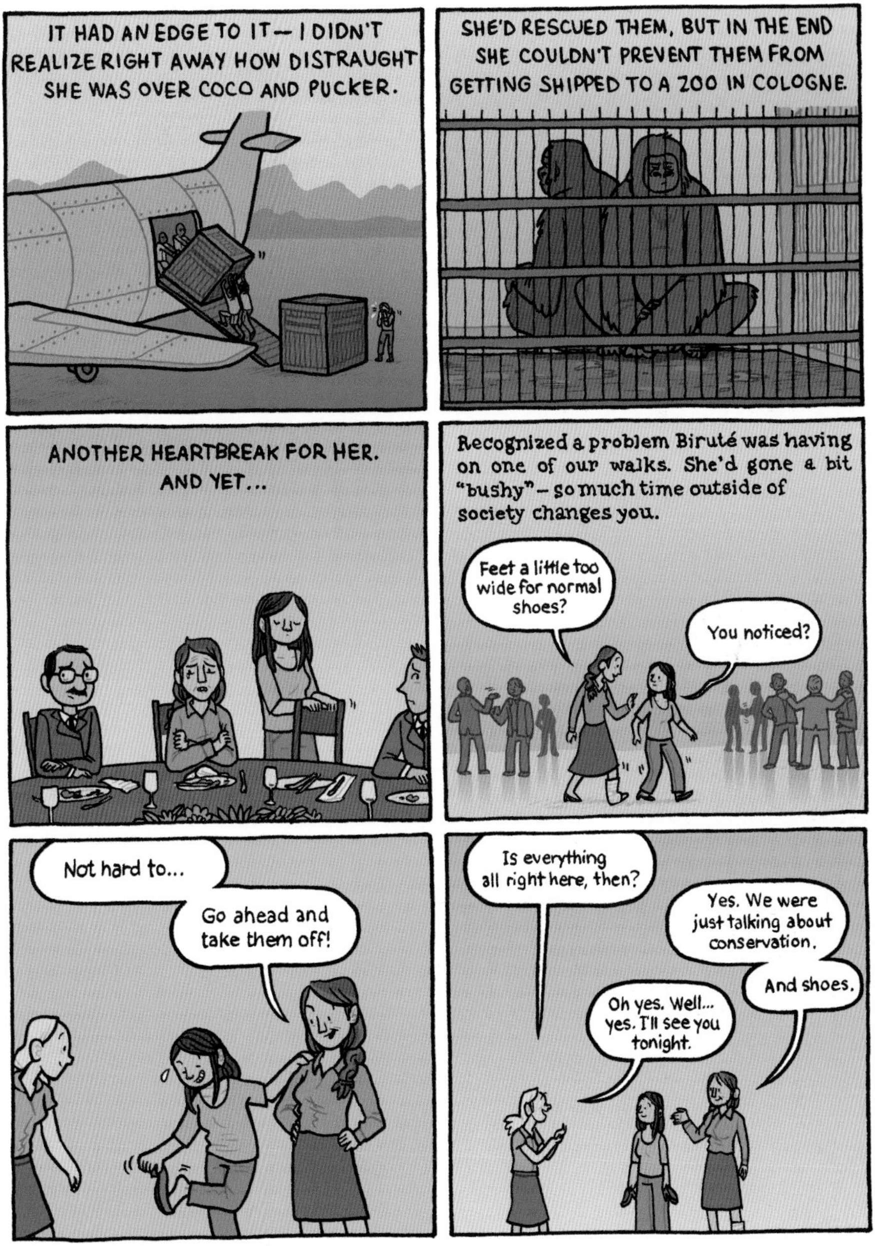
IT HAD AN EDGE TO IT—I DIDN'T REALIZE RIGHT AWAY HOW DISTRAUGHT SHE WAS OVER COCO AND PUCKER.
SHE'D RESCUED THEM, BUT IN THE END SHE COULDN'T PREVENT THEM FROM GETTING SHIPPED TO A ZOO IN COLOGNE.
ANOTHER HEARTBREAK FOR HER. AND YET...
Recognized a problem Biruté was having on one of our walks. She'd gone a bit "bushy"—so much time outside of society changes you.
Feet a little too wide for normal shoes?
You noticed?
Not hard to...
Go ahead and take them off!
Is everything all right here, then?
Yes. We were just talking about conservation.
And shoes.
Oh yes. Well... yes. I'll see you tonight.

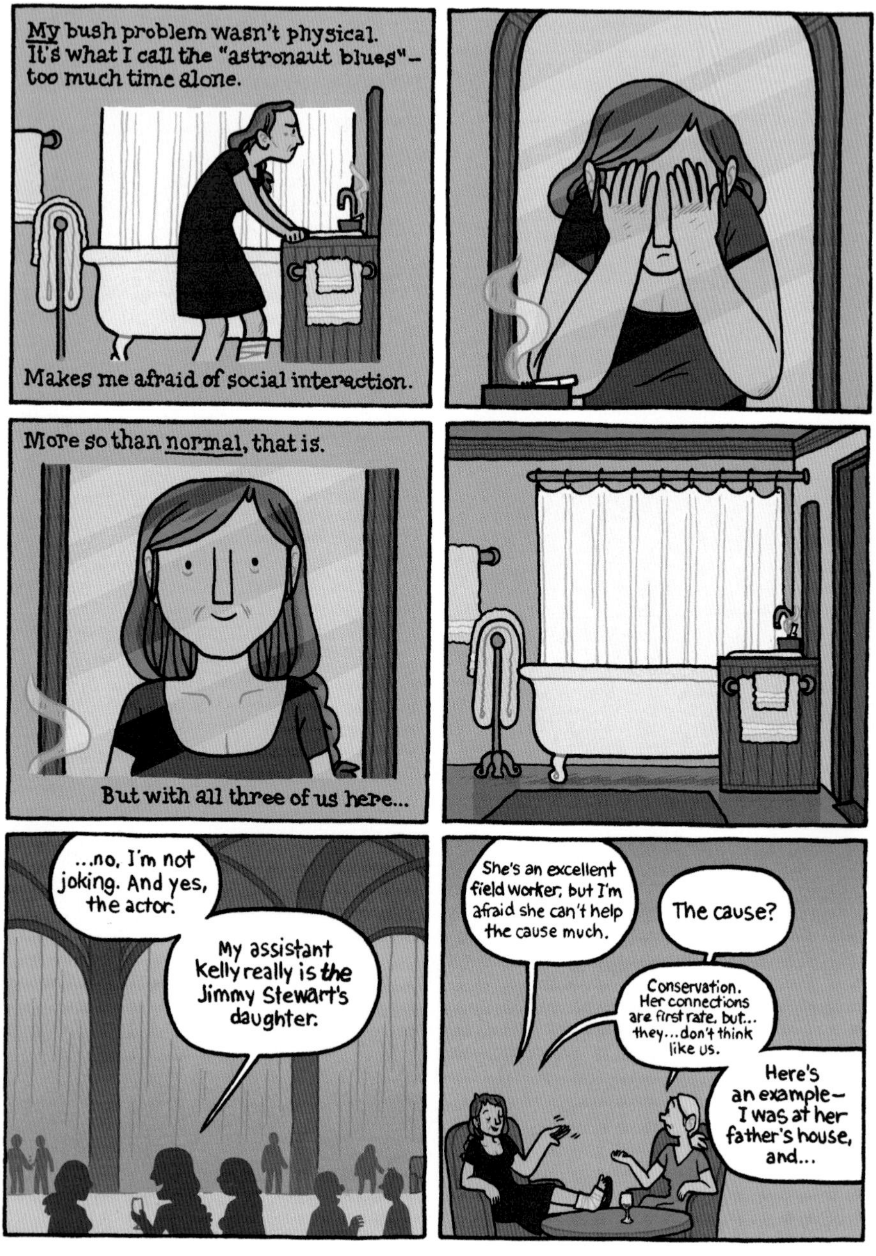

My bush problem wasn't physical. It's what I call the "astronaut blues"—too much time alone.
Makes me afraid of social interaction.
More so than normal, that is.
But with all three of us here...
...no, I'm not joking. And yes, the actor.
My assistant Kelly really is *the* Jimmy Stewart's daughter.
She's an excellent field worker, but I'm afraid she can't help the cause much.
The cause?
Conservation. Her connections are first rate, but... they... don't think like us.
Here's an example—I was at her father's house, and...

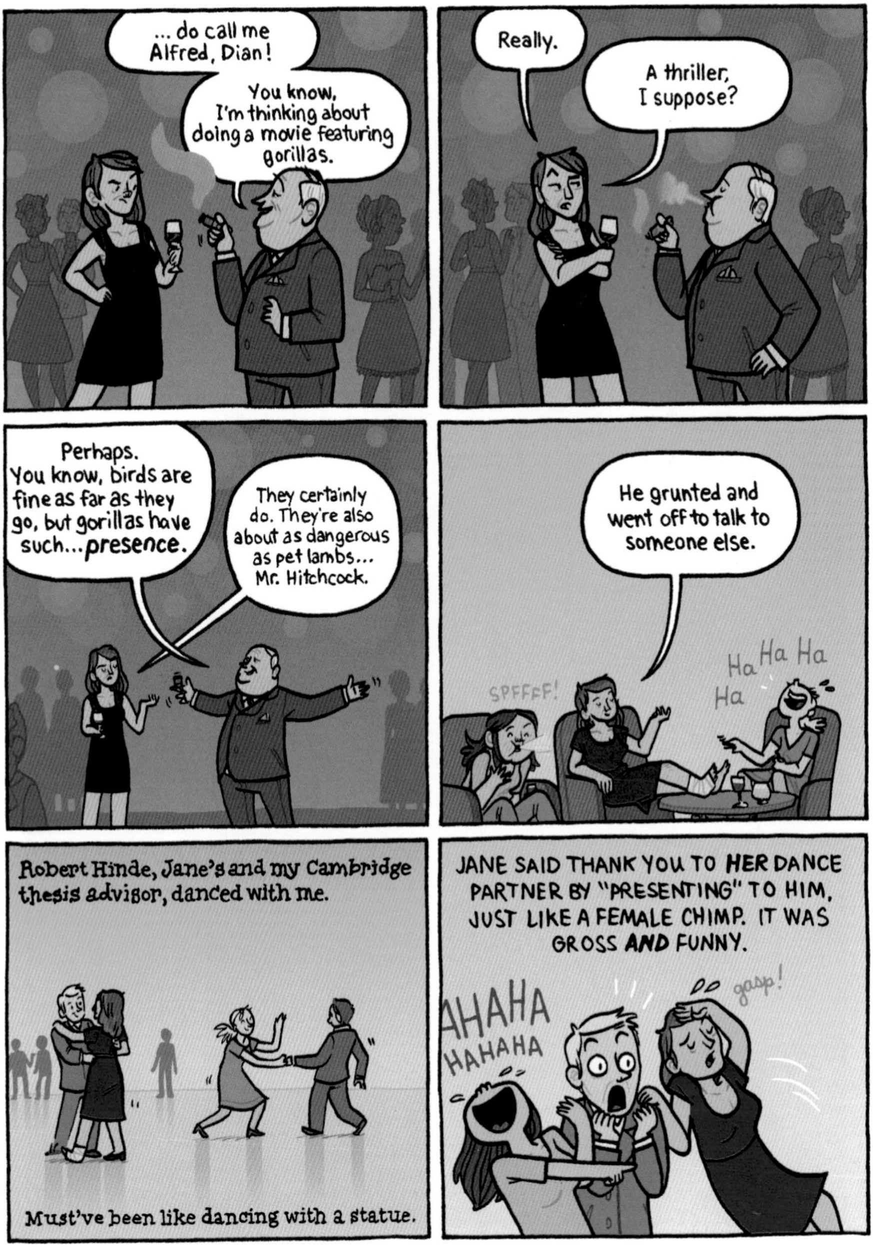

... do call me Alfred, Dian!
You know, I'm thinking about doing a movie featuring gorillas.
Really.
A thriller, I suppose?
Perhaps. You know, birds are fine as far as they go, but gorillas have such... presence.
They certainly do. They're also about as dangerous as pet lambs... Mr. Hitchcock.
He grunted and went off to talk to someone else.
SPFFFF!
Ha Ha Ha Ha
Robert Hinde, Jane's and my Cambridge thesis advisor, danced with me.
Must've been like dancing with a statue.
JANE SAID THANK YOU TO HER DANCE PARTNER BY "PRESENTING" TO HIM, JUST LIKE A FEMALE CHIMP. IT WAS GROSS AND FUNNY.
AHAHA
HAHAHA
gasp!

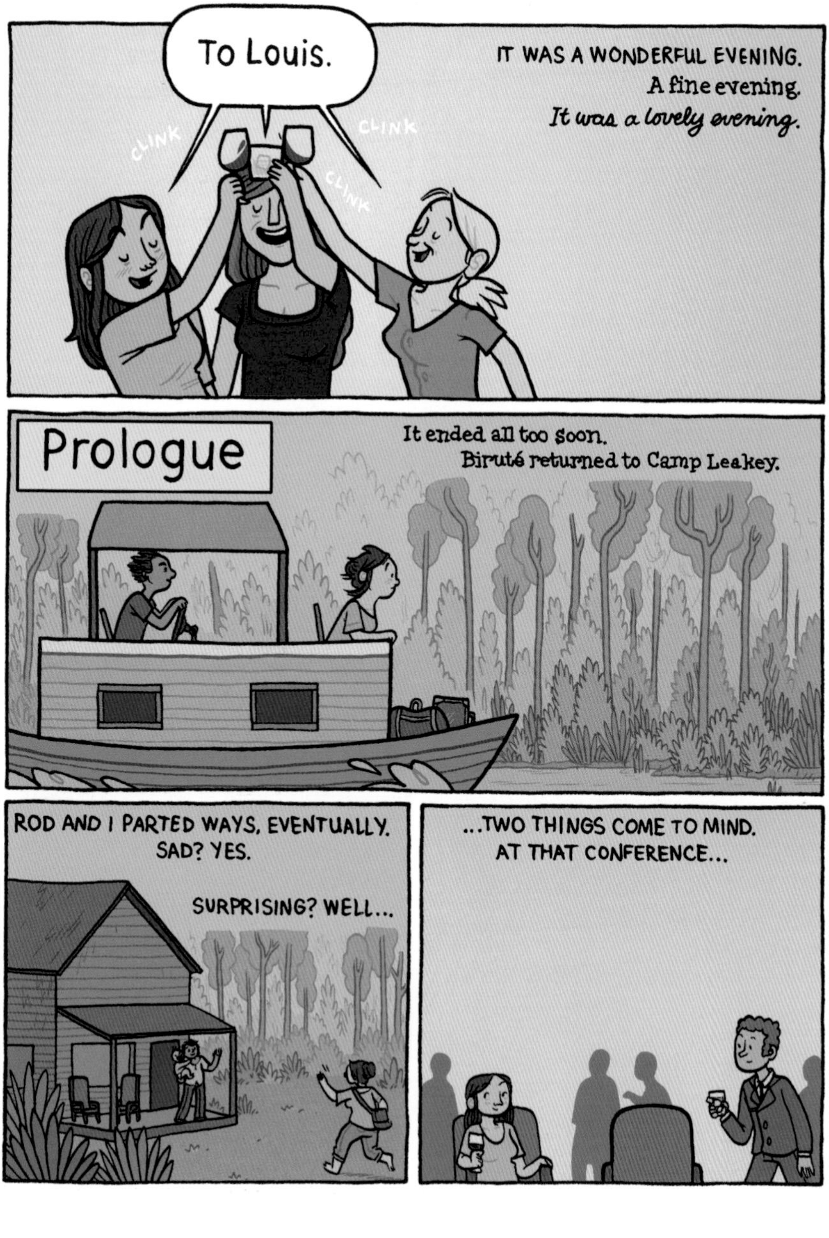
To Louis.
CLINK
CLINK
CLINK
IT WAS A WONDERFUL EVENING.
A fine evening.
It was a lovely evening.
Prologue
It ended all too soon.
Biruté returned to Camp Leakey.
ROD AND I PARTED WAYS, EVENTUALLY.
SAD? YES.
SURPRISING? WELL...
...TWO THINGS COME TO MIND.
AT THAT CONFERENCE...

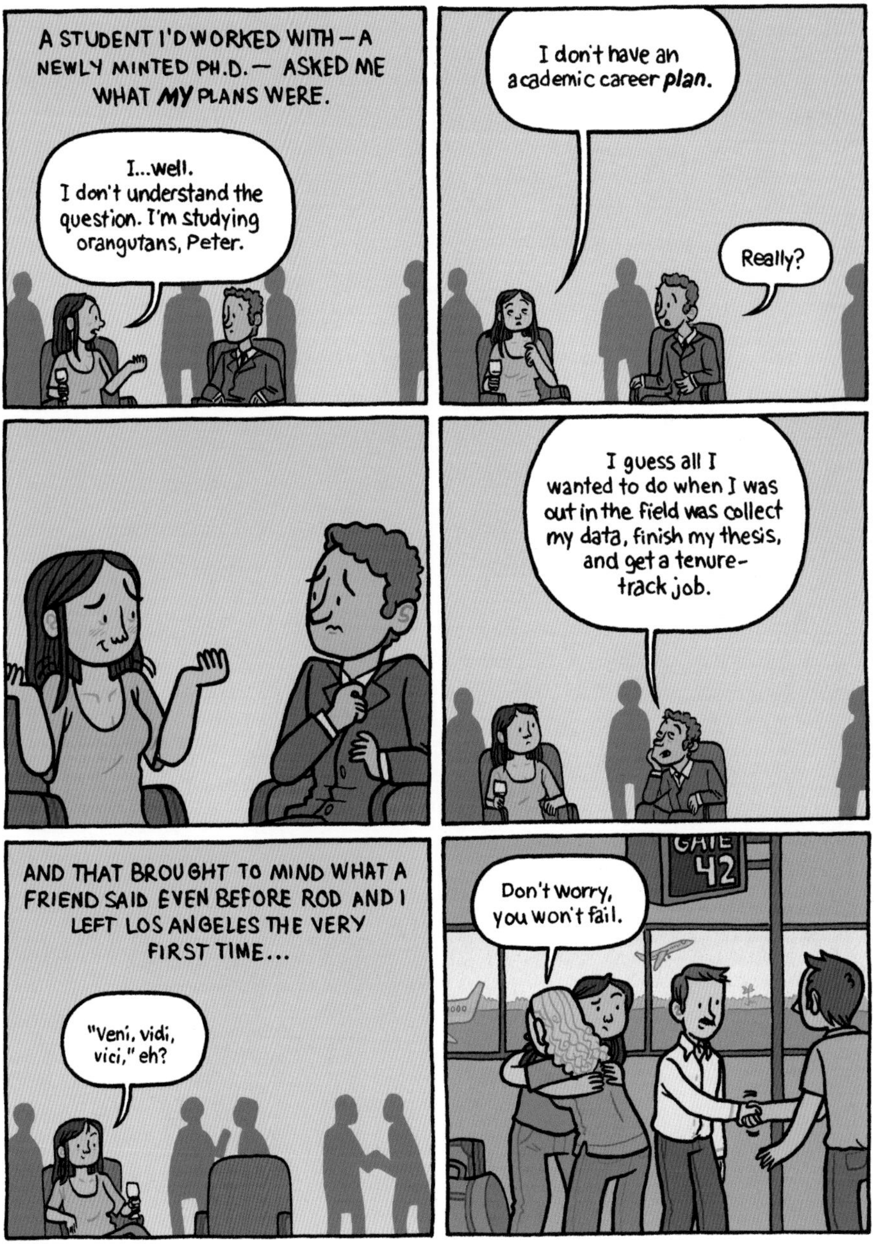
A STUDENT I'D WORKED WITH — A NEWLY MINTED PH.D. — ASKED ME WHAT MY PLANS WERE.
I...well. I don't understand the question. I'm studying orangutans, Peter.
I don't have an academic career plan.
Really?
I guess all I wanted to do when I was out in the field was collect my data, finish my thesis, and get a tenure-track job.
AND THAT BROUGHT TO MIND WHAT A FRIEND SAID EVEN BEFORE ROD AND I LEFT LOS ANGELES THE VERY FIRST TIME...
"Veni, vidi, vici," eh?
GATE 42
Don't worry, you won't fail.

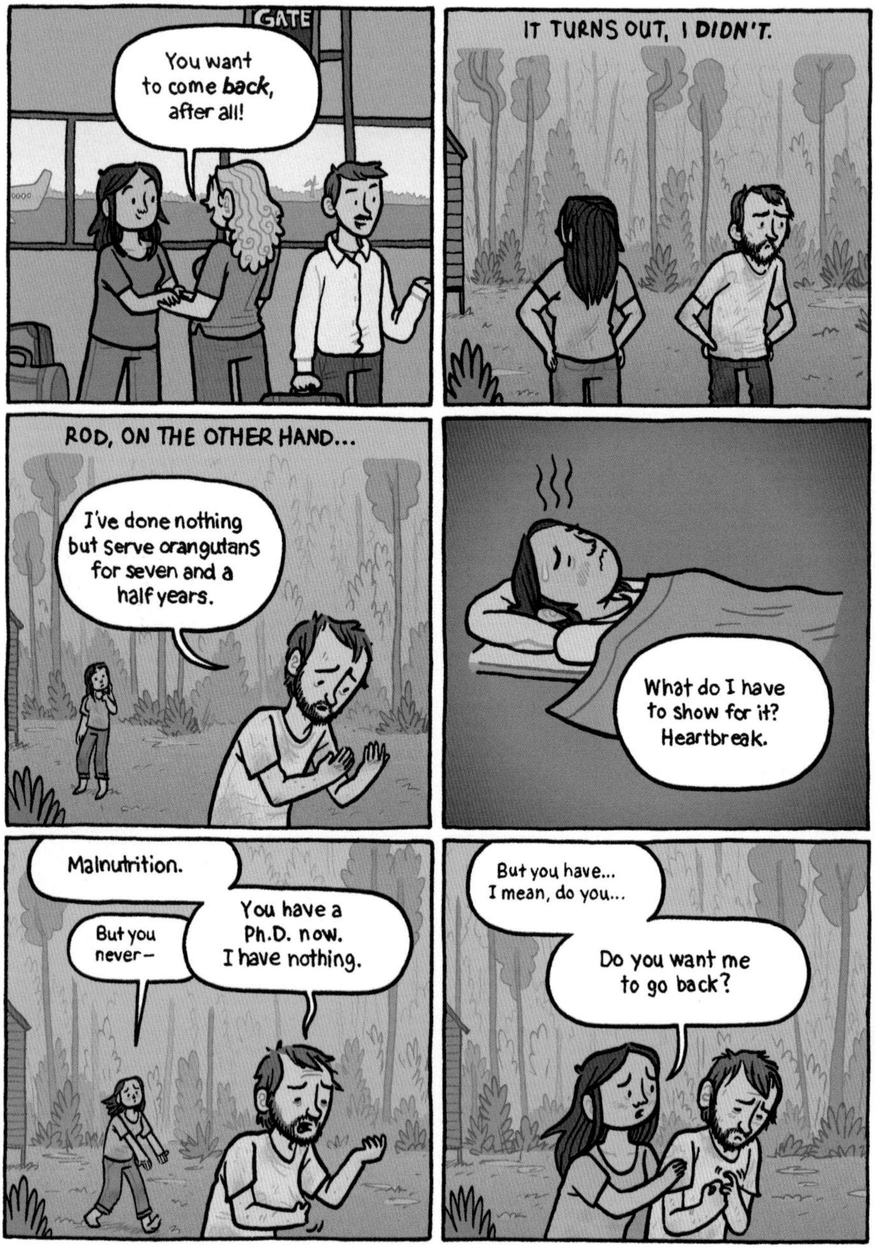
GATE
You want to come *back*, after all!
IT TURNS OUT, I *DIDN'T.*
ROD, ON THE OTHER HAND...
I've done nothing but serve orangutans for seven and a half years.
What do I have to show for it? Heartbreak.
Malnutrition.
But you never—
You have a Ph.D. now. I have nothing.
But you have... I mean, do you...
Do you want me to go back?

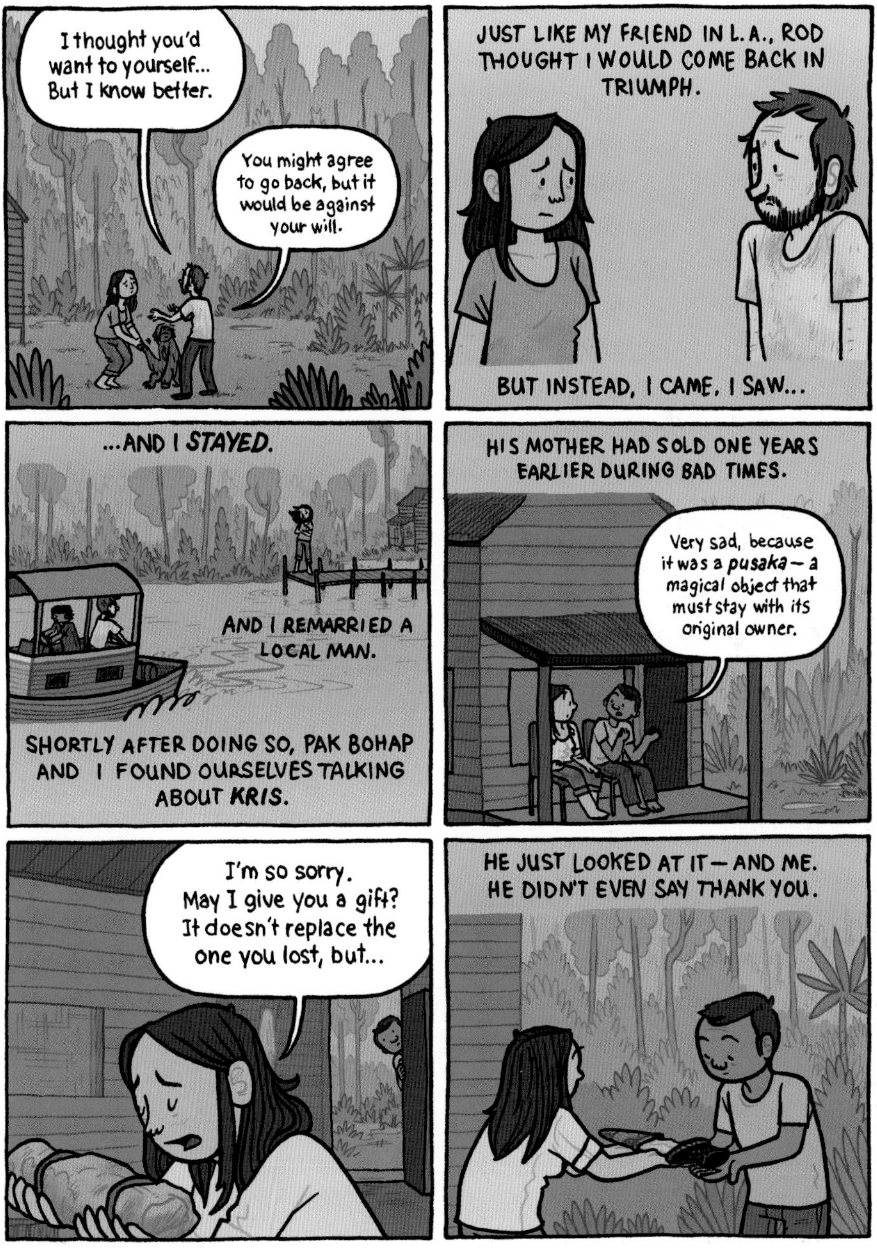
I thought you'd want to yourself... But I know better.
You might agree to go back, but it would be against your will.
JUST LIKE MY FRIEND IN L.A., ROD THOUGHT I WOULD COME BACK IN TRIUMPH.
BUT INSTEAD, I CAME, I SAW...
...AND I *STAYED.*
AND I REMARRIED A LOCAL MAN.
SHORTLY AFTER DOING SO, PAK BOHAP AND I FOUND OURSELVES TALKING ABOUT **KRIS.**
HIS MOTHER HAD SOLD ONE YEARS EARLIER DURING BAD TIMES.
Very sad, because it was a **pusaka** — a magical object that must stay with its original owner.
I'm so sorry. May I give you a gift? It doesn't replace the one you lost, but...
HE JUST LOOKED AT IT — AND ME. HE DIDN'T EVEN SAY THANK YOU.

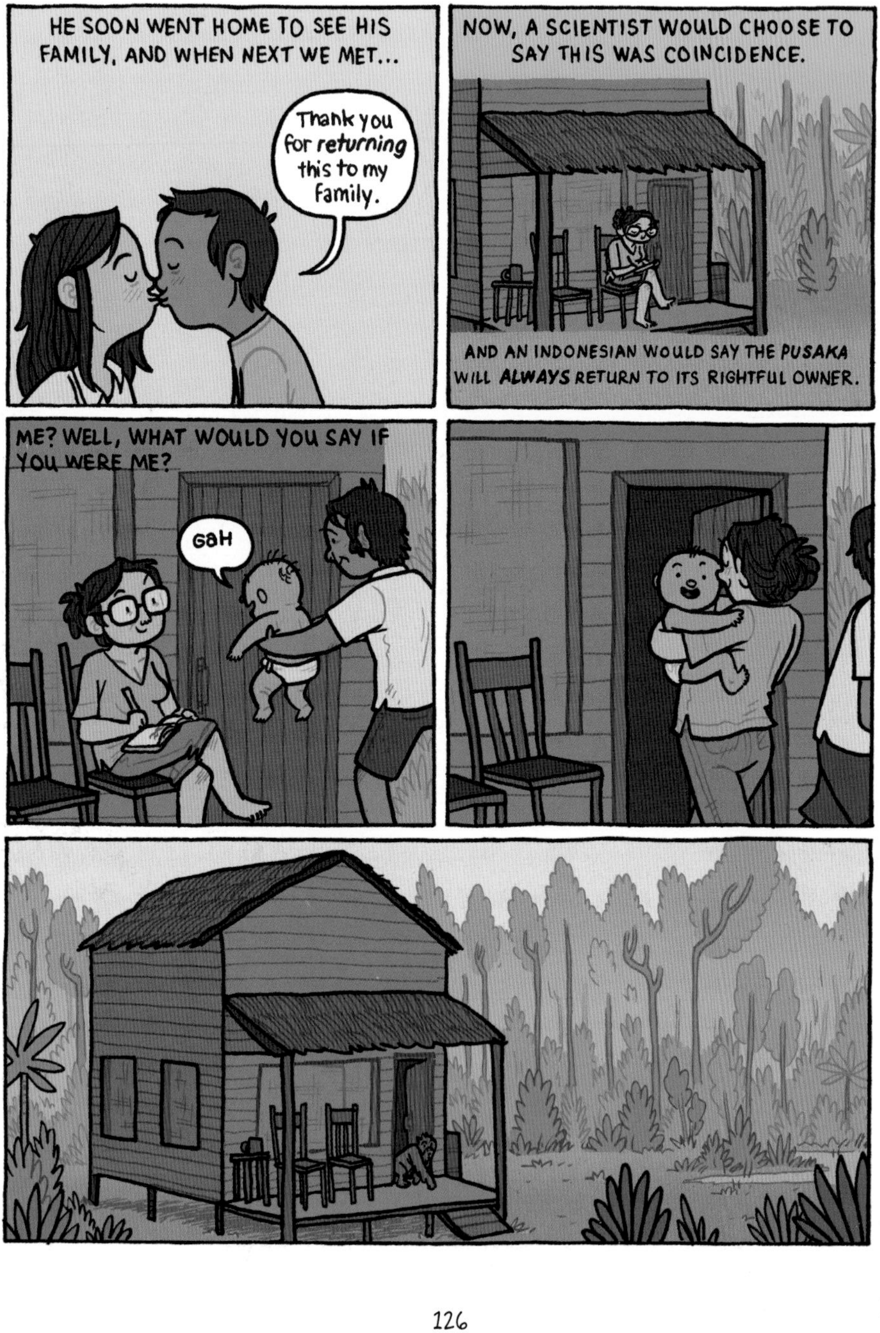
HE SOON WENT HOME TO SEE HIS FAMILY, AND WHEN NEXT WE MET...
Thank you for *returning* this to my family.
NOW, A SCIENTIST WOULD CHOOSE TO SAY THIS WAS COINCIDENCE.
AND AN INDONESIAN WOULD SAY THE *PUSAKA* WILL ***ALWAYS*** RETURN TO ITS RIGHTFUL OWNER.
ME? WELL, WHAT WOULD YOU SAY IF YOU WERE ME?
GAH

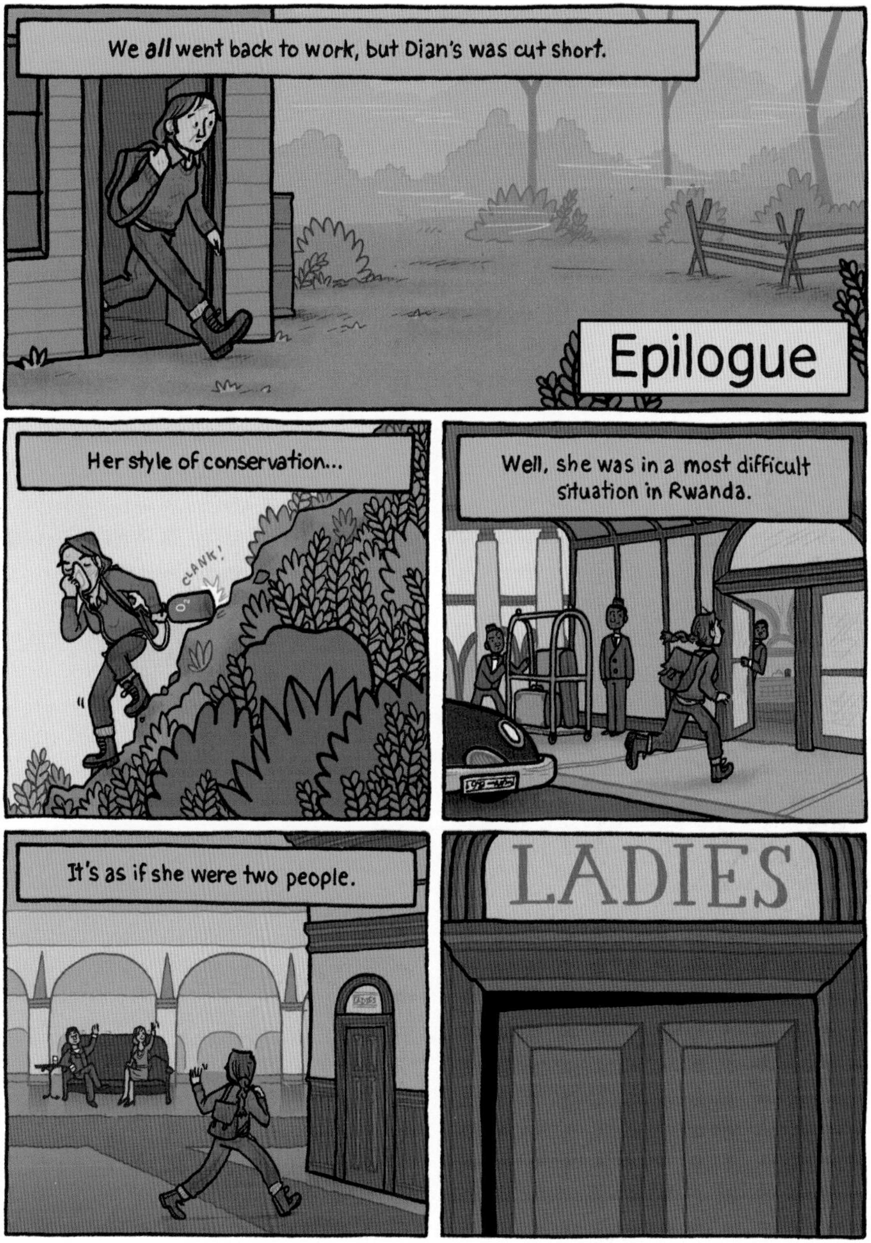
We all went back to work, but Dian's was cut short.
Epilogue
Her style of conservation...
CLANK!
Well, she was in a most difficult situation in Rwanda.
It's as if she were two people.
LADIES

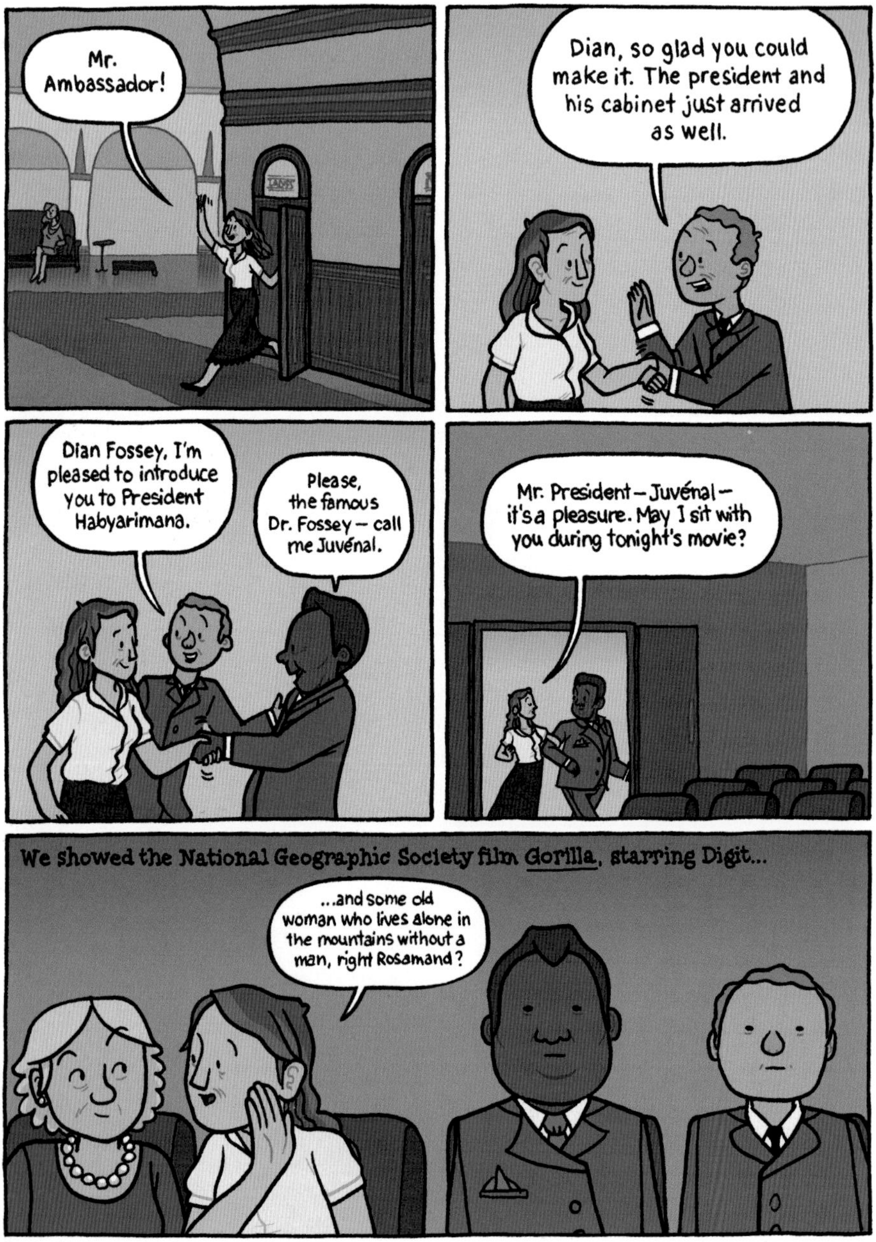
Mr. Ambassador!
Dian, so glad you could make it. The president and his cabinet just arrived as well.
Dian Fossey, I'm pleased to introduce you to President Habyarimana.
Please, the famous Dr. Fossey – call me Juvénal.
Mr. President – Juvénal – it's a pleasure. May I sit with you during tonight's movie?
We showed the National Geographic Society film Gorilla, starring Digit...
...and some old woman who lives alone in the mountains without a man, right Rosamand?

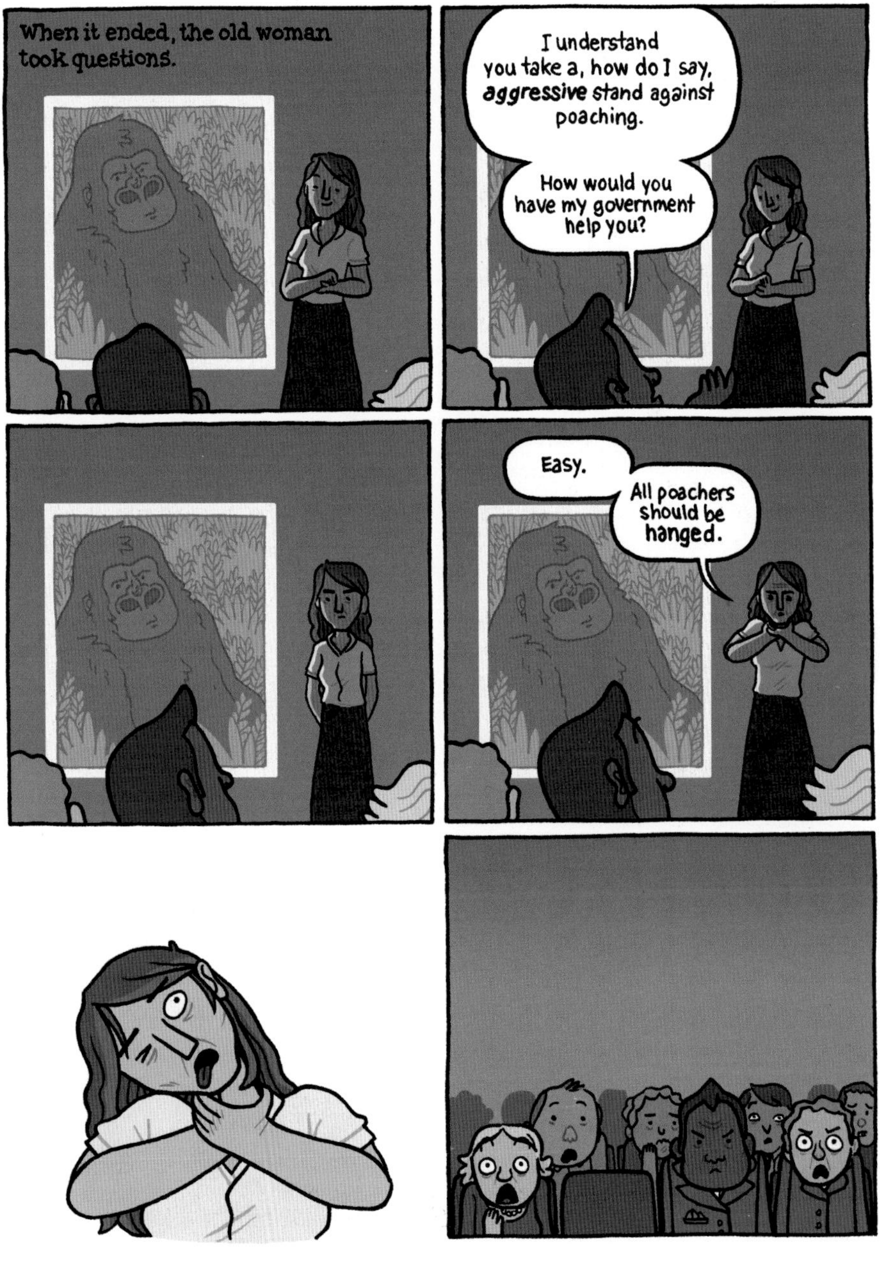

When it ended, the old woman took questions.
I understand you take a, how do I say, aggressive stand against poaching.
How would you have my government help you?
Easy.
All poachers should be hanged.

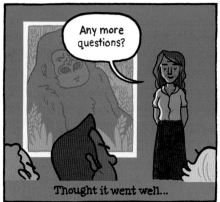

Any more questions?

Thought it went well...

...but apparently the event was <u>not</u> a diplomatic success.

Two Dians. One side *fascinating* and *delightful*.

The other side *fierce* and *unrelenting*.

Most people just didn't understand her.

Very few people tried.

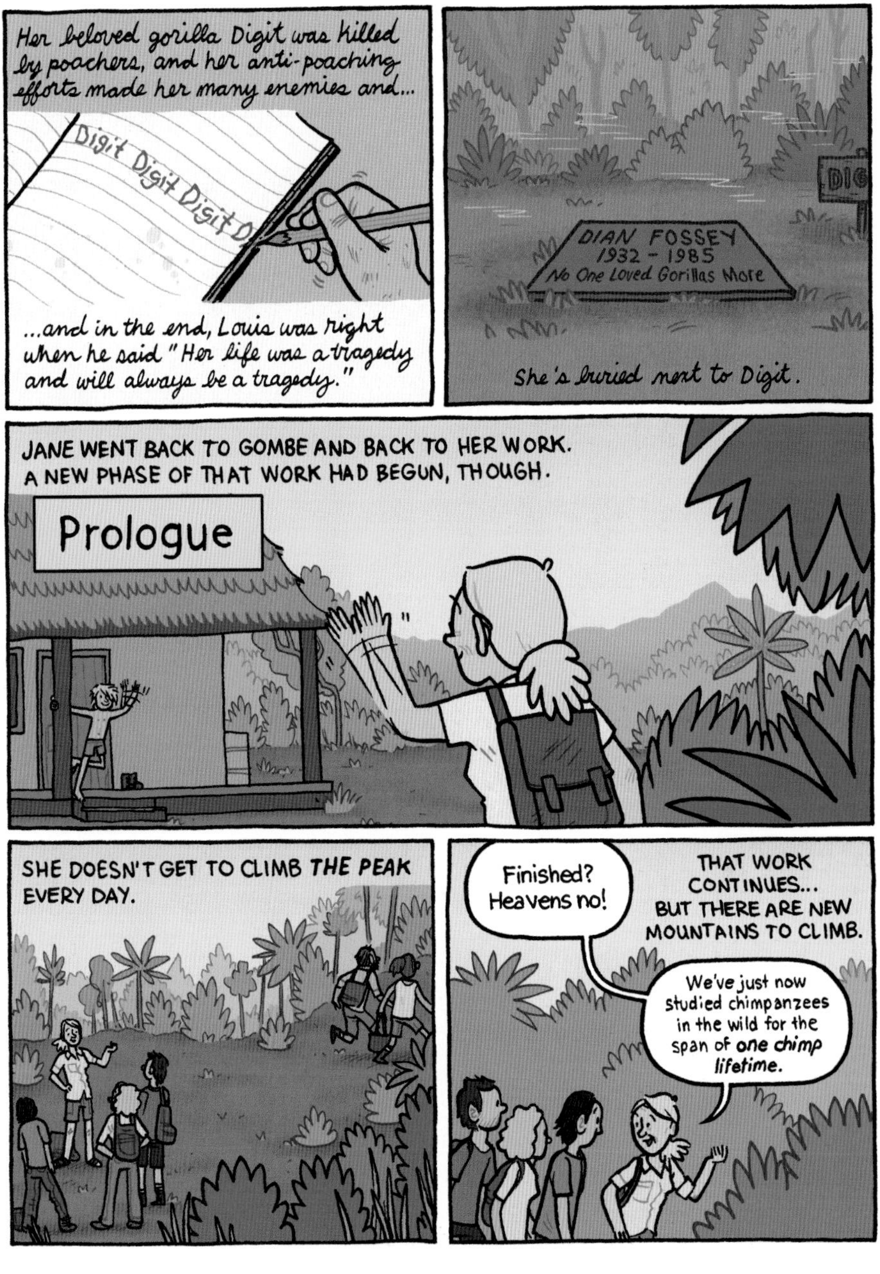
Her beloved gorilla Digit was killed by poachers, and her anti-poaching efforts made her many enemies and...
Digit Digit Digit D
...and in the end, Louis was right when he said "Her life was a tragedy and will always be a tragedy."
DIAN FOSSEY
1932 - 1985
No One Loved Gorillas More
She's buried next to Digit.
JANE WENT BACK TO GOMBE AND BACK TO HER WORK.
A NEW PHASE OF THAT WORK HAD BEGUN, THOUGH.
Prologue
SHE DOESN'T GET TO CLIMB *THE PEAK* EVERY DAY.
Finished? Heavens no!
THAT WORK CONTINUES... BUT THERE ARE NEW MOUNTAINS TO CLIMB.
We've just now studied chimpanzees in the wild for the span of *one chimp lifetime.*

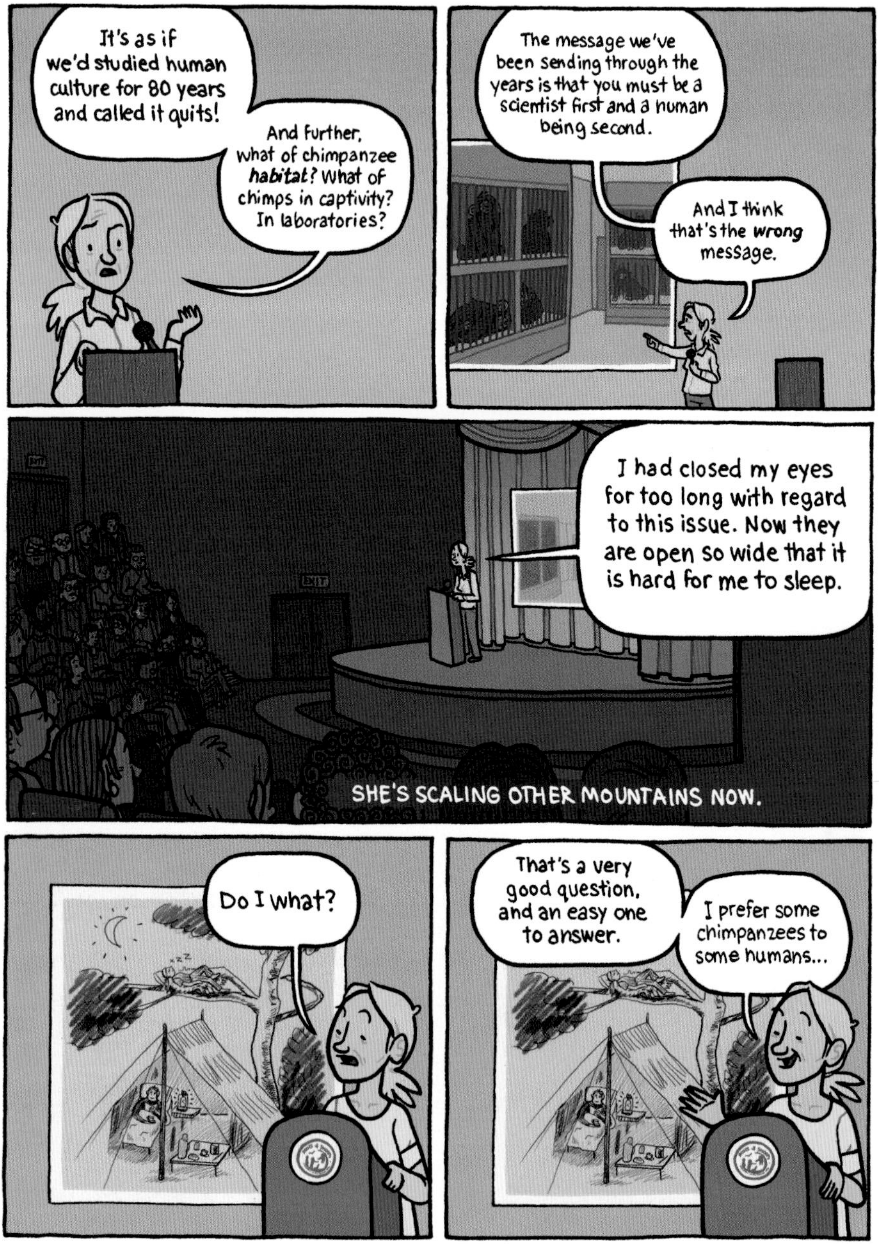

It's as if we'd studied human culture for 80 years and called it quits!
And further, what of chimpanzee *habitat*? What of chimps in captivity? In laboratories?
The message we've been sending through the years is that you must be a scientist first and a human being second.
And I think that's the *wrong* message.
EXIT
I had closed my eyes for too long with regard to this issue. Now they are open so wide that it is hard for me to sleep.
SHE'S SCALING OTHER MOUNTAINS NOW.
Do I what?
That's a very good question, and an easy one to answer.
I prefer some chimpanzees to some humans...

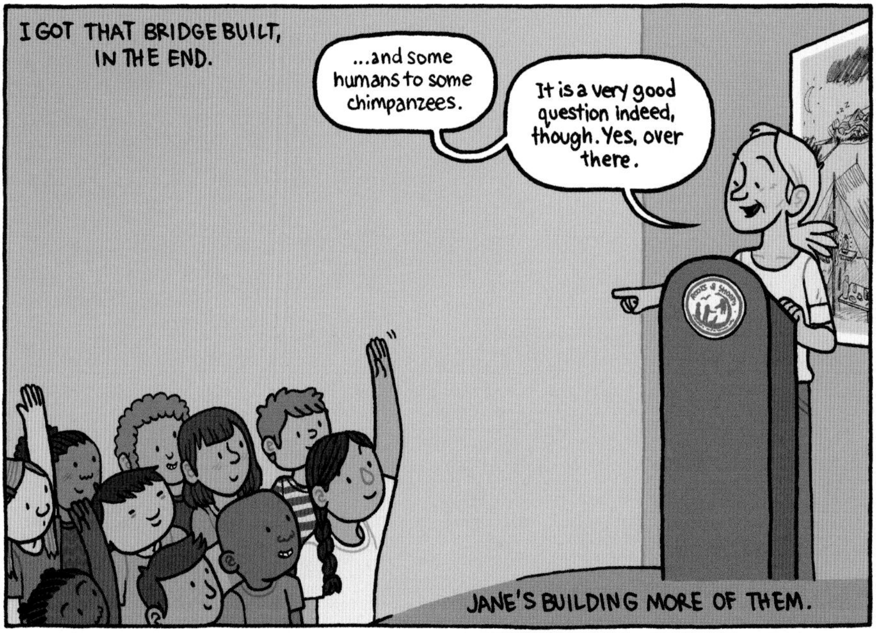
I GOT THAT BRIDGE BUILT, IN THE END.
...and some humans to some chimpanzees.
It is a very good question indeed, though. Yes, over there.
JANE'S BUILDING MORE OF THEM.

AFTERWORD

Maris and I didn't get up before dawn in the jungle, we didn't climb mountains, and we didn't wade through swamps either. So we didn't observe Jane Goodall, Dian Fossey, and Biruté Galdikas the same way they observed chimpanzees, gorillas, and orangutans.

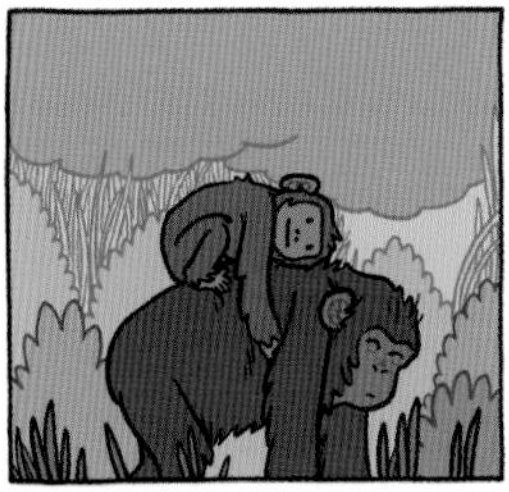

As a result, some of what you just read is fiction. You probably guessed that already, but some of it would have been fiction even if we had done all the things our heroes did. The reason is, real lives don't behave like stories, complete with tidy beginnings, middles, and ends. (Science doesn't even have an end!) And some of what I write now, late at night here in Michigan with the only animal of any size nearby being my cat, is probably fiction too, since I'm writing this long after finishing the script and sending it to Maris. Memories fade, and writing a story isn't science, so I didn't keep a lab notebook to remind myself of the failures, false starts, and occasional a-ha! moments that went into putting this book together.

So, can you trust what I wrote, or what Maris drew? Well, yes . . . mostly.

Here's what I mean: We did study their lives, read a lot about primates, and try to get all the significant details right. That's not to say that every single detail isn't important in science, but we wanted to tell a story and not make a textbook. So we had to pick and choose whether and when to leave something out, or compress a week's (or a month's, or a year's) worth of their hard work down to something you could read in much less

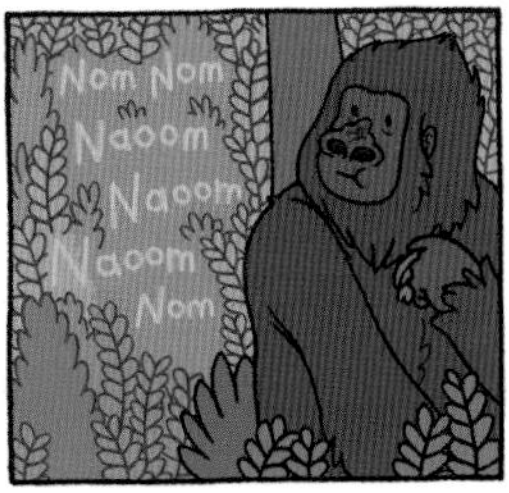
Nom Nom
Naoom
Naoom
Naoom
Nom

than a week or a month or a year. To do this I put together detailed timelines and looked for parts where events, discoveries—and just as important—themes and ideas complemented each other. Maris studied primate behavior, anatomy, and their environments. And we both listened to the sounds the animals make and studied the things the scientists said and did, in their own words whenever possible, and asked ourselves and each other lots of questions about how to weave three remarkable lives into one story.

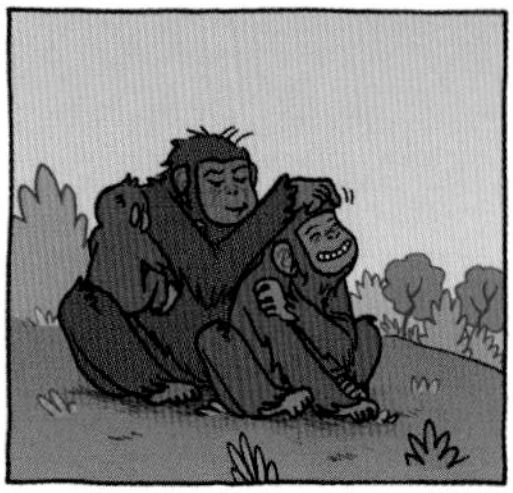

What kind of person does it take to do this kind of work? How hard is it? When did our understanding of what it means to be a primate begin? And why is it important? Those are the questions we hope you had when you started the book, and hope you've gotten some answers by the end.* But by now you've guessed, and guessed right, that the end of this book isn't the end of the story. There's a lot more you can learn about Jane Goodall, Dian Fossey, and Biruté Galdikas, and we recommend starting with the list that follows. It includes books we consulted all the time when we made this one, and we know you'll enjoy reading more about these three amazing women.

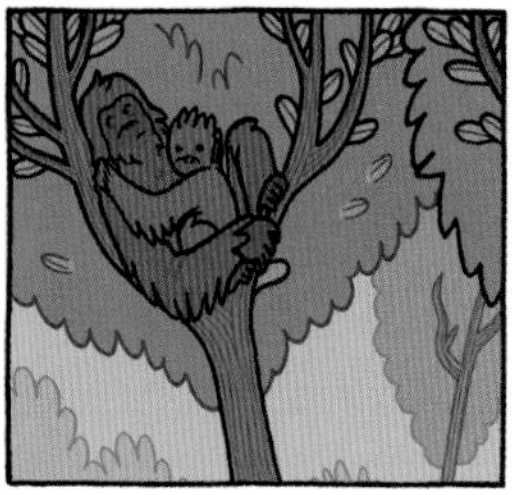

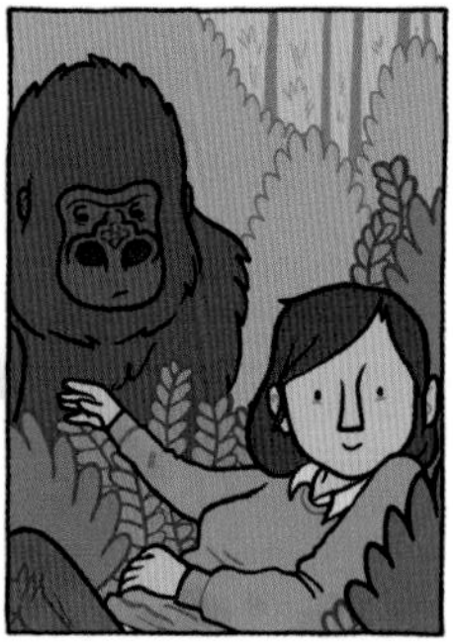

* My answers to the first three questions are: Smart and tough. Very. Not as long ago as you might think and we're not done yet. As for why this is important . . . visit www.gt-labs.com/blog/2013/05/primates.html and leave a comment. We want to hear what you think!

BIBLIOGRAPHY

JANE GOODALL: TRAILBLAZER
  In the Shadow of Man (NY: Mariner Books, 2000).
  Through a Window (NY: Mariner Books, 2000).
  Africa in My Blood: An Autobiography in Letters: The Early Years
    (NY: Mariner Books, 2001).
  Beyond Innocence: An Autobiography in Letters: The Later Years
    (NY: Mariner Books, 2001).
  Jane Goodall: The Woman Who Redefined Man, by Dale Peterson
    (NY: Houghton Mifflin, 2006).

DIAN FOSSEY: CONSERVATOR
  Gorillas in the Mist (NY: Mariner Books, 2000).
  Woman in the Mists, by Farley Mowat (NY: Warner Books, 1988).
  No One Loved Gorillas More: Dian Fossey, Letters from the Mist, by Camilla
    de la Bédoyère with photographs by Bob Campbell (Washington, DC:
    National Geographic, 2005).

BIRUTÉ GALDIKAS: AMBASSADOR
  Reflections of Eden (Boston: Little, Brown, 1995).
  Orangutan Odyssey, with Nancy Briggs, photographs by Karl Ammann
    (NY: Harry N. Abrams, 1999).
  Great Ape Odyssey, photographs by Karl Ammann (NY: Harry N. Abrams,
    2005).

Other good books to read include

*Ancestral Passions: The Leakey Family and the Quest for Humankind's
  Beginnings*, by Virginia Morell (NY: Simon & Schuster, 1995).
By the Evidence: Memoirs, 1932-1951, by Louis Leakey (NY: Harcourt Brace
  Jovanovich, 1974).
Leakey's Luck: The Life of Louis Seymour Bazett Leakey, by Sonia Cole
  (NY: Harcourt Brace Jovanovich, 1975).
Walking with the Great Apes: Jane Goodall, Dian Fossey, Biruté Galdikas,
  by Sy Montgomery (Boston: Houghton Mifflin, 1991).
. . . and many others, not to mention many magazine articles—those from
National Geographic are notable for their first-person accounts and great
photographs.

ACKNOWLEDGMENTS

Thanks to Maris, first and foremost.
Also: Tanya initially, Calista thoroughly,
Colleen graphically, Gina promotionally,
Mark editorially, and Kat, finally . . .
in all the best senses of the word.
—Jim Ottaviani

Thanks to Jim and all the folks at First Second (see above)
for making this happen. To Mum, for encouraging
my nerdy tendencies early on; Liz for the coffee;
Biggs for the purring; and Joe for, well . . . everything.
Lastly, thanks to everyone out there inspiring a
life-long love of all things art and science.
—Maris Wicks

JANE GOODALL, DIAN FOSSEY, and BIRUTÉ GALDIKAS
show us that knowledge brings compassion,
and compassion insists on action.
A portion of the author's proceeds will go to the following:

The Jane Goodall Institute
www.janegoodall.org

The Dian Fossey Gorilla Fund International
www.gorillafund.org

The Orangutan Foundation International
www.orangutan.org

SQUARE
FISH

An Imprint of Macmillan
175 Fifth Avenue
New York, NY 10010
mackids.com

Square Fish and the Square Fish logo are trademarks of Macmillan and
are used by First Second under license from Macmillan.

Square Fish books may be purchased for business or promotional use. For information
on bulk purchases, please contact the Macmillan Corporate and Premium Sales
Department at (800) 221-7945 x5442 or by e-mail at specialmarkets@macmillan.
com.

Photo of Birtuté Galdikas, Dian Fossey, and Jane Goodall on page 137 is used with
permission from the Orangutan Foundation International (www.orangutan.org).

Cataloging-in-Publication Data is on file at the Library of Congress

ISBN 978-1-250-06293-2 (paperback)

Originally published in the United States by First Second
First Square Fish Edition: 2015
Book designed by Roberta Pressel
Square Fish logo designed by Filomena Tuosto

10 9 8 7 6 5 4 3 2 1

AR: 3.6